Freud
and the
Passions

Literature & Philosophy

A. J. Cascardi, General Editor

This series publishes books in a wide range of subjects in philosophy and literature, including studies of the social and historical issues that relate these two fields. Drawing on the resources of the Anglo-American and Continental traditions, the series is open to philosophically informed scholarship covering the entire range of contemporary critical thought.

Already published:

J. M. Bernstein, *The Fate of Art: Aesthetic Alienation from Kant to Derrida and Adorno*

Peter Bürger, *The Decline of Modernism*

Mary E. Finn, *Writing the Incommensurable: Kierkegaard, Rossetti, and Hopkins*

Reed Way Dasenbrock, ed., *Literary Theory After Davidson*

David Haney, *William Wordsworth and the Hermeneutics of Incarnation*

David Jacobson, *Emerson's Pragmatic Vision: The Dance of the Eye*

Gray Kochhar-Lindgren, *Narcissus Transformed; The Textual Subject in Psychoanalysis and Literature*

Robert Steiner, *Toward a Grammar of Abstraction: Modernity, Wittgenstein, and the Paintings of Jackson Pollock*

Sylvia Walsh, *Living Poetically: Kierkegaard's Existential Aesthetics*

Michel Meyer, *Rhetoric, Language, and Reason*

Christie McDonald and Gary Wihl, eds., *Transformations in Personhood and Culture after Theory*

Charles Altieri, *Painterly Abstraction in Modernist American Poetry: The Contemporaneity of Modernism*

John C. O'Neal, *The Authority of Experience: Sensationist Theory in the French Enlightenment*

Freud
and the
Passions

Edited by
John O'Neill

The Pennsylvania State University Press
University Park, Pennsylvania

Library of Congress Cataloging-in-Publication Data

Freud and the passions / edited by John O'Neill.

     p.   cm.—(Literature & philosophy)
    Includes bibliographical references and index.
    ISBN 0-271-01529-2 (cloth: alk. paper)
    ISBN 0-271-01530-6 (paper: alk. paper)
    1. Affect (Psychology)   2. Freud, Sigmund, 1856–1939.
   3. Psychoanalysis and literature. I. O'Neill, John, 1933–
  II. Series: Literature and philosophy.
  BF175.5.A35F74   1996
  152.4'092—dc20   95-22441
                                             CIP

It is the policy of The Pennsylvania State University Press to use acid-free
paper for the first printing of all clothbound books. Publications on uncoated
stock satisfy the minimum requirements of American National Standard for
Information Sciences—Permanence of Paper for Printed Library Materials,
ANSI Z39.48-1992.

For
Chris and Ken
and
Freud

Contents

The Question of an Introduction: Understanding and the Passion of Ignorance

JOHN O'NEILL

Nowadays, given the state of the art in psychoanalytically driven literary criticism, an editor can hardly hope to impose structure, flow, and clarity upon essays whose delight the reader finds in their transgressions of such canons. And so these essays are not in any simple sense a collection. They need not be read in sequence. All the same, to point to the paradox of editing—*editor/traditor*—involves more than that act of bad faith committed in untitled works of art. These essays do not analyze the passions of hatred, envy, or domination simply by turning them into their opposites: hatred to love, envy to admiration, submission to domination. This would parody psychoanalysis just as much as if the passions were set into stories so strange that we think we have understood them from their resistance to intelligibility. If we thwart the expectation of a dispassionate survey of the contributions, do we not risk the reader's impatience? I think not. The reader is not a machine. The reader does not have any instincts to be pleasured or angered by the text. The reader is more likely a passionate reader; that is, one moved both to incorporate the text and to be incorporated by it. So an introduction to the texts that follow could never settle on one side of the interaction between reading and writing that is suffered in each of us. Rather, as Montaigne saw, the reader/writer is a deranged body whose quest for order, narrativity, and history feeds upon

itself—consubstantially—without ever achieving closure.[1] It is not only
the critics but Freud himself who saw that he could never get beyond
the series of passion plays in which he had cast himself and his patients.
At best, he might try to keep psychoanalysis to the far side of the language of the passions, hiding his own body from their assault but not
without revealing his own passion for carnal knowledge, power, and
perversion, as shall be evident from several of the following essays.

I might have set each essay in alphabetical order. Roland Barthes has
argued that this is not a logical device but a psychological one, so to speak.
Because the alphabet represents no natural order, it liberates the reader to
pursue texts that operate their own seduction. It serves readers' pleasure
by allowing mood, purpose, curiosity, or use to engage them. For this
reason, any introduction can hardly look better than the wrapping on a
present, which in our culture we do not enjoy for itself (another primal
scene of sibling rivalry?) but tear off to get at our desire. Still, an introduction might serve the reader's forepleasure and so I have placed "first"
William Kerrigan's exploration of the Renaissance shift in the rate at
which we seek cultural (dis)content. This is the tradition of Bacon, Shakespeare, and Milton and, of course, of Hobbes. All these thinkers understood the restlessness and insecurity of the modern world as a self-
consuming artifact analogous to the mechanism of forepleasure operative
in poetry and philosophy, in science as in economics: "The competitive
drive for infinite glory or infamy is, as Milton and others saw, an infirmity
because it is like the drive for knowledge. You get a little fame. If you are
not going to get any more, if that is all the fame you will have, the grandiose individual will feel his fixed amount of fame as an insufficience, an
injustice, a slight. Fame is little foreplay. When it is not increasing, it leads
to the unpleasure of frustration" (Chapter 1).

By the same trope of forepleasure, I risk challenging the reader to sustain the seduction of the "following" essays until a climax is reached and is
repeated in Laurence Rickels's extraordinary reflections on how the twin
passions of love and hatred revolve around the maternal lost-object. So, to
repeat the question of the beginning: I then thought that having raised the
issue of a pleasurable start, I should play off the pleasure principle in Kerrigan's essay with Donald Carveth's essay on how Freud needed to find his
way from a biological to a culturological model of the conflict between
life and death that the passionate body lives from its first to last breath:

> on the margins of his final ego psychological model in which the
> subject's passions are ultimately reduced to sexual and aggressive
> drives and drive-related affects and fantasies together with their

various combinations or compromise-formations are such, by no means incompatible, notions as: the subject's desire to reestablish the oceanic bliss of primary narcissism (Freud 1930, chap. 1); to recapture the omnipotence and perfection of the "purified pleasure ego" (Freud 1914, 1915) in which everything that is good or pleasurable is "me" while everything unpleasurable or bad is "not-me"; to find an object that always represents the "re-finding" of the primary object, the maternal breast (Freud 1905, 222); to finally circumvent the paternal prohibition and achieve the longed-for (and dreaded) incestuous consummation; to bask in the secure protection of an idealized, all-powerful father image transferred unto the universe at large (Freud 1927); or even to reestablish the Nirvana-like quiescence of inorganic life (Freud 1920). (Chapter 2)

Whether Freud marginalized the pleasurable passions or allowed them to break the dike of aggressive rationality only late in life—on the model of the decline of civilization—is an issue pursued in Kathleen Woodward's remarks on Freud's *Moses and Monotheism* (1934–38) as well as in my own essay on Freud's *Leonardo da Vinci*. The issue here concerns the role of sublimation and the possibility of transcending conflict on the levels of sexuality and society through a third-order sublimation of the mastery of science and the mystery of art. Since my own essay deals with the detail of this argument, especially the complex question of sublimation, I shall simply put the conclusion that the passionate mind is not driven by repression but is rather opened up through a sexualization that is in turn opened up to mind—each escaping the economy of scarcity and dissatisfaction that for the most part Freud believed to be the human condition. But for this to occur, as it does in Leonardo's portraits of Leda or of John the Baptist, for example, there must also occur a recognition of the circulation of sexual difference in oneself through the other's difference. This is necessary so that the struggle between the sexes is overcome in the reconciliation of their desire of one another: "These pictures breathe a mystical air into whose secret one dares not to penetrate. . . . The figures are still androgynous, but no longer in the sense of the vulture-phantasy. They are beautiful youths of feminine delicacy and with effeminate forms; they do not cast their eyes down, but gaze in mysterious triumph, as if they knew of a great achievement of happiness, about which silence must be kept" (*Penguin Freud Library* 14:210; *SE* 11:117).

Now I cannot resist narrativizing the essays by Kathleen Woodward, Claire Kahane, and Mary Jacobus. In view of the contemporary ideology of the passions as those desirable, searchable, and unavoidable moments of self-discovery, knowledge and empowerment, it is startling to see how Kathleen Woodward sets limits to the feminist appropriation of male anger as an "emotion of choice" by showing how Freud struggled to reveal man's passion for the restraint of passion:

> for Freud the regulating emotion of guilt emerges inevitably from a primal psychology of the emotions, from the tension or ambivalence between hate and love, the emotional representatives of the two basic drives: the drive to aggressivity (power) and the libidinal drive (sexual desire). In Freud's view guilt is both genetic and structural to the human psyche from the moment of the constitution of civilization that is, the founding moment of the sons revolting against the father). If love and hate are the two primary emotions, guilt is a secondary emotion, entailing self-consciousness. Guilt is the third term, unsettling and oppressive yet paradoxically also stabilizing.... Like a point on a nuclear thermostat, guilt works homeostatically to maintain a fluctuating equilibrium between love and hate, to regulate the temperature, to keep things cool. (Chapter 4)

Woodward is not appealing to guilt in order to reject the simple sexist inversion expressed in feminization by anger. She is calling for a civilized sublimation of anger in any human being. Here, as I have said, Freud's studies of Michelangelo's Moses and Leonardo da Vinci's Madonnas, as well as Freud's own self-analysis, are especially important.

Yet we know that Freud—above all in his principal case histories—hardly managed to maintain his ideal of a dispassionate stance upon the passions that otherwise gripped his patients. As Claire Kahane shows, the Dora case nicely reveals how Freud fell into the trap of a sexual discourse in which he was as much seduced as his young patient. Dora's story weaves into his own case, pushing back into a primal scene that is completely schizzed by Freud's fantasy of fellatio imposed upon the "kiss scene" between Dora and Herr K. Even while drifting off around his own cigar/phallus, Freud was determined to impose a heterosexual frame upon events that resisted such interpretation. Increasingly he expresses anger at Dora for maintaining resistance to psychoanalysis:

> Although Freud, in his quest for scientific status, attempted to give dispassionate accounts of his patient's histories, intending them to

> serve as the ground for his metaphysical speculation, it was Freud
> who empowered us to hear the passions in the very act of enuncia-
> tion, to theorize enunciation itself as a form of passion, an eroti-
> cally compelling oral/aural exchange between voice and ear,
> speaker and listener. Indeed, Freud's talking cure specifically elic-
> its and utilizes the passions of that exchange in and through the
> discursive connection between analyst and analysand. (Chapter 5)

The passions are all spectacle and all-consuming. They rule us—we
subject ourselves to them—in a drama of the soul that reaches beyond
the countervailing political, social, and economic interests that reduce
us to civil conduct and our contentment with peace, order, and good
governance. By the same token, we are (like Dora) resistant to psychoanalysis because it, too, is ambivalently anarchic and authoritarian. We
want Dora's passionate struggle with Freud to survive her exhibition in
the clinic. We do not want her passion for Frau K to turn her into a
man—a stage-door Johnny or a courtier—because we want to see how
the passions transgress and override the sexes, seeking something beyond them. And like Dora we may yearn for passionate suspension
before the Madonna although we know very well that in the end the
dream will have to be all tidied up as in a Shakespearean play, so that
everyone can go home. Of course, we never quite return home. For it
is in the family that the passions brood and flare, or subside, unre-
solved. At home, we are not offstage but find ourselves on that other
stage where the pre- and post-Oedipal drama is a daily thing, at times
brilliantly clear, at others cruelly obscure. To escape, we lift the family
romance onto our own bodies like those great actors whose passions
fill our books, screens, and music, or like the Holy Family, the saints
and heroes to whom we devote a Sunday hour.

The scheme of things that rules the Dora case is very similar to that
revealed by Mary Jacobus in her essay on the case of homosexuality in
terms of the psychogenesis of the passions, the enigma of suicide, and
the delirium of censorship. Freud identifies the girl's passion for ladies
with a male pursuit while claiming that she is feminized by her display of
passion. The daughter's choice of a maternal object arouses in Freud a
feminine identification that he resists throughout the analysis—as he did
in the case of Dora. The patient's suicide attempt is analyzed in terms of
the pre-Oedipal organization of the passions in which love and hate are
not yet opposites. Thus the woman suffers from an inability either to
mourn the loss of the maternal body or to repudiate it entirely:

when it comes to Freud's discussion of the ways in which the girl resembles her father and his list of the girl's "masculine" intellectual attributes—"her acuteness of comprehension and her lucid objectivity, *in so far as she was not dominated by her passion*" (my emphasis; *SE* 18:154)—he tends to associate passion, to the contrary, with an aberration: She is masculine in her passion, but her passion makes her *less* masculine, *less* like her father. Passion turns out to be a form of masquerade (of courtly love, of masculinity) whose meaning is reversed—much as Lacan alleges, apropos of "the phallic mark of desire," that "virile display itself appears as feminine." In Freud's gender-scheme, it is masculine to desire the lady, but feminine to make a virile display a phallic desire. Loving a woman as a man might do (Freud's earlier definition of Dora's "gynaecophilia") takes on the paradoxical appearance of femininity. (Chapter 6)

If I may say so, the theme of homosexual resistance inhabits all of the present essays. I believe it constitutes the very basis of Freud's theory of the psychogenesis of the passions, should one try to systematize it. In the two previous cases, Freud was spurned even though he had identified with the woman-in-the-woman who had surrendered to such passion! Along these lines, we may also see Freud drawing upon his own body the stigmata of castration not only as loss but in a defiant rejection of the phallus—an enigma that brings psychoanalysis to its very limits. To put it another way, the limit question of psychoanalysis is, How do we want to be divided? This is how I read John Forrester's essay on the Judgment of Solomon upon the two mothers disputing ownership of the baby one had stolen from the other. Here nothing so divides us from ourselves and one another as the knife of envy:

> Envy as a fundamental fact of psychic life is well known in two different psychoanalytic theories, both of which have had rather mixed fortunes. The first is Freud's thesis that a little girl becomes a woman via the transformation of penis envy into the wish for a baby. Aligning his theory of general social envy with the specific theory of penis envy reveals immediately their closeness of fit, if I can put it like that. The primal scene of penis envy is very similar to the primal scene of envy in general: the girls, like the sibling, *see* the other child with an object that she thinks gives him complete satisfaction, and she falls prey to envy. What is missing when Freud discusses envy of the penis compared with envy in

general is the subsequent reaction-formation: the identification with the other child and the clamorous demand for equality. (Chapter 7)

Better no child than to envy another woman's motherhood—or better to lose one's motherhood than to envy another woman's child. Better, then, to lose the breast/penis than to see another devour it? Is that the underlying source of our passion for justice and equality, as Forrester suggests, in line with Freud and Nietzsche's naughty analysis of the transformation of the social passions?

Inasmuch as we also think of the passions—whether for food, knowledge, jewelry, or music—as never serviced by their objects but rather by our selves as their willing/unwilling servant, I think Jerome Neu's essay invites us to explore the phenomenology of ambivalence whose effect is to deprive our passions from completion:

> That we should hate people we love because they abuse or betray us presents no mystery. After all, people are mixed bags and so there is no problem about loving them in some respects while hating them in others. The interesting question is why we should hate people precisely because we love them (presuming even that they love us back, that it is not unrequited love). Part of the answer, I think, is that love brings with it dependence, and so vulnerability and risk—so we naturally come to resent those we love because we love them, because it makes us dependent. The next, deeper question is why or whether dependence should be thought of as hateful (rather than merely risky). So far as our identities are at stake in love, death enters the picture and helps make extreme fear (which so often functions as a source of hate) intelligible. The naturalness of ambivalent love and hate may thus connect with problems of self-identity. (Chapter 3)

To exceed ambivalence is to court death. Once this step is taken, we are swept up by passions that move us either by their quality or by their quantity. To hate greatly is better than to love lightly. Half in love with death, we want passions rid of moderation or of ambivalence: either to relive the fall from grace or else to assume a terrible divinity. In this mood we are not concerned with ethics or with practical reason in respect of the passions; the game is over by then. The passions are at work in mysticism, science, gambling, addiction, and love. The common element is the relation of absolute need that unites the subject with the object of passion rather than anything peculiar to their respective nature. Passion is a relationship that cannot be foregone, ignored, or abandoned. Most of us can never simply hate. We can never love and love alone. Hence our fascination with those figures of theater, opera, and film who appear to be nothing but an undivided passion, magnificently full—even to death.

Our collective refusal to believe what it might be better for us to know repeats on the level of the individual what Ellie Ragland-Sullivan, after Lacan, calls our passion for ignorance. Here she analyzes our passionate insistence upon suppressing our symbolic grasp of what would otherwise disrupt our imaginary self with the realization that it has been abandoned by the Other to whom it continues to address its love:

> Love, hate and ignorance are paths that concern *being* in terms of the three lines of division—real, symbolic, imaginary—in which any person is engaged when realizing himself symbolically in speech. Indeed, in the act of speaking, one homes in on the being of the other. Put another way, love wishes the unfolding of the being of the other, and hate, the debasement of the other's being (1988a, 276–77). But what does it mean to say ignorance— which aims at one's own being—is a passion? Trying to describe passion, Lacan calls it "something like a third dimension, the space, or rather the volume, of human relations in the symbolic relation." "But it is only in the dimension of being, and not in that of the real," Lacan says, "that the three fundamental passions can be inscribed—at the junction of the symbolic an imaginary, this fault line . . . called *love*—at the junction of the imaginary and the real, *hate*—and at the junction of the real and the symbolic, ignorance (1988a, 271). (Chapter 8)

Our passion for ignorance determines the fortitude with which we hold on to our suffering, as did Dora throughout her life, and more so Wolf Man. But for this suffering to be borne it must be deeply buried, or encrypted in memories, language, dreams, objects, and stories that serve to remind us of what must never otherwise come to mind—short of analysis. Perhaps, then, this ignorance is the enigma contained in Leonardo da Vinci's lone woman and doubled Madonna whose loss fueled in him the passion for scientific knowledge examined in my own essay. Did Leonardo encrypt in the smile and the story of the little bird his lifelong refusal to abandon the edible mother? Is that why Mona Lisa and John the Baptist smile to one another, if not at us? In such flights of fancy we encounter the inextricable knot of knowledge and error around which the passionate analyst must construct a truth as slowly as an oyster builds a pearl upon a grain of sand. No doubt this work begins in adolescence—or in a second infancy worked over after the fact (*Nachträglich*) of m(other) abandonment whose recapture by Freud constitutes the youth of psychoanalysis itself:

> In these primal moments, just as in the *Gradiva* novella, we find a kind of primal scene in which the passion for love and death stand together—Freud's love for the mother and other mother and their death through a double entombment, one of whom was very much a Gradiva at this time. The affects associated with these scenes are returned to Freud during his adolescence and produce within him both a fascination and a fear of young women. Death is the theme that ties all the figures, the nursemaid, the mother, the sister, the brother, Gisela, and Eduard, together. (Chapter 10)

Puberty or liberty? Tenderness and passion: a space between childhood and adulthood that we find so acutely analyzed in Miles's essay on Freud's *Gradiva*. If only one could learn to love in youth as one had loved and lost in infancy, Freud seems to say. Or if only one could be saved forever in the seduction of an insouciant mother, the model of all passivity, pathos, and cool passion, resistant to the dividing Law. To experience passion we need to be wholly consumed by something other than ourself: by the loved one's beauty or by the enigma of her narcissistic self-absorption. At the same time, we demand that the beloved one love us for no other reason than that we love her: "When we meet again you may be disappointed on finding that I look different from the lovely picture your tender imagination has painted of me. I don't want you to love me for qualities you assume in me, in fact not for any qualities you assume in me, in fact not for any qualities; you must love me as irrationally as other people love, just because I love you, and you don't have to be afraid of it" (Freud to Martha Bernays, 16 January 1884).[2]

Freud's concept of the passions is entirely narcissistic. He regarded love's passion (to anticipate Lacan) as nothing but a *narcissisme à deux,* since a man's love for a woman is entirely a projection of his own, while a woman, as Freud believed, can love only herself. What fascinates a man is a woman's plenitude and his own emptiness. The bridge between the two is the child through whom the woman again loves herself while reawakening in the man his first lost love. Thus Freud's passion for his mother remained the analytic model of all the passions, even the libido itself, as is evident from his study of Leonardo da Vinci. *Carpe matrem!* Like Leonardo and other youths, Freud brooded more than he loved, bound forever to listening to the mother-body, to catch Nature's secrets and to repress her death. What of the father, then? Dead meat—the substitute mother-meal—prepared by jealous brothers hiding Freud who put them up to the primal murder. *Trauerspiel*—tossing and retrieving the mother-body, that body a child loses each time there is another body in hers—another murder to be wished for and mourned ever after. The death wish is the brat's cover for the lost mother whose death Freud most feared and bore inside himself like a cancer owed to Nature rather than to God. Thus the passion play of psychoanalysis repeats itself throughout the case histories so brilliantly explored by Laurence Rickels as exhumations of passions buried alive, releasing ghosts and rats not laid to rest by the dead father:

> In the case study of Rat Man and in Freud's own case we find the motive force of the unmournable—and doubly unacknowl-edged—death of child and sibling which is the rehearsal, and, then, repetition of the death of the father, the guarantor of proper mourning. Thus in many cases—Rat Man, Schreber, and Wolf Man, for example—Freud encountered difficulties on two fronts, specifically in superimposing the dead sibling onto the father's corpse. And yet both deaths, the mournable and the unmournable, pressed to find simultaneous broadcast. Other-wise psychoanalytic theory would have been left to founder on the two deaths on which it was founded. (Chapter 11)

At another level, of course, Freud's case histories derive their appeal from the very same theater of the passions that Charcot had presented every Tuesday at the hospital of Saltpêtrière attended by Freud in the early days of his career.[3] There Freud was caught up in the same chal-lenge that the uncontrollable fits and rages of hysterical bodies offer to the devotees of reason, order, and control. By the same token, the prac-tice of psychoanalysis was from the outset trapped in the erotics of a male science imposing itself upon a female body (see Chapter 6)—not that Freud was unaware of male hysteria, especially in himself. Precisely because of these transgressive possibilities, it was essential to the profes-sional future of Freud's science that the passions be removed from the scene of psychoanalysis. For however outrageous Freud's theory of sexu-ality may appear to readers, it is still quite distant from the passions that are the unanalyzed/unanalyzable residue of hysteria, neurosis, and psychosis. What was Dora's fixation before the Madonna; what was the passion for bottoms in Wolf Man and Rat Man, or Freud's own passion for cigars? We might also ask about the repression of the passion for madness and for the occult that is never quite complete in Freud's struggle with their effects. And so they return, however cryptically.

At the end of the day, perhaps we ought to speak of our ignorance of the passions rather than insist upon our knowledge of them, especially if we do not hold that the passions are molecular forces that explain our behavior without belonging to the same grammar of understanding through which we ordinarily account for ourselves. This, I think, is the insight in Lacan's account of our need to go beyond our denial of the family events that constitute the passions from which we suffer by demanding that others confirm our obstinacy. We are passionate because we are ignorant and we are ignorant because we desire not to know how we love, hate, envy, submit, or dominate. The pain of such ignorance constitutes its bliss, and our endurance of it represents a mode of *jouissance.* The blindness of the passions lies in our ability to look away from ourselves even when we look into the eyes of other selves whom we love whom we hate.

NOTES

1. John O'Neill, *Essaying Montaigne: A Study of the Renaissance Institution of Writing and Reading* (London: Routledge and Kegan Paul, 1982).

2. *The Letters of Sigmund Freud,* selected and edited by Ernest L. Freud, translated by Tania and James Stern (New York: Basic Books, 1960).

3. William J. McGrath, *Freud's Discovery of Psychoanalysis: The Politics of Hysteria* (Ithaca: Cornell University Press, 1986).

1

Macbeth and the History of Ambition

WILLIAM KERRIGAN

As Gordon Braden and I finished our recent book *The Idea of the Renaissance,* I realized that we were in a position to make an interesting psychological observation about this period. The considerable materials of our study dovetailed so neatly with a particular Freudian mechanism of forepleasure that I would have to claim, if our notions about how to organize the period's preoccupations were sound, that the Renaissance was the great age of this mechanism, a time when culture, politics, and even the sexual life were reimaged so as to install forepleasure in the fundamental ambitions of European man.

The mechanism I have in mind is by no means center stage in Freud's work. Its best-known appearance comes at the end of "Creative Writers and Day-Dreaming," where Freud, noting how the formal properties of literature give us a certain degree of pleasure but also prompt us to seek more pleasure, speaks of an "incentive bonus" or "forepleasure"—a yield of largely formalistic fun that like a bonus inspires us to work for more fun.[1]

A fuller discussion occurs in the *Three Essays on Sexuality.* Here Freud offers a quite straightforward and unobjectionable account of foreplay, the same old story, the standard plot of sexual excitement. I look; I am excited, so I touch; I am still more excited, so I kiss; and so on, with many delightful detours, until intercourse and orgasm. Such forepleasure, Freud maintains, is in its incremental structure importantly unlike the pleasure principle. In the pleasure mechanism tension and disequilibrium are followed by satiety and renewed equilibrium, the model being an infant getting hungry, crying out, being fed, and then, equilibrium regained, going to sleep. But the pleasure in sexual foreplay serves to increase, not reduce tension, just as the offer of an incentive bonus will increase the amount of work. I touch, I receive a certain amount of pleasure. But if I am not going to get more, if the plot is for some reason arrested, this pleasure quickly becomes the unpleasure of frustration. At the end of the same old story, orgasm's discharge reestablishes the calculus of the pleasure principle, but the earlier pleasure is sufficiently different from the tension-discharge model to require its own name; Freud proposes to call it the mechanism of forepleasure or the forepleasure principle (*SE* 7:210–12). But he has surprisingly little use for it, perhaps because he does not have much to say about the passion to which this mechanism is wed in the history of Western culture: ambition. The intellectuals of the Renaissance were the first explorers of the kinds and styles of forepleasure.

In new conceptions of knowledge, for example. It is one of the recurrent features of Greek, and later of medieval thought, that stillness, rest, immutability, and the like, are signs of perfection. Thus Aristotle in *De anima:* "Thinking has more resemblance to a coming to rest or arrest than to movement" (407A). Most of us think of romanticism as having made a concerted effort to uproot this old conviction. To take examples from both ends of romanticism, we have Blake projecting energy and desire into the realms of transcendence, and Wallace Stevens sardonically implying that no one (certainly no hedonist) could bear the traditional heaven, where the ripe fruit never falls. Contemporary theorists often present us with a series of dichotomies pitting terms like closure, determinacy, and product against terms like openness, indeterminacy, and process, where the first set of terms is assumed to be conservative, stodgy, or cowardly, and a great rhetorical effort is made to convince us that we really do prefer indeterminacy and process to their opposites. If such a preference has come to seem matter-of-fact rather than preposterous, it is in part because seductive intellectuals over the last five hundred years have sold us on the grandeur of voyages beyond comprehension.

The figure with whom intellectual histories of the Renaissance customarily begin, Nicholas of Cusa, spun the conceptual apparatus of the Middle Ages in just this direction. Geometry for Plato was a prime example of still perfection; Nicholas asks us to imagine a circle, then, introducing explosive motion, asks us to blow it up to infinity. The intellect, he maintained, desires the incomprehensible, not the fixed or the delimited. Here is Nicholas imagining beatitude:

This enjoyment does not pass away into a past, because the appetite does not fade away during the enjoyment. [The situation is] as if—to use an illustration from the body—someone hungry were seated at the table of a great king, where he was supplied with the food he desired, so that he did not seek any other food. The nature of this food would be [such] that in filling him up it would also whet his appetite. . . . And so, he would always be able to eat; and, after having eaten, he would still be able to be led to the food with whetted appetite.[2]

This Cusan food both satisfies and whets the appetite. The very domain of Freud's pleasure principle—food's satisfaction of appetite—here makes room for the incremental increases of the forepleasure principle. The Gargantua of Rabelais is born crying "Drink, drink, drink!" and the wanderings of his troubled son, Pantagruel or "Allathirst," conclude at the Oracle of the Holy Bottle, whose advice is to drink: the entire work is a prolonged comic tribute to the divinity of appetite. One also thinks inevitably of Cleopatra:

> Age cannot wither her, nor custom stale
> Her infinite variety. Other women cloy
> The appetites they feed, but she makes hungry
> Where mosᵗ. she satisfies.
>
> (2.2.234–37)[3]

We have gone from heavenly to earthly knowing. But Shakespeare, too, cannot imagine perfect love without removing satiety from appetite. Love is transformed into unending hunger.

Milton locates the paradox of satisfaction and excess in the mind of man. Though God commands us to observe the limits of "temperance, justice, continence," yet he "pours out before us, even to profuseness, all desirable things, and gives us minds that can wander beyond all limit and satiety."[4] Such is the condition of our virtue and our vice. The narrator's address to Adam and Eve in *Paradise Lost* resounds with the wish for limitation. After making love our general parents have fallen asleep, the daily concession to satiety:

> Sleep on,
> Blest pair; and O yet happiest if ye seek
> No happier state, and know to know no more.
>
> (4.773–75)

"Sleep on" stands for the status quo of happiness. This happiest state seems to contain its own fortification against change, as the "on," reversed, becomes the temperate "no" to apparently happier states. Three audacious cannon shots of "no" in "know to know no" confound the very enunciation of "more" in echoing refusals. But if there is indeed more to know, how can the human mind not wander beyond all limit and satiety? The forepleasure structure implicit in knowing is our doom in paradise. To wit: you get some knowledge; if you are not going to get more knowledge, the amount you have will be felt as unknowledge or ignorance, a painful limitation betraying what the mind was made to do. In fallen history we don't know to know no more no more.

Were there world enough and time I would discuss the equilibrium of utopia and the persistent disturbance of this equilibrium by dystopian irony, but I move on from knowledge to fame.

Fame was of course a major preoccupation of the cultures of antiquity, especially the Roman. One of the things I remember best from high school Latin is Cicero's repeated emphasis on "honos et gloriae": his unquestioned assumption that life is really about honor and glory. This is precisely the worldly culture that Saint Augustine, the great architect of medieval Christianity, attacked so decisively in *The City of God.* The revival of this theme in the Renaissance is one of the clearest instances of a break with the Middle Ages, much of whose literature is so uninterested in individualized fame as to be anonymous. Renaissance authors, educated by humanists, openly thematized their immortal longings. What did it mean, after all, to be learned? To know who was famous, and for what, and to gain fame for oneself by continuing their fame.

Eventually the educational program of Renaissance humanism would produce John Milton, its ideal pupil, whose lifelong ambition was to leave something so written to aftertimes that they would not willingly let it die. Fame, he wrote in "Lycidas," is that last infirmity of noble mind; and the emphasis in this famous line probably falls on "noble," the implication being that ignoble minds are distraught by lesser infirmities. Yet as Jakob Burckhardt realized, fame in the Renaissance had its black wing in the deliberate cultivation of infamy, which in Italy produced a new style of criminality: the vendetta brought Seneca to life in dire acts of vengeance demanding recognition for their artfulness. Burckhardt's great chapter on the modern idea of fame ends with the cautionary tale of Herostratos.[5] He burned to the ground the temple of Artemis at Ephesos (according to Herodotus one of the seven wonders of the ancient world), and when asked under torture why he did it, replied, "To make my name known." It was immediately agreed by those present that his name would never be spoken, but somehow the ancient media learned of his crime, and thus we know his name today. No story could reveal more clearly that, despite the emphasis in humanist education on the goodness of fame-lust, the logic of renown is not the logic of virtue.

The competitive drive for infinite glory or infamy is, as Milton and others saw, an infirmity because it is like the drive for knowledge. You get a little fame. If you are not going to get any more, if that is all the fame you will have, the grandiose individual will feel his fixed amount of fame as an insufficiency, an injustice, a slight. Fame is like foreplay. When it is not increasing, it leads to the unpleasure of frustration.

Finally, a word about power. Bacon distinguishes empire from other forms of the state on the basis of its capacity for continual enlargement. But it was Hobbes, a writer much attuned to Renaissance themes, who saw the mechanism most clearly in his analysis of political power. "For the nature of power is in this point like to fame, increasing as it proceeds; or like the motion of heavy bodies, which the further they go, make still the more haste."[6] The career of power is restlessness itself. You gain some. You must then gain more, lest the amount you have be felt as insecure. There's beggary in the power that can be reckoned. To secure itself, power must always be in a state of escalation.

Knowledge, fame, love, power. All of them in their Renaissance forms are driven by the insistent need for *more.* It looks as if the mechanism of my own argument should force me to adduce evidence that the Renaissance preferred foreplay to orgasm. I can. There is a minor genre in the seventeenth-century lyric called the "anti-fruition" poem, in which males indicate their disappointment with the design of the sexual act.[7] In these not altogether playful lyrics, way off in the corner of Renaissance poetry, I read the signature of the age: a preference in expressly sexual terms for the incremental pleasure of foreplay. The main complaint against orgasm in these poems is precisely that it *is* a limit, settling for some finite satisfaction: an outcome governed by the pleasure principle.

Romantic culture normalized the various expressions of the Renaissance mechanism. Lyrics plumbed bottomless griefs and soared to topless exultations. The boundless, more than beautiful, announced the sublime. Philosophy welcomed all varieties of infinity. Kant cannot conceive of history without the pressure of relentless dissatisfaction:

> if we assume there to be a constant progress and approach to the supreme good (that is set out as his goal), mankind still (even with such consciousness of the unchangeableness of his char-

acter) cannot connect *contentedness* with the prospect of his
state (both moral and physical) lasting through eternal change.
For the state in which he is now always remains an evil one by
comparison with the better one into which he is preparing himself to enter, and the representation of an unending progress
toward the ultimate end is nonetheless at the same time one
prospect in an unending sequence of evils, which, though they
will surely be outweighed by the greater good, do not yet allow
contentedness to prevail, a contentedness he can think of only by
finally attaining the ultimate end.[8]

In this, as in other liberal conceptions of progress, self-repudiation is
history's engine. The evil to be avoided above all others is contentment.
But during the Renaissance moral strictures inherited from medieval
Christianity were still strong enough to condemn, however ambivalently, the new experiments in drivenness. Most of the great writers of
the period were deeply divided over the mechanism that in other contexts constituted their vision of excitement. Thus Petrarch, though suffering from a well-documented case of fame-lust, was still ashamed of
this immoderation, and often sounds the notes of medieval moralism:

> Sleep is driven away by sleeping, weariness
> by repose, and hunger by food, while thirst
> is quenched by moderate drinking.
> Astonishing as this may be, greed alone is
> whetted by acquiring.[9]

What is true of greed ought to be true, he adds, undoing his own moral
clarity, of our "desire for knowledge and passion for letters." Petrarch is
mistaken to suppose that happiness lies in the proper location of the
mechanism. For the mechanism itself wherever it is encouraged breeds
an unhappy restlessness, as Petrarch elsewhere realizes: "Moderation in
all kinds of fortune is like gold; and human happiness without setting a
limit to itself is eager to advance, and extending into infinity brings with
it not only a great deal of anxiety, but nothing enduring, nothing certain,
nothing peaceful."[10] Nonetheless, despite such wavering awareness, we
find throughout the best work of the period an imaginative indulgence
in limitless ambitions. Something in the Renaissance mind resisted what
little nature has given us of stillness, rest, and peace.

If this thesis about Renaissance culture has merit, there ought to be a
Shakespeare play that is centrally and unmistakably about the fore-

pleasure mechanism. It would scarcely make sense to offer a description of Renaissance culture that had no fix on its greatest writer. This play, I submit, is *Macbeth,* his tragedy of "vaulting ambition."

The first of several moments of great epochal force in this play is Lady Macbeth's promise that she would, if sworn to do it, pluck her nipple from the boneless gums of an infant at her breast, "while it was smiling in my face," and dash its brains out (1.7.54–59). On the one hand, she means that she would, if she were sworn to do it, as Macbeth is sworn to murder Duncan, commit the most terrible crime imaginable for her gender. Her violent fantasy also betrays her contempt for softened manhood. I feel sure that baby she has in mind is a male, too full of milk and therefore in danger of becoming an unambitious or feminine male. In Holinshed we are told that Scottish mothers often denied the breast to their infants in order to produce superior warriors.[11]

Her vow is heavy with decision. The infant smiling at the breast is the pleasure principle's supreme benefactor. She will dash its brains out because another mechanism is to drive their ambitions, and its fuel is blood, not milk. The fantasy strikes at satiety, ambition's earliest enemy. Her husband's best-known fantasy completes in masculine terms the logic of the murdered infant. The dagger that Macbeth sees before him, handle toward his hand, is the hallucinated embodiment of his murderous will. Insofar as Lady Macbeth has excited that will, you do not need to be all that much of a Freudian to regard the dagger, when "gouts of blood" begin to stream from it, as an ejaculating penis—the penis, I would call it, of the Renaissance mechanism, insatiate, pumping ever more blood, inundating blood, multitudinous seas of it, blood so thick that Macbeth will feel that he is wading in it. Once shed, the blood just won't stop flowing, and won't, of course, be washed away. Freud wrote of this play in an essay whose title has hovered unmentioned over my essay: "Those Wrecked by Success."[12]

The anguish of Macbeth is particularly germane to the transformation in Western ambition I have been trying to discuss. Gaining the crown, which would seem to be the zenith of worldly ambition, is as nothing to him without the perpetuation of his power through succession. The great vision of Banquo's children occupying the throne in an unbroken line stretched out to doomsday is received by Macbeth as utter annihilation:

> They hailed him father to a line of kings.
> Upon my head they plac'd a fruitless crown,
> And put a barren sceptre in my grip,
> Thence to be wrench'd with an unlineal hand,

No son of mine succeeding. If't be so,
For Banquo's issue have I fil'd my mind,
For them the gracious Duncan have I murther'd,
Put rancors in the vessel of my peace
Only for them, and mine eternal jewel
Given to the common enemy of man,
To make them kings—the seeds of Banquo kings!

(3.1.60–70)

It strikes me that the emotion in this speech is very close to that of the cuckold. It is as if Banquo has seized Macbeth's bed rights, and fashioned children in the womb of his queen. Fame-lust, with its driven need for more, here confronts tragic limitations. Macbeth holds a barren scepter: his barren phallus is fused with his kingship, and no seed of his will inherit it. There is only, as it were, the ongoing orgasm of blood, which brings no peace, but rather sleeplessness, hunger, guilt. Macbeth has murdered the pleasure principle, and with its demise all satiety, all joys of limitation and enoughness, die too.

In the character of Macbeth, then, Renaissance fame-lust has been denied one of its customary channels. Fame, as Jonson suggests in a epithalamion, fused readily with the desire to procreate:

Haste, haste, officious sun, and send them night
    Some hours before it should, that these may know
All that their fathers, and their mothers might
    Of nuptial sweets, at such a season, owe,
        To propagate their names,
            And keep their fames
            Alive, which else would die,
For fame keep virtue up, and it posterity.[13]

Blocked in this area, Macbeth might express his fame-lust through a calculus of infamy—the way of Herostratos. But unlike Richard III, whose self-delighted villainy would "put the murderous Machevil to school," Macbeth (I suspect this is what critics mean when they sometimes remark that he is a "good" man) lacks any sense of a competitive magnificence in his villainy. He is never anything but grim. He is never done with bloodly deeds that cannot be undone. Bearing this desperation in mind, let's turn to the peculiar nihilistic numbness that overtakes Macbeth at the end of the play.

Driven Hobbes-like to commit murder upon murder to secure the

future of his present power, Macbeth in the end achieves something
oddly akin to the invulnerability he has ever craved:

> I have almost forgot the taste of fears.
> The time has been my senses would have cool'd
> To hear a night-shriek, and my fell of hair
> Would at a dismal treatise rouse and stir
> As life were in't. I have supp'd full of horrors.
> Direness, familiar to my slaughterous thoughts,
> Cannot once start me.
>
> (5.5.9–15)

"I have supp'd full of horrors." At the close of his career the hero of
vaulting ambition discovers an equilibrium resembling the peace of the
pleasure principle. But this is closer to desiccation than to ordinary
fullness, less the satisfaction of appetite than its death. "I have almost
forgot the taste of fears." In the end, there is no more pleasure in
forepleasure, and ambition's slave is incapable of arousal.

A servant informs Macbeth that the female shrieks unable to rouse him
marked the death of his queen. He then delivers his great speech on life's
meaninglessness, a famous crux in the historical understanding of literature. From the time I was an undergraduate, nearly thirty years ago, I
wondered, as I now know many have, how this writer, filled as he had to
be with Renaissance presuppositions and Renaissance experiences, was
able to imagine the unyielding nihilism of Macbeth. I believe now that I
have found a piece of the puzzle, a fragment of the subterranean Renaissance logic that arrives at this remarkable speech:

> She should have died hereafter;
> There would have been a time for such a word.
> To-morrow, and to-morrow, and to-morrow,
> Creeps in its petty pace from day to day,
> To the last syllable of recorded time;
> And all our yesterdays have lighted fools
> The way to dusty death. Out, out, brief candle!
> Life's but a walking shadow, a poor player
> That struts and frets his hour upon the stage
> And then is heard no more. It is a tale
> Told by an idiot, full of sound and fury,
> Signifying nothing.
>
> (5.5.17–28)

His huge disillusionment regards the meaninglessness, not of life in general but of *staged, told, heard, signified* life, and not of time in general but of *recorded* time. Why do these mean nothing? The recording of time, the actor being heard, the tale being told—these constitute the Renaissance media, the system within which fame is spread. Macbeth's empty tomorrows creep in their petty pace to the end of recorded time; which is to say, they measure out the entire future, the precise space of fame's possibility or *potentia.* Human lives are still registered for an audience, but the recording, staging, and telling no longer preserve the unique individuality of the dead; hence the total absence here of a eulogy for Lady Macbeth that would give some summary form to her existence and launch her memory into "tomorrow," the sphere of posthumous fame. Unlike Hamlet and Othello, who die profoundly intent on having their stories told properly, Macbeth is numb to recognition, and finds no comfort whatsoever in the anticipation of being remembered accurately. Fame (Latin *fama,* the spoken) becomes the sound and fury of an idiot's tale. Thus the nihilism of the speech can be understood more precisely as an attack on the futility of fame: a last despairing realization that he and his queen cannot succeed themselves through fame, that even this symbolic form of issue is not to be theirs. In *Macbeth* Shakespeare reckons the psychic cost of infamy's career as a disengagement from fame-lust.

But to catch the deepest nuance here we must think behind the speech, to a possible comfort that this mind could, but does not, allow itself. "Renown and grace is dead" (2.3.94), he discerns after the murder of Duncan. Yet his bloody deeds, which cannot be undone, might still achieve a dark celebrity. Macbeth's fundamental inability to revel in the thought of being remembered for his supremacy in villainy (what I earlier called, somewhat ironically, his goodness) plays a key role in producing this terminal vision. As A. C. Bradley remarked, Macbeth's unconscious "inner being is convulsed by conscience."[14] To that extent at least, Macbeth's nihilism is touched with a certain dogged nobility. The curse of the murdered pleasure principle brooks no exceptions: he can take no pleasure in his evil.

To behold the very preconditions of fame emptied of significance is despair of a distinctly Renaissance kind. How much it takes, in the imagination of this playwright, to construct a hero who will give voice to a complete dismissal of fame! He must commit heinous and damning murders, slaughtering the pleasure principle for the sake of ambition; he must suffer from the fate of childlessness; and finally he must retain enough conscience to repudiate the temptations of herostratic renown. Fame dies hard. The drives of Renaissance ambition are so tenacious and so compelling that only their supreme victim can hope to be free from them.

At this late date it is probably impossible for us to disengage our ambitions from the Renaissance mechanism. The magnificence of strife, the lure of beyondness, the romance of the ever-changing: passions driven by the forepleasure mechanism allow us to dream that we are, might once have been, or may one day be, gods, with "thoughts that wander through Eternity" (*Paradise Lost* 2.148). But we also inherit from the Renaissance an examination of the demonic futility of this brand of heroism. If we no longer believe in the supernatural or in damnation, we should still take away from the tragedy of Macbeth a healthy suspicion of vaulting ambition. As I look about me to the intellectual life in America today, I see a widespread political condemnation of our ways and traditions so fierce and unrelieved that it means to sicken us at the very thought of ourselves. I see theoreticians striving for a more and more powerful mastery of language and literature. I see careerism gone totally out of control, generating new jargons that seem to exist only to supply a place of dignity (lucrative dignity) for a priesthood able to manipulate them. I see minds desperate to overturn all certainties and expose the scandal in all assumptions. I see rampant dishonesty, as converts to the newest truth silently abandon yesterday's truth without admitting that they fell victim to an intellectual fad.

The thought of Nietzsche enjoys in our day the preeminence to which it aspired. He understood, as our designated prophet should, the terms of modern ambition:

> What is happiness?—The feeling that power *increases*—that a resistance is overcome.
>
> *Not* contentment, but more power; *not* peace at all, but war; *not* virtue, but proficiency (virtue in the Renaissance style, *virtu,* virtue free of moralic acid).[15]

Virtue as power, in other words, free of moral limits. Our heritage of contentment is in danger of being eclipsed altogether by the tradition of strife sublime.

Now is a good time to remind ourselves that we do not really need this continual agitation to secure our intellectual happiness. So kick back, American literati. Give littleness a place. Be content with less than everything. Make ambition the companion of self-deflating humor. Negotiate with immoderation: the road to excess leads also to the crumbling palace of despair. Hold in suspicion the rhetoric of escalating ambitions.

The true story of every age need not be the history of its moral contempt for itself. Guilt is real. We have no doubt envied and hated the great writers of the past. But have we killed these mighty Duncans who sleep in our castles? No. We are important, but not so important as that. Learn once again to be strong and self-contained. Our contentment may in the end require nothing more than sober observation, sharp wits, and sound learning, perennial virtues that have seen many happy minds through times of romantic extravagance.

NOTES

1. *The Standard Edition of the Psychological Works of Sigmund Freud,* ed. James Strachey (London: Hogarth, 1953–74), 9:152–53. Hereafter cited as *SE.*

2. *Nicholas of Cusa on Learned Ignorance,* ed. and trans. Jaspar Hopkins (Minneapolis: Arthur Banning Press, 1985), 155–56.

3. All references to Shakespeare in this essay use *The Riverside Shakespeare,* ed. G. Blakemore Evans et al. (Boston: Houghton Mifflin, 1974).

4. *Areopagitica* is quoted from *Complete Poems and Major Prose,* ed. Merritt Y. Hughes (New York: Odyssey, 1957), 733.

5. *The Civilization of the Renaissance in Italy,* trans. S. G. C. Middlemore, 2 vols. (New York: Harper, 1958), 1:162. For the conception of Fame as having two wings, one white and one black, see *Samson Agonistes* 973–74 in *Complete Poems,* 574.

6. *Leviathan* (Oxford: Clarendon Press, 1909), 66.

7. For details see Braden and Kerrigan, *The Idea of the Renaissance* (Baltimore: Johns Hopkins University Press, 1989), 182–88.

8. *Perpetual Peace and Other Essays,* trans. Ted Humphrey (Indianapolis: Hackett, 1983), 99.

9. *Rerum familiarum* 17.8, trans. Aldo S. Bernardo (Baltimore: Johns Hopkins University Press, 1985), 27.

10. *Rerum familarum* 3.7, trans. Aldo S. Bernardo (Albany: State University of New York Press, 1975), 131.

11. *The Description of Scotland* in *Holinshed's Chronicles of England, Scotland and Ireland,* 6 vols. (New York: AMS, 1965), 1:23–24.

12. This is the second section of "Some Character-Types Met with in Psycho-Analytic Work," in *SE* 14:316–24.

13. *Under-Wood* 75 in *The Complete Poems,* ed. George Parfitt (New Haven: Yale University Press, 1975), 222.

14. *Shakespearean Tragedy* (London: Penguin, 1991), 324.

15. *The Anti-Christ* 2 in *Twilight of the Idols and The Anti-Christ,* trans. R. J. Hollingdale (Harmondsworth: Penguin, 1968), 115–16. Nietzsche is no doubt thinking of his colleague Jakob Burckhardt, but on the subject of the endlessly restless will he may also be remembering Schopenhauer's pessimistic version of Platonic desire: "For all striving springs from want or deficiency, from dissatisfaction with one's own state or condition, and is therefore suffering so long as it is not satisfied. No satisfaction, however, is lasting; on the contrary, it is always merely the starting-point of a fresh striving." *The World as Will and Representation,* trans. E. F. J. Payne, 2 vols. (New York: Dover, 1969), 1:309.

2

Psychoanalytic Conceptions of the Passions

DONALD L. CARVETH

passion n. 1. strong emotion; outburst of anger (flew into a passion); sexual love; strong enthusiasm (for thing, for doing), object arousing this. 2. (P~). the sufferings of Christ on the Cross . . .

—Sykes (1982)

During the first of the four stages through which Freud's theory of resistance and repression gradually evolved "there were no fundamental passions, no irreducible forces determining our human nature. What mattered was simply what grew out of particular interpersonal encounters" (Greenberg and Mitchell 1983, 27). In this period during the 1890s psychic conflict was conceptualized as tension between the "dominant mass of ideas constituting the ego" (Breuer and Freud 1895, 116) and any impulses, affects, wishes, ideas, or memories that in some way threaten or contradict the self-concept. At this stage in Freud's thinking the *Ich* or "ego" referred not to the hypothetical control apparatus of his later structural ego psychology (Freud 1923), but rather to the "I"; that is, the subject's sense of self, self-image or self-representation.

How does the dominant mass of ideas become dominant? Freud is almost totally silent on this point during the early phase of his theorizing, yet his argument has some clear implications. What

become dominant are what we might today think of as "proper"
ideas, those which fit well with our view of ourselves as we
would prefer to be. They are socially sanctioned ideas which fit
well with our own values, standards, and morality. (Greenberg
and Mitchell 1983, 33)

In this first model, then, a socially conditioned self-image seeks to
preserve itself in the face of "incompatible ideas" (Breuer and Freud
1895, 167) through the repression of the latter. Social values and socialization pressures are associated with the repressing forces; and the
repressed is very loosely defined as a range of "incompatible" psychological and emotional contents associated with various interpersonal
situations. "The particular culture in which we live, its values and
standards, is crucial in determining which affects we find acceptable . . .
[and] which cannot be adequately discharged. . . . The theory is not
specific as to the fundamental nature of the stimuli with which the
psychic apparatus must deal" (Greenberg and Mitchell 1983, 27).
    In the second phase of his thinking regarding the nature of mental
conflict, Freud shifts away from the model in which "the tension between one's impulses and the social structure into which one must fit is
what determines repression" (Greenberg and Mitchell 1983, 34) and
begins, for a time, to conceptualize the repressing forces as biological
rather than social in nature. Although the repressed contents are themselves still broadly defined and not yet conceived in instinctual terms,
repression itself now comes to be seen as biologically based: " 'defense'
in the purely psychological sense has been replaced by organic 'sexual
repression' " (Freud 1906, 278).
    In keeping with his radical modification of the so-called seduction
theory of neurosis,[1] Freud now shifts the accent away from the role of the
social environment in neurosogenesis onto biological factors in his conceptualization of both the nature of the repressed (infantile sexual drives
and drive-related fantasies versus memories of abuse) and of repression
(an "organic" repression versus one motivated by the socially conditioned self-image). "In the same way that seduction has been replaced by
impulse, so has social restraint been replaced by innate aversion" (Greenberg and Mitchell 1983, 35). In the *Three Essays on the Theory of Sexuality,* Freud writes: "One gets an impression from civilized children that the
construction of these dams is a product of education, and no doubt education has much to do with it. But in reality this development is organically
determined and fixed by heredity, and it can occasionally occur without
any help at all from education" (Freud 1905, 177–78).

In the third phase of development of the theory of resistance and repression, Freud introduced his first instinctual dualism, the sexual and the self-preservative drives ("love versus hunger") (Freud 1905) as distinct from his later dualism of the life and death instincts ("love versus hate") (Freud 1920). After a period in which the repressed was conceived in largely noninstinctual and personalistic terms as composed of a wide range of situationally determined affects, impulses, ideas, and memories felt to be "incompatible" with the "ego" as self-image, Freud now becomes much more specific as to the instinctual nature of the repressed. Furthermore, in suggesting that "what he had earlier termed the self-preservative instincts might be thought of as 'ego instincts,' thus replacing the identification of the ego with the 'dominant mass of ideas' with an instinctual definition" (Greenberg and Mitchell 1983, 37), Freud continues his tendency, evident in phase 2 in the concept of an "organic repression," to see instinctual forces at work on both sides of the repression barrier (Freud 1910). "With this concept Freud defined the field of conflict (impulse versus repression) totally in instinctual terms" (Greenberg and Mitchell 1983, 37).

In the fourth and final phase of his development of the theory of resistance and repression, in his structural ego psychology Freud in one sense returns to his earliest model of psychic conflict as composed of socially conditioned forces in tension with "incompatible" elements of the personality (Freud 1923, 1926) But whereas in the earliest model the repressed was conceived in unspecific, personalistic terms, it is now composed of the psychic manifestations of Eros, the sexual or life instinct on the one hand and Thanatos, the death instinct or its outward manifestation as the aggressive drive on the other. Both serving and yet frequently opposing the sexual and aggressive drives is an "ego"—now no longer conceptualized in phenomenological or experiential terms but redefined as a hypothetical control apparatus—the task of which is to somehow reconcile the often conflicting demands of an "id" governed by the "pleasure principle" with a "superego" and "ego ideal" mediating what might be called a "morality principle" (albeit a primitive and often sadistic pseudo-morality) while seeking above all to adhere to the claims of the "reality principle."

Thus, from the earliest phase in which socially conditioned forces clash with a range of incompatible elements of our emotional life, to a second phase in which such elements are opposed by an "organic repression" and a third phase in which instinctual forces operate on both sides of the repression barrier, we arrive at the fourth and final phase in which a socially conditioned ego resorts to a range of defensive operations in the face of anxiety (Freud 1926). The latter is associated with a series of infantile danger-situations to which the ego feels itself exposed by the sexual and aggressive instinctual drives of the id, the reproaches and attacks of the superego, and the objective difficulties that face it in reality.

Although it is true up to a point to say that in this final theory Freud has produced a model of instinct versus society, it is important to avoid succumbing to the "oversocialized" (Wrong 1961) conception of the superego characteristic of the sociological assimilation of psychoanalytic ego psychology (see, e.g., Parsons 1962, 1964). While the superego, for Freud, certainly did involve the internalization of social morality via the parental conscience, as "heir to the Oedipus complex" (Freud 1923, 36) the superego more fundamentally represents the turning against the self of id aggression toward the Oedipal rival with whom the subject has come to identify.

It would be misleading to imply that Freud's conception of the passions could be limited to his final model of the sexual and aggressive drives and drive-related affects and fantasies as the fundamental motivating forces of human behavior—or even, more broadly, to the conceptions that represent earlier phases of his evolution of this metapsychological model. For although this certainly represents the end-result of his developing metapsychology, Freud's thinking always exceeded such formalization. For many of his interpreters it is precisely those elements of his thought that exist "on the margins" of the main line of his theoretical development that represent the most interesting aspects of Freudian theory.

Hence, on the margins of his final ego psychological model in which the subject's passions are ultimately reduced to sexual and aggressive drives and drive-related affects and fantasies together with their various combinations or compromise-formations are such, by no means incompatible, notions as: the subject's desire to reestablish the oceanic bliss of primary narcissism (Freud 1930, chap. 1); to recapture the omnipotence and perfection of the "purified pleasure ego" (Freud 1914, 1915) in which everything that is good or pleasurable is "me" while everything unpleasurable or bad is "not-me"; to find an object that always represents the "re-finding" of the primary object, the maternal breast (Freud 1905, 222); to finally circumvent the paternal prohibition and achieve the longed-for (and dreaded) incestuous consummation; to bask in the secure protection of an idealized, all-powerful father image transferred unto the universe at large (Freud 1927); or even to reestablish the Nirvana-like quiescence of inorganic life (Freud 1920).

In focusing in the following on Freud's explicit metapsychological model of the passions there is no intention to deny the existence or importance of such additional narrative lines in Freudian theory. It is merely to insist that the dominant story cannot be dismissed merely on the grounds that it is manifest. In my view, its critique is warranted if for no other reason than that it enjoyed for many years a hegemonic position in psychoanalytic discourse, at least in North America.

For anyone schooled in the oversocialized conceptions of the subject as a social product and performer that have tended to predominate in social theory, the major initial appeal of psychoanalysis might well be in its guise as an id psychology and instinct theory.[2] It is interesting to note that this aspect of the theory has figured large in the academic assimilation of psychoanalysis, even while the analysts themselves were extending Freud's later initiatives in the areas of ego psychology (A. Freud 1936; Hartmann 1939, 1964; Blanck and Blanck 1974) and object-relations theory (Guntrip 1971; Kernberg 1976; Greenberg and Mitchell 1983). Hence, psychoanalytic philosophers, such as Brown and Marcuse, neglecting the alternative Freuds upon whom mainstream psychoanalysis was building, chose to focus exclusively upon Freud the instinct theorist and endeavored to modify the Freudian psychobiology in the direction of Rousseauean romanticism and away from the Hobbesian pessimism of the master.

More than three decades have now passed since Wrong first drew attention to the fact that the social sciences have tended to portray the personality as either all superego (the moral subject of internalized norms; Riesman's inner-directed subject guided by an internal moral gyroscope) or all ego (Goffman's manipulator of impressions; the diviner of and conformer to social expectations in pursuit of self-esteem through attaining status in the eyes of significant others; Riesman's "other-directed" radar personality). But far from transcending the social determinism and sociological reductionism that characterized these earlier schools of thought, it can be argued that more recent paradigms, such as structuralism and poststructuralism, have merely represented the old sociologism in a different, albeit a fashionably Continental guise.

By offering a theory of instincts as countervailing forces in the personality clashing with the socially produced components of character and thus accounting for the experience of intrapsychic conflict, psychoanalysis has held great appeal for the critics of such sociologism. For now the socially internalized aspects of the self have to be seen as pitted against an unruly and essentially asocial and passionate instinctual core of the personality: the Freudian id. In the resulting conflicts between the ego-superego and the id, many have found a plausible explanation for psychic conflict, various types of deviant behavior, the inner costs of outward adjustment, problems of conscious and unconscious guilt, anxiety and self-punishment and many other hitherto incompletely comprehended human phenomena.

In the words of Rieff: "Freud, himself—through his mythology of the instincts—kept some part of character safe from society, restoring to the idea of human nature a hard core, not easily warped or reshaped by social experience" (Rieff 1959, 34–35). In this way, psychoanalysis was seen to offer a conception of nature (human nature) as a counterpart to culture, an instinctual individual self in tension with the social self and, hence, an initially appealing (and seductive) conceptualization of socialization as a struggle between the collective domesticating pressures and the willful and imperious drives of the "natural man." Here it seemed was a theory suited to the task of drawing attention to the pain and sacrifice entailed in submission to civilization, the socialized subject's enduring ambivalence regarding the bargain it reluctantly strikes with the social order, and the threat to individual liberty represented by the collectivity (Freud 1930).

In the psychoanalytic dualism of culture versus nature and ego versus instinct (Yankelovich and Barrett 1970), the libertarian thinker appeared to find a basis for his defense of the embattled individual and his critique of an oppressive and repressive social order. Such a defense of nature against the demands of culture could take the form, depending upon the theorist's view of human nature, either of a neo-Rousseauean call for the liberation of the healthy instincts of the "noble savage" (as in Reich and Brown), or of that far more subtle, ambivalent and tragic-ironic perspective that was Freud's own and that recognizes in human nature both the inclination toward libidinal exuberance and a degree of destructiveness incompatible with the existence of a viable human community (Freud 1927, 1930; Herberg 1957; Niebuhr 1957; Kaufmann 1963; Schafer 1976). In this latter perspective both the terrible price exacted by civilization from the instinctual individual and the need for him to pay it are represented.

In the work of Marcuse, there was an attempt to avoid the romanticism of the former view as well as the ambivalent conservatism of the latter through an elaboration of Freud's own distinction between a "basic repression" necessary for the very existence of civilized order and a "surplus repression" above and beyond this unavoidable minimum induced by the exigencies of class exploitation (Freud 1927, 10–12). But whereas Marcuse accepted Freud's view of the subject's sexual and aggressive passions as instinctual, he overlooked the fact that for Freud it was sublimated or aim-inhibited (as opposed to simply released) Eros that was capable of binding aggression. Furthermore, Marcuse's whole attempt to relativize as a product of specific socioeconomic conditions human conflicts and discontents that, although they may not arise from "instinctual" sources are certainly irreducible to sociohistorical factors alone, is characteristic of that more subtle variety of romanticism (disguised as hardheaded realism), which is utopian Freudo-Marxism.

But without entering any further into such philosophical and political arguments, it is sufficient to notice that, despite their profound ideological differences in other respects, these perspectives shared a common acceptance of some version of the Freudian theory of the instincts and, hence, rested upon an instinctivist view of human nature. Whether "natural man" was conceived in terms of innate innocence or innate depravity, or some combination of the two, and whether the solution was seen to be instinctual liberation or the more temperate path of sublimation and rational suppression, all these outlooks operated within the culture versus nature duality that Freud enshrined in his structural theory of the mental apparatus as the duality of ego-superego versus id.

According to Erikson, Freudian theory embodies a *centaur model of man:*

> The id Freud considered to be the oldest province of the mind, both in individual terms—for he held the young baby to be "all id"—and in phylogenetic terms, for the id is the deposition in us of the whole of evolutionary history. The id is everything that is left of our organization of the responses of the amoeba and of the impulses of the ape, of the blind spasms of our intra-uterine existence, and of the needs of our postnatal days—everything which would make us "mere creatures." The name "id," of course, designates the assumption that the "ego" finds itself attached to this impersonal, this bestial layer like the centaur to his equestrian underpinnings: only that the ego considers such a combination a danger and an imposition, whereas the centaur makes the most of it. (Erikson 1950, 192)

While agreeing with Erikson's characterization, Guntrip regards the theory as "astonishing and unrealistic, in its assumption that human nature is made up, by evolutionary 'layering,' of an ineradicable dualism of two mutually hostile elements" (Guntrip 1971, 50). He takes

the seeming plausibility of the centaur model as evidence both of
"how far back in history human beings have suffered from split-ego
conditions" and of "how tremendous has been the struggle to disentan-
gle the two elements in Freud's original thought, the physiological and
biological impersonal-process theory of id-drives and superego controls, and the personal object-relational thinking that has always been
struggling to break free and move on to a new and more adequate
conceptualization of human beings in their personal life" (Guntrip
1971, 51–52).

Suffice it to say that these premises—the instinct theory and the
centaur model—upon which so many towering philosophical and political *Weltanschauungen* have been erected are, to say the least, highly
questionable. Freud himself half recognized this when he wrote that "the
theory of the instincts is so to say our mythology" and admitted that
"instincts are mythical entities, magnificent in their indefiniteness." His
statement that whereas "in our work we cannot for a moment disregard
them, yet we are never sure that we are seeing them clearly" (Freud
1933, 95) surely justifies our skepticism concerning the psychoanalytic
"biologizing" of human passion. There is no need to deny the embodied
nature of our humanity or the existence of certain innate or "instinctual"
behavioral patterns released by environmental stimuli of various types
(Bowlby 1969–80), in order to reject the outmoded biologism of
Freud's hydraulic conception of the instinctual drive grounded in a somatic source as the basis of human motivation.

Having attempted to preserve the instinct theory for a considerable
time, I am familiar with the standard ploys. As many writers have
pointed out (Fenichel 1945, chap. 2; Waelder 1960, chap. 5; Parsons
1962; Hartmann 1964, chap. 4; Carveth 1977a, 1977b), Freud did not
use the German word *Instinkt,* implying fixed and unchangeable animal "instinct," but the term *Trieb,* conveying the idea of an impulse or
drive influenced in aim and object by the social environment. Certainly
psychoanalysis is all about such social, especially familial, influences
upon the "instinctual drives." However, when Freud states that an instinct, though having its source somewhere in the body, can only be
known via its attached mental representation (Freud 1915a, 122;
1915b, 177), we are led to suspect that the mental representation that
supposedly betrays the presence of an instinct might well be the essence of the phenomenon: that what Freud refers to in his concept of
instinct is nothing other than motivated human action of an affective
sort carried on either overtly or in imagination and either consciously,
preconsciously, or unconsciously.

Freud described human passion and desire as if they were fundamentally grounded in biologically based drives of sex and aggression. Owing to his commitment to nineteenth-century scientific materialism and positivism (Yankelovich and Barrett 1970), Freud sought to "materialize" human purposes by somehow grounding them in physiology. While recognizing that many of such "instinctual drives" were entirely learned or acquired and describing the interpersonal situations and events that shaped them in aim and object—and, in addition, implicitly understanding that a range of our passions arise from our existential predicament as time-binding beings burdened with consciousness of our mortality (Freud 1930)—Freud still felt the need to speculate about their alleged somatic sources and claim for them the sort of material as opposed to psychological reality that, despite his establishment of the idea of psychic reality, remained for the positivist the only form of the really real. While this approach appeared to have a certain plausibility insofar as the sexual drive was concerned given conventional (but in my view highly questionable) assumptions about the physiological sources of human sexuality, it ran into serious difficulty with respect to the aggressive drive for which no convincing somatic sources could be identified.

In recent years, the argument has been revived that the view of Freud as a positivist, mechanist, and reductionist is a distortion of his essential humanism brought about by Strachey's attempt to transform Freud's "soul-study" into a medically respectable positive science of psychoanalysis by the miracle of free translation (see Bettelheim 1982, among others). The argument has its appeal, but it won't wash. Although I myself have supported the theoretical strategy of deliteralization or metaphorization of concretized psychoanalytic concepts (Carveth 1984b), from a scholarly point of view it is simply too easy to set aside Freud's positivism, materialism, and mechanism in favor of a humanistic reading that interprets such concepts as the instinctual drive metaphorically as referring to human passion and desire in the broadest sense. This, no doubt, is what Freud *should* have meant and, perhaps at times, what he did mean. But it is nevertheless quite clear that he often meant his materialistic metapsychology to be taken quite literally. Like the cultural milieu in which he worked, Freud suffered from the problem of "two souls in one breast": the romantic-humanist lived in continual tension with the positivist-reductionist. The result is the "mixed discourse" (Ricoeur 1970)—or "broken speech"—of psychoanalysis.

Far from being a merely semantic distinction and philosophical nicety, this difference between the conception of human motivation as biologically based instinctual drive or as meaningful personal action is theoretically crucial and has wide-ranging implications. Take as merely one example the nature of human sexuality. It is evident that the conventional way of thinking of sexuality as primarily a bodily, animal, biophysiological, and instinctual phenomenon, rather than as a primarily mental or psychological process, has obscured the fact that in this metaphor-mad, symboling animal, far from "bubbling up from the body," human sexuality is more accurately a process that "trickles down from the mind."

Contrary to the misleading implications of such psychoanalytic terms as those of the oral, anal, phallic, and urethral *zones,* rather than *meanings*—terms that imply that a human passion arises from its somatic vehicle rather than expressing itself through the body as the instrument of a human project (Sartre 1943; Fairbairn 1952)—it is quite evident that the real somatic origin of Eros in *animal symbolicum* (Cassirer 1944) lies somewhere in the cerebral cortex. For therein lies the material foundation for the multifaceted erotic imagery and complex and subtle personal and interpersonal plots, in the service of which we enlist our bodies as props, and so exploit their capacity for sensual and sexual responsiveness in our pursuit of purposes that range from the temporary loss of an intolerable individuality, to aggressive domination or masochistic submission, to friendly play, the reproduction of the species, or the pursuit of self-esteem.

Fortunately, Freud and his followers have always demonstrated a healthy capacity to disregard the biologistic metapsychology in the interests of psychoanalytic psychology and to prevent abstract theoretical preaching from seriously hampering concrete analytic practice. If this were not the case and analysts actually took the instinct theory seriously, analysis would necessarily cease whenever it encountered what it believed to be the manifestations of an irreducible and unanalyzable instinctual drive. The hermeneutic psychoanalytic enterprise, this relentless probing for subtle and secret meanings and motives would, if metapsychology were valid, be rendered futile in the face of the instinctual "bedrock" (Freud 1937) of human nature.

But the fact that metapsychology is anti-analytical has seldom deterred the analyst from analysis. Hence, rather than interpreting a young man's passion for a married woman as a natural expression of the sexual instinct, analysis is alive to possibilities such as that what appears to be a sexual passion for a woman might, in addition, reflect an aggressive aim toward the cuckolded man, or even a homosexual wish for sexual contact with the man by means of the bridge provided by the woman he possesses. Things are often not what they seem. Aggression often disguises itself as love and vice versa. Psychoanalytic psychology teaches us this; psychoanalytic metapsychology obscures it.

Despite their many other differences, theorists as diverse as Sartre, Fairbairn, Lacan, and Kohut all tend to agree that the human body, rather than being the natural source of instinctual drives, is an ensemble of means for the expression of diverse ends, some of which may entail the most "unnatural" uses of this vehicle or even its destruction. Far from being instinct-dominated creatures, human beings are meaning- and metaphor-ridden animals (Bruyn 1966; Burke 1968; Carveth 1984b; Duncan 1968, 1969; Lakoff and Johnson 1980; Mills 1939, 1940)—which is to say that communication and communion are constitutive of the very structure of *Dasein* or human *being-in-the-world* (Heidegger 1927). While certainly *also* seeking pleasure, the human subject is nevertheless—at least in health—essentially oriented toward the other and fundamentally motivated to seek attachment (Bowlby 1969–80) to a good or "optimally responsive" (Bacal 1985) object or "selfobject" (Kohut 1977) as the essential foundation for a viable sense of self. In this view, the Freudian model of the person as an essentially narcissistic pleasure-seeker reluctantly oriented toward others as necessary means to the end of instinctual discharge is a description of a pathological state of disintegration—however accurate such a picture of our "fallen" humanity may be.[3]

Despite his so-called return to Freud, Lacan in one sense offers what amounts to a self psychology through his "narcissization" of human desire. For Lacan, unlike Freud, desire is not for the object as a means to the end of consummatory instinctual discharge. On the contrary, as distinct from organic "need" human desire is "the desire of the other"; that is, my desire is to be desired by the other, to be, as it were, the apple of his/her eye. This is not essentially different from Fairbairn's object-relations psychology in which "libido" is fundamentally object-seeking, or from Kohut's psychology of the self in which the subject's desire is fundamentally for mirroring and empathically attuned responsiveness from its "selfobjects."

It is interesting that, while overtly embracing Freud's concept of the death instinct in his metapsychological explanations of the roots of human self-destructiveness, most of the illustrative clinical material presented by Menninger in *Man Against Himself* seems clearly to emphasize the role of what he himself calls "thwarting" in the early development of the patient. He writes that

> unendurable thwartings lead to unendurable resentment which, lacking the opportunity of a justification or the proper psychological set-up for external expression, is repressed, directed inward, absorbed for a time by the administration of the ego but with the ultimate result of an overtaxing of its powers of assimilation. This is an elaborate way of saying that unmastered self-destructive impulses insufficiently directed to the outside world or insufficiently gratified by external opportunities are reflected upon the self, in some instances appearing in this form of constantly maintained anxiety which, in the end, produces the very result which had been anticipated and feared, namely annihilation. (Menninger 1938, 319)

Naturally, Menninger himself would most likely have said that such thwartings are not themselves the *cause* of the aggression that turned against the self, results in self-destruction of various types. For him, thwarting merely interferes with the normal binding of Thanatos by Eros, resulting in an environmentally caused failure of instinctual fusion resulting in unmodulated hate derived, not from thwarting but from the death drive, being turned against the self. However, it is possible to argue, against Menninger, that the environmental failure or thwarting of the child does not merely lead to failure to bind innate aggression, but evokes aggression as a secondary reaction to frustration. This, of course, is the frustration-aggression hypothesis which, in varied forms, informs the thinking of many of those who reject the Freudian and Kleinian notions of a death drive and of a primary aggressive drive.

In re-reading Menninger one is reminded that there exist two, quite distinct, versions of the classical drive-structure theory. Even after Freud embraced the death instinct in 1920, the mainstream Freudian tradition continued to view the sexual drive as the main focus of repression and symptom formation (Greenberg and Mitchell 1983, 32). As late as 1926 Freud could write: "We have always believed that in a neurosis it is against the demands of the libido and not against those of any other instinct that the ego is defending itself" (Freud 1926, 124). In contrast, Menninger and his co-workers (Menninger et al. 1963) clearly saw sex as more of the solution than the problem. Like the later Klein, Menninger felt that the real root of humanity's difficulties lies in human aggression, in the problem of hate. Sex, for Menninger, only becomes a problem when it is pathologically infected by aggression. The antidote to hate is love. In Menninger's version of the drive-structure model the defenses are directed primarily against aggression or aggressively infected sexuality.

Regarding Freud's relatively late introduction of the death drive and its outward manifestation as the aggressive drive, Menninger et al. (1963) write:

> This sudden and belated discovery of evil is a psychological phe-nomenon Freud never analyzed. Its most famous exemplar was Gautama Buddha, from whom—according to the story—the sight of evil was artificially hidden until the day of his enlighten-ment. The British philosopher C.E.M. Joad, who long held to the hypothesis of a single life force, recorded his similar insights thus: "Then came the war, and the existence of evil made its impact upon me as a positive and obtrusive fact. All my life it had been staring me in the face; now it hit me in the face.... I see now that evil is endemic in man." (115)

In overtly embracing a drive theory of sex and aggression on the level of metapsychology, even while unintentionally offering some clinical support for a theory of environmental failure or thwarting as the cause of psychopathology, Menninger remained caught on the horns of the nature/nurture dilemma that has bedeviled psychoanalytic thinking from the beginning and still haunts it today, despite almost universal acknowl-edgment that it rests on a false dichotomy. Menninger et al. (1963, 119–20) review five theories of human nature ranging from, at one extreme, the monistic theory of human nature as all-bad (which they attribute rather unfairly to Hobbes); to, at the other extreme, the monistic theory of humanity as all-good (the "see no evil/hear no evil/speak no evil" position), which they imply no known theorist has been so naive as to embrace.

Between these paranoid-schizoid (all-bad or all-good) extremes and moving toward Klein's depressive position or Mahler's self and object constancy, but with a marked bias toward the all-good pole, lie two environmentalistic approaches that I do not see their grounds for distin-guishing. In each of these, human destructiveness is acknowledged but explained (or explained away) on the basis either of a theory of the corruption of the natural goodness of the "noble savage" by society as in Rousseau and Marx—the question as to how society becomes corrupt when human beings are naturally good being left unclear—or through a theory that views the child's destructiveness as entirely secondary to frustration, abuse, or deprivation.

In these types of environmental or sociological reductionism and their psychoanalytic counterparts (the works of Fairbairn, Guntrip, and Kohut come to mind, with the writings of Miller representing the almost monomaniacal extreme of this tendency), the fact of evil is seen, but its inevitability and deep roots in our very nature are denied. Rejecting such naively environmentalist theories of aggression in which "there are no bad boys, only bad parents," Menninger et al. (1963, 120) embrace the Freudian and Kleinian position of instinctual ambivalence, Eros versus Thanatos, which Freud himself acknowledged to be a modern equivalent of the pre-Socratic philosopher Empedocles' theory of the universe as the outcome of the clashing forces of *philia* (love) and *neikos* (hate) (Freud 1937).

The strength of Freud's, Klein's, and Menninger's position on this issue lies in its rejection of the sort of theoretical splitting that regards human nature as either all-bad or all-good. Unfortunately, it grounds its vision of human ambivalence (both good and evil) in a dual drive theory that, from a Judeo-Christian point of view, is unacceptable both in its biologism and in its gnostic dualism or Manichaeanism. Naturally, I am not arguing that instinctual dualism is unacceptable because it deviates from biblical teaching. Rather, it is that, in demythologized form (Bonhoeffer 1953; Bultmann 1958, 1961; Macquarrie 1973; Tillich 1952), the Judeo-Christian anthropology with its implicitly existential understanding of the human situation as irreducible to the terms of heredity and environment is simply more subtle, sophisticated, and insightful, on psychological and philosophical grounds alone, than any psychoanalytic anthropology I know of—except for certain readings of Kleinian and Lacanian theory that are to a degree at least compatible with an existential, if not a specifically biblical, framework.

According to Nietzsche: "Whoever fights monsters should see to it that in the process he does not become a monster. And when you look into an abyss, the abyss also looks into you" (Nietzsche 1886, epigram 146, p. 89). Hence, one ought to choose one's enemies carefully; in the course of the ensuing struggle, one inevitably comes to resemble them. There is no doubt that in their attempts to preserve monotheism ("Hear, O Israel: The Lord our God is one Lord" [Deut. 6:4]) against the dualistic Manichaean heresies, various tendencies within both Judaism and Christianity came to be infected to various degrees with the very dualism they sought to reject. One need only think for a moment of those tendencies in which the devil, rather than being merely a fallen angel, takes on a status almost equal in power to that of the Almighty; and in which the human being, rather than being created "in the image of God" with a body that, as a part of the creation, is fundamentally good is conceived, on the contrary, as an intrinsically corrupt creature—not through a fall into sin through the prideful exercise of free will as the Bible essentially maintains, but (in the gnostic distortions) through his very involvement as a material and biological being in a creation that is itself represented as essentially evil.

Setting such gnostic distortions aside, the main tendency of Judeo-Christianity is clearly discernable (Niebuhr 1941). However, in tracing human destructiveness to the essentially asocial and antisocial sexual and aggressive drives (which even as *Trieb* as opposed to *Instinkt* Freud insists arise from a somatic source) (Freud 1915a); in its mind/body dualism and centaur model of man in which, as in Plato, reason (ego) and morality (superego) constitute the human rider who seeks to tame the appetites of its "beastly" counterpart (id); in its representation of the system unconscious or the id as "a chaos, a cauldron full of seething excitations" (Freud 1933, 73), a kind of swamp needing to be drained for the sake of civilization ("Where id was, there ego shall be. It is a work of culture—not unlike the draining of the Zuider Zee") (Freud 1933, 80); and in its metapsychology (or metaphysics) of Eros versus Thanatos—Freudian psychoanalysis represents one of the major expressions of the gnostic heresy in our time. It represents a regression from the essentially more mature level of object relations reflected in the Judeo-Christian anthropology (that transcends both paranoid-schizoid splitting as well as dualism by recognizing both the fact and the inevitability of evil but, at the same time, subsuming it within a superordinate affirmation of the fundamental goodness of the creation) by understanding it (evil) as a consequence of a universal and inevitable "fall" from innocence into narcissism intrinsic to the emergent, existential structure of human selfhood.

Freud's critique of narcissism, his insistence upon the need to develop beyond narcissistic object-choice and to achieve a capacity for mature object love (for "in the last resort we must begin to love in order not to fall ill, and we are bound to fall ill if . . . we are unable to love") (Freud 1914, 85)—together with his related commitment to science, which also represents a demand to overcome narcissism, to distinguish between fantasy or projection and empirical actuality, between what we want to believe about reality and what is really real (Freud 1933, lecture 35)—might well have constituted the basis for his understanding of human destructiveness. Unfortunately, instead of developing a conception of aggression (as distinct from vital assertion) as composed essentially of narcissistic rage in the face of both the unavoidable narcissistic injuries intrinsic to the human condition as such, together with the *surplus frustration* arising from environmental failure of various types, he opted instead for a drive-theoretical explanation that essentially biologizes human destructiveness and attributes it to our animality rather than our humanity.

Despite attempts to displace the blame for Freud's regrettable bio-logism unto Strachey's translation of *Trieb* as "instinct" instead of "drive," the fact remains that the *Triebe* are, for Freud, ultimately grounded in a somatic source (Freud 1915a). The very concept of the *Triebe* as exist-ing on the "frontier" between the psyche and the soma is an instance of Freud's dualism and his centaur model of man: the aims and objects represent the human side and the somatic source the animal. However shaped in aim and object by social influences, human motivation, in this view, including human destructiveness, arises fundamentally from the body; that is, from our animality.

By way of contrast, in a Judeo-Christian anthropology informed by and demythologized in terms of Heideggerian, Meadian, and Lacanian perspec-tives, both human desire and destructiveness are seen to arise primarily from our uniquely self-conscious, ontological predicament as language-animals who, beginning with entry into the symbolic order (certainly by eighteen months, if not considerably earlier), must live with the often painful awareness of our separateness, vulnerability, incompleteness, and essential helplessness in the face of ultimate extinction. There is no need to resort to varieties of existentialism that as one-sided philosophies of free will deny the biological, environmental and unconscious determi-nants of human experience and behavior, or that embrace a nihilistic attitude of despair that denies the possibilities of human love, joy, and fulfillment—thus privileging crucifixion over resurrection, Good Friday over Easter Sunday—in order to recognize the origin of many of our uniquely human passions and desires, as well as of our various defensive strategies, in the tragic and fearful dimension of human existence.

I find it curious that Karl Menninger, whose psychoanalytic writings fre-quently contain a Christian subtext, should in his theory of evil have fallen into a fundamentally non-Christian, gnostic dualism that departs from Judeo-Christian monotheism both by embracing two "gods" (drives, prin-ciples, or forces) of equal power and by abandoning the biblical under-standing that, unlike the fundamental goodness of the creation, evil is not a primary phenomenon, but represents humanity's "fall" from the good brought about by the sin of pride, described in psychoanalytic discourse as (secondary) narcissism, the overcoming of which in favor of mature object love it is our developmental task—and our moral responsibility—to achieve (Freud 1914).

I assume it was Menninger's lifelong devotion to Freud that distracted him from what, in certain contexts, he saw clearly enough. For example, writing in *Man Against Himself* of the forces that inhibit our capacity to love and in this way mitigate our hate, Menninger writes that

> first and foremost among the inhibitions of the erotic development are the stultifying and deadening effects of narcissism. Nothing inhibits love so much as self-love and from no source can we expect greater ameliorative results than from the deflection of this love from a self-investment ... to its proper investment in outside objects. ... Narcissism chokes and smothers the ego it aims to protect—just as winter protection applied to a rosebed, if left on too late in the spring, prevents the roses from developing properly, or even growing at all. Thus again psychoanalytic science comes to the support of an intuitive observation of a great religious leader who said, "He who seeketh his own life shall lose it but whosoever loseth his life for my sake shall find it." We need only read in place of "for my sake" an expression meaning the investment of love in others, which is presumably what Jesus meant. (Menninger 1938, 381–82)

In referring to a convergence between psychoanalytic science and Christian religion, Menninger points to the so-called U-tube theory of inverse libidinal investment in objects or the ego that Freud held during the years between 1914 when his original instinctual dualism (sexual versus self-preservative or ego-instincts) broke down on the shoals of narcissism until his introduction in 1920 of his final instinctual dualism of Eros versus Thanatos. Thus, for six years Freud was forced, despite himself, to abandon his preferred instinctual dualism or Manichaeanism for a libidinal monism and an ethic privileging object love over narcissism that has clear parallels to the Judeo-Christian monotheism toward which, for a host of personal reasons, he was intensely ambivalent (Vitz 1988).

The U-tube theory has been the subject of much criticism. Fromm, for example, argued that, contrary to its implication that the more one loves oneself the less able one is to love others, the facts are just the reverse: only the person who loves himself is able to love others (Fromm 1947, 123–45). However, this dispute is easily resolved if one posits that whereas Fromm is speaking about something like Winnicott's "true self" (Winnicott 1960) and about a sense of authentic self-worth, Freud is speaking about libidinal investment, not in the true self, but rather in the self-image (Freud 1914).

Even after the introduction of the structural theory in 1923, the term "ego" in Freud's writings often referred, as we have seen, not to the hypothetical construct of a control apparatus, or to the self, let alone the authentic self, but rather to what Lacan referred to as the "specular ego" or self-image (Lacan 1977, chap. 1). If, giving Freud the benefit of the doubt, we interpret him to mean that the more energy and attention we feel we have to devote to shoring up or polishing our "images" (because, as we would now say, they are so prone to devaluation or fragmentation) the less we have available to invest in other people, then his U-tube theory begins to take on a good deal of plausibility. In theological terms, it is even recognizable—like Lacan's Catholicized version of psychoanalysis—as entailing a critique of the idolatry of the self reflected on the individual level in narcissism and, on the collective level, in the anthropocentric outlook characteristic of secular humanism.

Menninger's critique of narcissism is founded on the idea that "when love is largely self-invested the gradual flow of the softening, fructifying essence of the erotic impulse over the stark arms of aggression . . . is stayed" (Menninger 1938, 382). In other words, self-invested libido is unavailable to bind and neutralize the aggressive instinct. Interestingly, however, Menninger's own metaphors are suggestive of a very different, noninstinctual view of the origins of human destructiveness. He writes:

> It is as if the personality were like a growing tree over whose dark bare branches as we see them in winter there creeps the soft verdure of spring and summer, clothing the skeleton with living beauty. But were such a tree to be so injured near the base that the sap flowed out in large quantities to promote the healing and the protection of this stem injury, an insufficient supply would be left for the development of the foliage of the branches. These, then, would remain bare, stark, aggressive—and dying, while the sap fed and overfed the basal wound. (Menninger 1938, 382)

Here, in addition to suggesting that narcissism prevents love from neutralizing hate, is the suggestion that hate itself stems not from an aggressive instinct, but from a basal wound to the self that narcissism seeks to cover and to heal. Here, of course, we are in the domain of the contemporary "psychology of the self" (Kohut 1977).

Now I, for one, am just as happy Menninger did not exchange his drive theory of aggression for such an environmentalist alternative. For while I reject Freud's and Menninger's biologism, I find the opposing environmentalism equally one-sided and naive. Such is the grip that binary oppositional thinking has over the human mind, that an enormous difficulty is faced by anyone who seeks to get psychologists to comprehend a theory of human nature that refuses not only to embrace nature at the expense of nurture, or vice versa, but that also refuses the pseudo-sophistication of the *both* nature *and* nurture position, in favor of a theory that, while not denying the contributions of either biological or environmental factors, resorts to an *existential* perspective that posits a uniquely human situation or predicament irreducible to heredity and environment.

I take this as evidence that, despite our arrogance, we psychosocial scientists are as yet far from achieving the sophistication of the theological tradition we have tended to despise. Menninger himself, who certainly did not despise this tradition, was nevertheless unable to utilize its insights fully in a psychoanalytic context. If he had, he would have been forced to abandon both his explicit metapsychological embrace of the biologistic theory of the death drive, as well as his implicit clinical leaning toward an environmentalistic theory in which aggression is merely a secondary reaction to early "thwarting" of the child— as well as any pseudosophisticated explanations in terms of the interaction of heredity and environment (the both/and position that, while refusing to privilege one pole of the dichotomy over the other, fails to transcend the binary opposition)—in favor of the Judeo-Christian understanding of sin.

In the biblical perspective, human destructiveness has little to do with man's animality. Despite our misrepresentation of human evil as "bestial" the fact is that animals are incapable of evil, precisely because they lack the cognitive capacity for that uniquely human type of empathy which, in enabling one to imagine what it is like to be the other, establishes the psychological basis for both sadism and sainthood. Nor does human destructiveness arise from the natural drives of the body that, however assertive they may be in the service of survival, do not primarily seek the destruction or suffering of the self or others, although these may at times be unavoidable by-products of survival aims. Neither, fundamentally, does it have to do with environmental thwartings that although certainly exacerbating the problem, do not cause it.

Rather, in the biblical framework, human destructiveness is intimately associated with the problem of idolatry, the worship of images

(Deut. 5:8) of the self or others. In this view, sin arises from a universal and inevitable "fall" into narcissism (idolization of the self or the other) that every child is fated to undergo, even in the presence of the most "optimally responsive" (Bacal 1985) "selfobjects" (Kohut 1977) imaginable. It entails the turning away from or misuse of the distinctively human capacity for empathy with others in favor of the idolatrous worship either of the self (the manic, grandiose, and sadistic strategies) or of an idealized other (the hysterical, depressive, and masochistic solutions).

Freud's concept of secondary narcissism; Klein's conception of the manic defense and the subject's relative imprisonment within its own projections; Lacan's conception of narcissism as fixation upon the "specular ego" formed in the "mirror stage"; Winnicott's conceptions of infantile omnipotence and the early period of relations with "subjective objects" prior to access through relations with "transitional objects" to the world of "objective objects"; and the early Kohut's conception of a "grandiose self" (Freud 1914, 1915a; Klein 1986; Lacan 1977, chap. 1; Winnicott 1969; Kohut 1971)—all suggest the inevitability of the ego-centric illusion of the self as the center of the universe, "His Majesty, the Baby, as once we fancied ourselves to be" (Freud 1914, 84). Even if we reject, as I do, the notions of primary narcissism and primary omnipotence (in my view, ignorance of impotence is not omnipotence) in favor of a view of grandiosity and omnipotence as secondary, manic defenses in the face of early anxieties of various types, we may nevertheless insist on the inevitability and universality of such defensive omnipotence, or its inversion in the idealization of the other rather than the self, in the face of the unavoidable anxieties intrinsic to the human condition, however much these may be intensified by environmental or selfobject failure of various types.

Here we have the beginnings of a psychoanalytic interpretation of what in religious myth is the doctrine of "original sin." This has always referred to the sin of pride or self-centeredness: narcissism on the individual plane and anthropocentrism on the collective. Of course, what needs to be added to this account is recognition of the fact that in addition to the traditionally "masculine" pattern of idolatrous worship of the self (god-playing), there is the traditionally "feminine" strategy of defensive idealization (god-making) in which the god-image is transferred to an idol to whom the subject surrenders her agency and responsibility.[4]

When the idea of original sin is subjected to psychoanalytic demy-thologization and understood to refer to such idolatries of the self and others, it ceases to be "original" in any literal, developmental sense.

For—*pace* gnostic Christians, Freudians, and Kleinians—far from being sinful at the beginning, the infant is in a state of "original innocence," which I think is what is implied in the myth of Eden in the first place; it is "asleep in the bosom of the Father" or Mother (i.e., the early selfobjects). If in original sin the human creature either usurps the position of the Creator (Niebuhr 1941), or subordinates the self to another creature as Creator, then from a developmental perspective it is clear that for either self-aggrandizement or self-abasement to occur it is first necessary for a self to be developed to be idolized or negated.

Although, since Stern's differentiation of several different "senses of self" the sense of a verbal self can no longer be equated with the self as such, there are nevertheless grounds for identifying the so-called rapprochement subphase of separation-individuation as a kind of "fulcrum" in cognitive and emotional development.[5] If I had to pinpoint developmentally the normal, as opposed to the pathogenically premature (Tustin 1986) timing of "the fall," the period around eighteen months would appear to be the most likely candidate. The fact that Freud's observations of his grandson's *Fort!/Da!* game took place when the latter was at the age of eighteen months (Freud 1920), which corresponds with Piaget's timing for the beginnings of symbolic functioning and the emergence of "object permanence" (Piaget 1955) and with Mahler's timing of the "rapprochement crisis," strikes me as evidence for the important "existential" transformation that occurs around the time of the child's accession to "the word." ("In the beginning was the Word, and the Word was with God, and the Word was God" [John 1:1].)

In the thought of Mead, the ability to "take the role of the other" and in this way discover the other as a subject, not merely an object, simultaneously enables one to discover oneself as an object (i.e., to become "objective") by viewing oneself, through empathy, from the standpoint of the other. For Mead, these capacities for role-taking and reflexive role-taking arise with and are dependent upon symbolic functioning. ("And the eyes of them both were opened, and they knew that they were naked" [Gen. 3:7].) Mead's analysis of psychosocial, as distinct from biosocial, communication on the uniquely human level of symbolic interaction has, in my view, provided the sociopsychological foundation for the biblical doctrine of charity. It is because being human necessarily entails the ability to take the role of the other that to refuse to be guided in one's treatment of others by one's capacity to imagine *being* them—that is, to identify with their feelings and to care—is the essence of sin.

However inappropriately they theorize the insight in biologistic rather than existential terms, the mainstream psychoanalytic theories of Freud, Klein, Winnicott, and Mahler at least enable us to understand that, however exacerbated by environmental failure, there is a basic level of disturbance that is an unavoidable feature of the human condition, even where parental selfobject responsiveness has been ideal. In contrast, the environmentalism of much contemporary post-Freudian and post-Kleinian psychoanalytic thinking has prevented it from recognizing the higher wisdom achieved in both the psychoanalytic and the biblical traditions in this regard.

The sad fact is that every human being is destined to undergo a kind of "fall from paradise," from an original state of innocence, faith, and trust into some degree of existential anguish, self-consciousness, frustration, reactive narcissistic rage, and consequent persecutory anxiety or guilt leading either to a defensive pretention to omnipotence or a parasitic dependency, or both, in the face of the fearful reality of separateness and death. Even under the best circumstances imaginable, reality is sufficiently frustrating and frightening to generate both "masculine" defensive grandiosity (the pathological extremes of which are seen in narcissistic disorders) and "feminine" defensive clinging (the extremes of which are seen in "borderline" conditions), each of which must be transcended if healthy emotional development is to occur.

Whereas contemporary self and object relations theory offers understanding of the environmental conditions necessary for the transcendence of both defensive grandiosity and clinging and for development of confidence in the integrity, value, and viability of the authentic self, it has tended to view the problems of the self as entirely pathological rather than existential. Since it downplayed or abandoned altogether the early Kohut's notion of a normal "grandiose self" that must experience optimal disillusionment,[6] self psychology, for example, has embraced an increasingly romantic outlook in which environmental failure is no longer seen as exacerbating or failing to alleviate a universally human problem but as the entire cause of the difficulty in the first place. Naturally, it attempts to mask the naïveté of this position by stressing that some degree of environmental failure (and, hence, defensive grandiosity and dependency) is inevitable. However, this merely assists in the evasion of the deeper truth that, even if the selfobject environment were perfect, the reality of separateness and death is enough in itself to drive us more than a little mad.

Self psychology recognizes the inevitability of empathic failure on the part of both the parents and the analyst, but its theory provides no adequate account of why such failure is inevitable. As it stands, the theory implies such failures result from the parents' or analyst's own pathology resulting from his caretakers' failures of him, and so on back through the generations. In contrast, a psychoanalytically demythologized version of the Judeo-Christian doctrine of "the fall" accounts for this inevitability, but not in terms either of environmental or biological reductionism, but rather in light of our uniquely human condition and of the existential structure of human selfhood.

There is a sense in which self psychology has failed as yet to achieve the depressive position. Lacking any tragic perspective—despite Kohut's reference to the psychology of "Tragic Man" (Kohut 1977)—it remains caught up in an excessive, paranoid-schizoid tendency to blame. For where "the fall" is not acknowledged, a "fall guy" (or girl) must inevitably be found. Of course, recognition of the tragic dimension of human existence in no way requires one to be blind to the ways in which inevitable human suffering fails to be mitigated or is made worse by the ways in which we chronically fail in our "response-abilities" to one another. In contrast to the naturalistic mystification of the passions in biologistic terms by Freud and in environmentalistic terms by much of post-Freudian and post-Kleinian self and object relations theory, an existential psychoanalytic perspective might yet enable us to recall their true origin—above and beyond the "surplus frustration" characterizing individual lives—in the "passion" that it is the fate of each of us to have suffered and to have to suffer.

NOTES

1. Freud (1896). The fact that, until fairly recently, a theory specifying the cause of neurosis as the sexual abuse of children has been known in psychoanalytic discourse as the "seduction theory" is not without significance.

2. The following section draws upon a previously published essay. See Carveth (1984a).

3. To say that we are essentially oriented toward the other, as both Meadian social psychology and various object-relations theories insist, is in no way to deny or devalue the importance of solitude (see Storr 1988). It is merely to recognize, with Winnicott (1958), that the very "capacity to be alone" depends on having so internalized a positively responsive other that in solitude one does not *feel* isolated or uncomfortably alone.

4. It should go without saying (but obviously does not) that "masculine" and "feminine" are placed within quotation marks to indicate that they are not being employed here in any essentialist sense. While there is no necessary connection between being male and playing god, or being female and worshiping, as Gilligan (1982) has pointed out, fundamental attitudes and orientations of this type are profoundly en*gender*ed in our patriarchal society.

5. Mahler et al. (1975); Blanck and Blanck (1974, 72). This is not the place to enter into a

discussion of the critique of the idea of an early phase of undifferentiation between self and object that Freud's, Winnicott's, and Mahler's thinking assumes. Whatever Freud may have meant by "primary narcissism" and Mahler by "autism" and "symbiosis," by "secondary narcissism" and the "subjective object" Freud and Winnicott do not mean to refer to absolute undifferentiation at all; they are refering to a state in which the *cognitively* differentiated object is *emotionally* experienced primarily through projections of the subject's own fantasies and self and object representations and predominantly in terms of the subject's pressing needs. And they mean to contrast this sort of narcissistic object-relation to one in which the subject is more able to get beyond such projections and egocentric demands for need-satisfaction and to recognize and make empathic contact with the real *otherness* of the object.

6. For the reasons given earlier, unlike the early Kohut (1971), I regard the grandiose self as a defensive formation, but also as both universal and inevitable in light of the universal need to defend against the frustrations and terrors of the human condition, even when these are not pathologically intensified by significant selfobject failure and other factors.

REFERENCES

Bacal, H. A. 1985. "Optimal Responsiveness and the Therapeutic Process." In *Progress in Self-Psychology,* edited by A. Goldberg, 202–26. New York: Guilford.
Bettelheim, B. 1982. "Freud and the Soul." *New Yorker* (1 March 1982).
Blanck, G., and R. Blanck. 1974. *Ego Psychology: Theory and Practice.* New York: Columbia University Press.
Bonhoeffer, D. 1953. *Letters and Papers From Prison.* London: Collins.
Bowlby, J. 1969–80. *Attachment and Loss.* Vols. 1–3. New York: Basic Books.
Breuer, J., and S. Freud. 1895. Studies on Hysteria. In Freud, *SE* 2.
Brown, N. O. 1959. *Life Against Death: On the Psychoanalytical Meaning of History.* Middletown, Conn.: Wesleyan University Press.
Bruyn, S. T. 1966. *The Human Perspective in Sociology.* Englewood Cliffs, N.J.: Prentice-Hall.
Bultmann, R. 1958. *Jesus Christ and Mythology.* New York: Scribner.
———. 1961. *Kerygma and Myth.* Edited by W. Bartsch. New York: Harper and Row.
Burke, K. 1968. *Language as Symbolic Action.* Berkeley and Los Angeles: University of California Press.
Carveth, D. L. 1977a. "The Hobbesian Microcosm: On the Dialectics of the Self in Social Theory." *Sociological Inquiry* 47:3–12.
———. 1977b. "The Disembodied Dialectic: A Psychoanalytic Critique of Sociological Relativism." *Theory and Society* 4:73–102.
———. 1984a. "Psychoanalysis and Social Theory: The Hobbesian Problem Revisited." *Psychoanalysis and Contemporary Thought* 4, no. 1:43–98.
———. 1984b. "The Analyst's Metaphors: A Deconstructionist Perspective." *Psychoanalysis and Contemporary Thought* 7, no. 4:491–560.
Cassirer, E. 1944. *An Essay on Man.* New Haven: Yale University Press.
Duncan, H. D. 1968. *Communication and Social Order.* New York: Oxford University Press.
———. 1969. *Symbols and Social Theory.* New York: Oxford University Press.

Erikson, E. 1950. *Childhood and Society.* Revised and enlarged edition. New York: Norton, 1963.

Fairbairn, W. R. D. 1952. *An Object-Relations Theory of the Personality.* London: Routledge.

Fenichel, O. 1945. *The Psychoanalytic Theory of Neurosis.* New York: Norton.

Freud, A. 1936. *The Ego and the Mechanisms of Defence.* New York: International University Press, 1946.

Freud, S. 1896. "The Aetiology of Hysteria." In *SE* 3.

———. 1900. *The Interpretation of Dreams.* In *SE* 4 and 5.

———. 1905. *Three Essays on the Theory of Sexuality.* In *SE* 7.

———. 1906. "My Views on the Part Played by Sexuality in the Aetiology of the Neuroses." In *SE* 7.

———. 1910. "The Psychoanalytic View of Psychogenic Disturbances of Vision." In *SE* 11.

———. 1914. "On Narcissism: An Introduction." In *SE* 14.

———. 1915a. "Instincts and their Vicissitudes." In *SE* 14.

———. 1915b. "The Unconscious." In *SE* 14.

———. 1916–17. *Introductory Lectures on Psycho-Analysis.* In *SE* 15–16.

———. 1920. *Beyond the Pleasure Principle.* In *SE* 18.

———. 1921. *Group Psychology and the Analysis of the Ego.* In *SE* 18.

———. 1923. *The Ego and the Id.* In *SE* 19.

———. 1926. *Inhibitions, Symptoms and Anxiety.* In *SE* 20.

———. 1927. *The Future of an Illusion.* In *SE* 21.

———. 1930. *Civilization and Its Discontents.* In *SE* 21.

———. 1933. *New Introductory Lectures on Psycho-Analysis.* In *SE* 22.

———. 1937. *Analysis terminable and interminable.* In *SE* 23.

Fromm, E. 1947. *Man For Himself: An Inquiry into the Psychology of Ethics.* New York: Holt, Rinehart and Winston.

Gilligan, C. 1982. *In a Different Voice: Psychological Theory and Women's Development.* Cambridge: Harvard University Press.

Goffman, E. 1959. *The Presentation of Self in Everyday Life.* Garden City, N.Y.: Doubleday.

Greenberg, J. R., and S. A. Mitchell. 1983. *Object Relations in Psychoanalytic Theory.* Cambridge: Harvard University Press.

Guntrip, H. 1971. *Psychoanalytic Theory, Therapy and the Self.* New York: Basic Books.

Hartmann, H. 1939. *Ego Psychology and the Problem of Adaptation.* New York: International University Press, 1958.

———. 1964. *Essays on Ego Psychology.* New York: International University Press.

Heidegger, M. 1927. *Being and Time.* Translated by J. Macquarrie and E. S. Robinson. New York: Harper, 1962.

Herberg, W. 1957. "Freud, the Revisionists and Social Reality." In *Freud and the 20th Century,* edited by B. Nelson, 143–63. Cleveland: World Publishing.

Kaufmann, W. 1963. "Freud and the Tragic Virtues." In *The Faith of a Heretic,* 331–52. Garden City, N.Y.: Doubleday.

Kernberg, O. 1976. *Object-Relations Theory and Clinical Psychoanalysis.* New York: Jason Aronson.

Klein, M. 1986. *The Selected Melanie Klein.* Edited by J. Mitchell. Harmondsworth, Middlesex: Penguin.

Kohut, H. 1971. *The Analysis of the Self.* New York: International University Press.

———. 1977. *The Restoration of the Self.* New York: International University Press.

Lacan, J. 1977. *Ecrits: A Selection.* Translated by A. Sheridan. New York: Norton.

Laing, R. D. 1960. *The Divided Self: An Existential Study in Sanity and Madness.* Harmondsworth, Middlesex: Penguin Books, 1965.

Lakoff, S., and M. Johnson. 1980. *Metaphors We Live By.* Chicago: University of Chicago Press.

Macquarrie, J. 1973. *An Existentialist Theology.* Harmondsworth, Middlesex: Pelican. (Originally published 1955)

Mahler, M. S., F. Pine, and A. Bergman. 1975. *The Psychological Birth of the Human Infant.* New York: Basic Books.

Marcuse, H. 1955. *Eros and Civilization.* New York: Random House.

Mead, G. H. 1934. *Mind, Self and Society.* Edited by C. Morris. Chicago: University of Chicago Press.

Menninger, K. 1938. *Man Against Himself.* New York: Harcourt, Brace.

Menninger, K., with M. Mayman and P. Pruyser. 1963. *The Vital Balance.* New York: Viking.

Miller, A. 1984. *Thou Shalt Not Be Aware: Society's Betrayal of the Child.* New York: Farrar, Straus and Giroux.

Mills, C. W. 1939. "Language, Logic and Culture." *American Sociological Review* 4:670–80.

———. 1940. "Situated Actions and Vocabularies of Motive." *American Sociological Review* 5:904–13.

Niebuhr, R. 1941. *The Nature and Destiny of Man.* Gifford Lectures. Vol. 1, Human Nature. New York: Scribner, 1964.

———. 1957. "Human Creativity and Self-Concern in Freud's Thought." In *Freud and the 20th Century.* Edited by B. Nelson, 259–76. Cleveland: World Publishing.

Nietzsche, F. 1886. *Beyond Good and Evil.* Translated by W. Kaufmann. New York: Vintage, 1966.

Piaget, J. 1955. *The Language and Thought of the Child.* New York: Macmillan.

Parsons, T. 1962. "Individual Autonomy and Social Pressure: A Reply to Dennis H. Wrong." *Psychoanalysis and the Psychoanalytic Review* 49:70–79.

———. 1964. *Social Structure and Personality.* New York: Free Press.

Reich, W. 1973. *Selected Writings.* New York: Farrar, Straus and Giroux.

Ricoeur, P. 1970. *Freud and Philosophy: An Essay on Interpretation.* Translated by D. Savage. New Haven: Yale University Press.

Rieff, P. 1959. *Freud: The Mind of the Moralist.* Garden City, N.Y.: Doubleday.

Riesman, D., N. Glazer, and R. Denney. 1950. *The Lonely Crowd: A Study of the Changing American Character.* New Haven: Yale University Press, 1961.

Sartre, J.-P. 1939. *Sketch For a Theory of the Emotions.* Translated by P. Mairet. London: Methuen, 1962.

———. 1943. *Being and Nothingness: A Study in Phenomenological Ontology.* Translated by H. E. Barnes. New York: Philosophical Library, 1953.

Schafer, R. 1976. *A New Language For Psychoanalysis.* New Haven: Yale University Press.

Stern, D. 1985. *The Interpersonal World of the Infant: A View From Psychoanalysis and Developmental Psychology.* New York: Basic Books.

Storr, A. 1988. *Solitude.* London: Collins.

Sykes, J. B., ed. 1982. *The Concise Oxford Dictionary of Current English.* Oxford: Clarendon Press.

Tillich, P. 1952. *The Courage to Be.* London: Collins.

Tustin, F. 1986. *Autistic Barriers in Neurotic Patients.* New Haven: Yale University Press.

Vitz, P. 1988. *Sigmund Freud's Christian Unconscious.* New York: Guilford.

Waelder, R. 1960. *Basic Theory of Psychoanalysis.* New York: International University Press.

Winnicott, D. W. 1958. "The Capacity to be Alone." In *The Maturational Processes and the Facilitating Environment.* London: Hogarth, 1965.

———. 1960. "Ego Distortion in Terms of True and False Self." In *The Maturational Processes and the Facilitating Environment.* London: Hogarth, 1965.

———. 1969. "The Use of an Object and Relating through Identifications." In *Playing and Reality.* London: Tavistock, 1971.

Wrong, D. H. 1961. "The Oversocialized Conception of Man in Modern Sociology." *American Sociological Review* 26:188–93. Repr. *Skeptical Sociology,* 31–46. New York: Columbia University Press, 1976.

Yankelovich, D., and W. Barrett. 1970. *Ego and Instinct: The Psychoanalytic Theory of Human Nature.* Revised ed. New York: Vintage.

3

Odi et Amo: On Hating the Ones We Love

JEROME NEU

C atullus, in the midst of his un-
happy affair with the woman he called Lesbia, wrote a two-line poem,
beginning in Latin "Odi et amo": "I hate and love. Why I do so, perhaps
you ask. I know not, but I feel it, and I am in torment."[1] He is not alone in
his experience, his pain, or his confusion. How can it be, and why should
it be that, to vary Oscar Wilde's formulation, each man (and woman)
hates the thing he or she loves?

CYCLES

Hatred is supposed to be the opposite of love, and doubtless (in some
sense) it is. But what does that mean? One thing it surely does not mean
is that the two emotions are incompatible, if that is supposed to entail
that they cannot be experienced toward the same object or at the same
time. What is it then for one emotion to be the "opposite" of another?
Putting that question aside for the moment, how is it that hatred, in
particular, is so tied to its putative opposite, love, that it seems natural
for them to occur together, if not simultaneously, then in constant alternation, in cycles?

Certainly relationships can go wrong, and do so for all sorts of reasons. There are possessive lovers, there are abusive lovers. Such relationships may be painful to *both* parties, and lead each to resent the
other. We hate people for the evil they do us, but more interestingly if

less justifiably, we also hate people for the evil we do them. If we become possessive and abusive, in addition to hating our victims for the real or imagined harms that led to our possessiveness and abusiveness toward them in the first place, we naturally hate those who harm those we loved (in this case, ourselves), and we naturally reciprocate the hatreds (even those of which we are the cause) of those who hate us. Spinoza works out some of these points in his logic of identification (what he calls "imitation of the affects").[2] And prior love produces greater hatred when one passion displaces the other.[3] This can be seen in heightened form in connection with paranoia, which in Freud's account also involves a reversal from activity to passivity ("I love him" to "he hates me") that leaves the persecutor still an object of love.[4] The same is true from the other direction, when love displaces hate, as in the move from passivity to activity in defensive identification with the aggressor.[5] Such relationships and cycles may reveal pathology in love, though one must wonder whether there is a dynamic *within* love that tends to lead to such pathology. This is an important point, to which we will return.

But it is not difficult to understand how someone might love someone else *despite* their oppressive faults, especially if the faults are seen as aspects or outgrowths of love, albeit pathological ones. If someone loves another *because* they are abusive, the pathology is more complex, but the mixed feelings are not by themselves puzzling. Loving and hating different aspects of a person, or for different reasons, produces mixed feelings; but mixed feelings are by themselves puzzling only if one has some special theory suggesting they should cancel each other out, as in a chemical reaction in which acid and base neutralize each other. Some theories of mind (for example, Hume's)[6] do just that, making ambivalence inconceivable. Far from casting suspicion on the phenomenon, however, this should make such theories immediately implausible. A theory that sees no difference between the presence of two "contrary" passions and no passion at all is seriously defective. Ambivalence is a real and commonplace part of the fluctuation of our feelings, the fluid many-aspected character of our emotional lives. As Montaigne writes, "Whoever supposes, to see me look sometimes coldly, sometimes lovingly, on my wife, that either look is feigned, is a fool."[7] While Montaigne emphasizes the fleeting character of our emotions, and even Hume would allow the rapid fluctuation or alternation of conflicting feelings, there can be deep and simultaneous conflicts.[8] The pathological cases prove it. Freud makes the point a central feature of his picture of the human mind: "The logical laws of thought do not apply in the id, and this is true above all of the law of contradiction. Contrary impulses exist side by side, without canceling each other out or diminishing each other."[9]

But let us seek to go beyond pathology. Plato writes in the *Phaedrus:* "Suppose we were being listened to by a man of generous and humane character, who loved or had once loved another such as himself; suppose he heard us saying that for some trifling cause lovers conceive bitter hatred and a spirit of malice and injury towards their loved ones; wouldn't he be sure to think that we had been brought up among the scum of the people and had never seen a case of noble love? Wouldn't he utterly refuse to accept our vilification of Love?"[10]

Trifling (and not so trifling) causes abound. Others hate us for the imagined harms we do them and, perhaps more intriguing though more perverse, they hate us for the real harms they do us. And of course we hate them in return. There is no problem about understanding hatred of those we love because they seek to control or abuse us. Does it make sense for us to hate them because they love us or because we love them?

DEPENDENCE AND MIXED FEELINGS

The dialectic that Hegel elaborates in his famous description of the relation of master and slave, a dialectic of the development of self-consciousness and individual identity, is also the dialectic of our interactions (loving and otherwise) with others. At least that is the story Sartre tells in *Being and Nothingness.*[11] It is a story of the inherent futility of love. Aiming at the full possession of a free being, our desire must fail as possession insofar as the other is free, and it must fail in terms of freedom insofar as the other is possessed. Thus Sartre speaks of "the impossible ideal of desire," "the lover's perpetual dissatisfaction" and "the lover's perpetual insecurity." Love falls into masochism and sadism. In Sartre's account, these have little to do with pleasure and pain, and much to do with freedom and control. Love is embedded in conflict, a war for recognition, in which Sartre concludes "it is indifferent whether we hate the Other's transcendence through what we empirically call his vices or his virtues. . . . The occasion which arouses hate is simply an act by the Other which puts me in the state of *being subject to* his freedom."

While Sartre's somewhat overheated metaphysics of sadomasochism is oddly detached from action and real interaction, and while it imagines a peculiar transcendent freedom too much always at issue, it nonetheless fruitfully explores in other terms the intricacies of identification, of introjection and projection; the prosaic but important truth emerges and remains that the lover wants to be loved. Whatever may be the case for putative selfless loves on the one hand, or pure physical cravings on the other hand, it is true for erotic love that the lover wants to be loved.[12] And this has consequences.

Love brings with it dependence and vulnerability. And these are fertile grounds for hatred. The more dependent an individual is on another, whether for freely given love or for other things, the more opportunities there will be for disappointment. But possibility does not amount to actuality. Why should hatred be inevitable? No reason so far has been given unless dependence is in itself hateful. Is it? While men are often ready to assume that it is, that may be a gendered assumption. It may be that men in our society reject dependence as hateful while women accept it as a desirable aspect of relationships, and that their differing assumptions have to do with current and local conditions of psychological development. It has been argued that "for boys and men, separation and individuation are critically tied to gender identity since separation from the mother is essential for the development of masculinity. For girls and women, issues of femininity or feminine identity do not depend on the achievement of separation from the mother or on the progress of individuation. Since masculinity is defined through separation while femininity is defined through attachment, male gender identity is threatened by intimacy while female gender identity is threatened by separation."[13] Is the attitude toward dependence, whatever the facts of our particular society, in general socially formed and therefore variable? Why should dependence, especially interdependence, be experienced as a danger?

Dependence and vulnerability are problems of identity, of the self who is not self-sufficient, of who we are in relation to others. They are problems at the boundary.[14] The lover wants to be loved. If you want something, you risk not getting it. You also risk getting it. If your love is returned, you are open to reciprocal demands. And "you" are at risk. "You" may become "we." This might seem an unalloyed good; so much so that people are tempted to imagine it happens more often than it does, leading to illusions of commonality (of what Sartre, following Heidegger, calls the *Mitsein*). Merging has long been regarded as a valuable, not a hateful feature of love. But we should be aware that such merging involves the overcoming of individual separation and so the end of the beloved (as well as of oneself) as a separate individual, and so a kind of death. And that is what hatred also aims at accomplishing— even if by other means. This may be but one of many points at which love and hatred come together in their consequences, if not their nature. ("I love you so much that I could eat you up.") John Donne concludes in "The Prohibition":

> Lest thou thy love and hate and me undo,
> To let me live, Oh love and hate me too.

The intricacies are many, but it is in any case clear that dependence brings with it risks and dangers of various sorts. Risk and danger are the characteristic objects of fear, and it is to be remembered that fear is (arguably) the most common source of hate.

The desire to merge has infantile roots. Freud connects what he calls the "oceanic feeling" with the earliest undifferentiated period of development, and Plato speaks in mythopoeic terms (through Aristophanes in the *Symposium*) of finding one's other half and becoming one as a return to our ancient state.[15] We may bring other things back from our earlier condition. If dependence is not inherently hateful, infantile dependence, at least in adults, certainly is. And our later loves have infantile sources. Freud emphasizes how it is in the bosom of the family that we learn to love, how the finding of an object is always a refinding.[16] Freud sometimes takes the history of displacement of objects (as well as of aims and component instincts) as grounds for something like a Sartrean pessimism about love:

> It is my belief that, however strange it may sound, we must reckon with the possibility that something in the nature of the sexual instinct itself is unfavourable to the realization of complete satisfaction . . . the final object of the sexual instinct is never any longer the original object but only a surrogate for it. Psychoanalysis has shown us that when the original object of a wishful impulse has been lost as a result of repression, it is frequently represented by an endless series of substitutive objects none of which, however, brings full satisfaction. This may explain the inconstancy in object-choice, the "craving for stimulation" which is so often a feature of the love of adults.[17]

Of course, that there are infantile sources of love need not leave us stuck with infantile dependence as the central feature of mature love relations. Nonetheless, the desire for unconditional support (which may, when we were infants, have been met), and the desire to merge (which, when we were infants, may have been felt as an actual experience), continue to some degree, and their own history is one of conflict: conflict with the desires of others and with other of our own desires (including those for independence and individuation). Even the desire for unconditional love is itself internally conflicted. While some think God provides the unconditional love formerly bestowed by our mothers, God loves all indiscriminately. The lover in interpersonal contexts wants to be loved for himself in particular, and that means the love desired is conditional on his being him (whatever that involves); it must not be indiscriminate. So one wants the love to be unconditional and one wants it to be conditional. And the history of the development of our desires takes place in the midst of the family, in the midst of rivalry.[18] The ego itself is formed out of identifications and introjections. "The distinction between self and not-self is made by the childish decision to claim all that the ego likes as 'mine,' and to repudiate all that the ego dislikes as 'not-mine.'"[19] In love we are again in the midst of identifications, rivalries and conflicts (some old, some new). For Sartre this is a metaphysical point, for Freud a psychological one.

Where does the fact that love has a history leave us? In ambivalence, I think. In Freud's early theorizing, he treats sadism (one of the poles of the failure of love according to Sartre, a denial of the other's freedom, as merging is a denial of the other's otherness) as a component sexual instinct, related to nonsexual instincts for mastery. In his later theorizing, he attributes it to a blend of life and death instincts.[20] Freud's later thought postulates an inclination to aggression, a "primary mutual hostility of human beings," and he suggests that aggressiveness "forms the basis of every relation of affection and love among people (with the single exception, perhaps, of the mother's relation to her male child)."[21] This provides no special explanation for hating those we love, for so far as hatred is instinctual it would equally explain hatred felt toward anyone. And hate is no more a simple instinct than love is. Both are attitudes felt by whole persons toward whole persons. But they connect with the instinctual reversals of activity and passivity that Freud explores in his consideration of sadism and masochism. Love and hate have instinctual roots, the convergence of which contribute to ambivalence. Freud saw this clearly even in his early theorizing, before the postulation of an independent death instinct:

> The history of the origins and relations of love makes us understand how it is that love so frequently manifests itself as "ambivalent"—i.e. as accompanied by impulses of hate against the same object. The hate which is admixed with the love is in part

derived from the preliminary stages of loving which have not been wholly surmounted; it is also in part based on reactions of repudiation by the ego-instincts, which, in view of the frequent conflicts between the interests of the ego and those of love, can find grounds in real and contemporary motives. In both cases, therefore, the admixed hate has as its source the self-preservative instincts. If a love-relation with a given object is broken off, hate not infrequently emerges in its place, so that we get the impression of a transformation of love into hate.[22]

Despite its changes, Freud's instinct theory remains determinedly dualistic throughout; the conflict is essential.[23] While love often enough appears to turn into hate, they are perhaps more often simultaneously present—the lapsing of love merely making the presence of the hate apparent. The hate that is in fact present all along may be unconscious or it may be a neglected (though perhaps not quite repressed) aspect of the love.

AMBIVALENCE

It is one of the lessons of Freud that we should be suspicious of loves that appear too pure. When a love claims to be wholly unconflicted, the modern mind suspects denial or other forms of evasion (even in Freud's own favored case of "the mother's relation to her male child"). For all our loves have a history in the development of our patterns of loving, and that history has always involved conflict—with others and within ourselves.

While in fact normal (if universality is evidence of "normality"), ambivalence is especially pronounced in neurotics of the obsessional sort and Freud presents a graphic picture of ambivalence in an incident involving that classic obsessional-neurotic, the Rat Man, and his lady-love (who had, it should be remembered, previously rejected his proposals) at a summer resort: "On the day of her departure he knocked his foot against a stone lying in the road, and was *obliged* to put it out of the way by the side of the road, because the idea struck him that her carriage would be driving along the same road in a few hours' time and might come to grief against this stone. But a few minutes later it occurred to him that this was absurd, and he was *obliged* to go back and replace the stone in its original position in the middle of the road."[24] (One wonders even about the Rat Man's first thought, the thought of possible harm to his lady-love. Despite its protective cloak, one wonders: Where did *it* come from?) The Rat Man's ambivalence (and not just his) is also manifested in doubts of various sorts, and Freud tellingly points to their significance: "A man who doubts his own love may, or rather *must,* doubt every lesser thing."[25] When love is interfered with and inhibited by hatred (especially unacknowledged hatred), doubt often characteristically emerges.

Unconscious conflict can manifest itself also in the self-reproaches of mourning and the self-tormenting of depression and even in social practices and rituals such as taboos.[26] While Freud writes most often of repressed, unconscious, hatreds, it should be noted infantile sources may fuel ambivalences of which we are only too well aware. A wholly unconflicted erotic love is, after Freud, unbelievable: "The evidence of psycho-analysis shows that almost every intimate emotional relation between two people which lasts for some time—marriage, friendship, the relations between parents and children—contains a sediment of feelings of aversion and hostility, which only escapes perception as a result of repression."[27]

Think again of what comes with love and the dynamics that follow. Love (on most accounts) naturally includes a desire to be with the beloved. Does wanting to be with the beloved lead (naturally? necessarily?) to wanting the intimacy to be exclusive, exacerbating fear of loss, and leading ultimately to efforts at control? Does the overestimation and idealization involved (naturally? necessarily?) in love, lead to disappointment when (inevitably) confronted with the reality of the beloved? If it does, expecting more of those we love, we may come to hate more deeply when they disappoint. Possessiveness and idealization may not be the only sources of hatred in love. Some of the traps may be built on apparent strengths of love, the comforts of security and identification. All the usual psychological mechanisms (displacement, projection, etc.) are available. So we may hate the people we love and who love us because it seems safe: assured of their love, we trust we will not lose them so we displace onto them the animosity we feel toward others that it seems too dangerous to express directly. Or we see ourselves mirrored in our loved ones, and project our own hated characteristics or self-hatreds onto them. Other twists and turns vary with the features one regards as essential to love, and the vast literature of love shows these to be indefinitely various.

All of this may seem to bring us back to pathology; but have we ever left it? Can one ever leave it? In connection with sexual perversion,

Freud writes, "In the sphere of sexual life we are brought up against peculiar and, indeed, insoluble difficulties as soon as we try to draw a sharp line to distinguish mere variations within the range of what is physiological from pathological symptoms."[28] A similar point may be true for love. In his "Observations on Transference-Love," Freud spells out the ways in which transference-love, the patient's love for the analyst, is abnormal, emphasizing its role as resistance to the aims of therapy, its repetition of earlier patterns of reaction, and its disregard for reality. He immediately adds: "We should not forget, however, that these departures from the norm constitute precisely what is essential about being in love."[29] Even the rationalist Plato, in the *Phaedrus,* recognizes and ultimately embraces the divine madness of love.

EMOTIONAL OPPOSITION

What makes love "the opposite" of hate? Spinoza defines love as "a Joy [sometimes translated Pleasure], accompanied by the idea of an external cause," and hate as "a Sadness [sometimes translated Pain], accompanied by the idea of an external cause."[30] Perhaps the place for us to start is with the apparently natural opposition of joy and sadness, pleasure and pain. Certainly typically, and on some accounts necessarily, one attracts and the other repels. Is the opposition of love and hate derivative?

Unfortunately, it is simply not the case that love is always pleasant and hatred always painful. Despite Spinoza's definitions of love and hate, which ground them in beliefs about the sources of pleasure and pain, we must all know from our experience that whatever the sources of feelings of love and hate, their manifestations and effects are not uniformly and distinctively pleasant or painful. While we might like to think love pleasant, we all know unrequited love is painful. Worse, we also know that even requited love can (perhaps must) bring pain. With the attachment of love comes the anxiety of loss and the pain of loss (whether actual or merely feared). Love makes us vulnerable in ways that enhance the possibilities of pain. Worse still, erotic love may in its very nature depend on absence and obstacle, lack and rivalry. It is not for nothing that eros is known as "bittersweet."[31] And looking from the other side, it is not unheard of for individuals to revel in hatred, to enjoy the passion and intrigue directed at enemies. It may even be the case that it is the intertwining pleasures and pains of love and hate that create a kind of equivalence between them, so that love and hate become the same, or rather, love-hate constitute a kind of passionate involvement that re-mains of a piece despite its cycles. So that the real opposition is not between love and hate, but between the intense passionate involvement they signify and indifference, a distancing emotional neutrality.[32] De-tached, we neither love nor hate.

The possible equivalence of love and hate is worth pausing on. Such equivalence is, according to Freud in "The Antithetical Meaning of Pri-mal Words," characteristic of many of our most basic concepts.[33] It emerges in the double and opposed meanings carried by many words in the oldest languages, as well as in the factors in the dream-work that allow an element in a dream to represent its contrary. At one level, this can be understood as a simple matter of association of contraries: so high makes us think of low, day of night, joy of sorrow. At a deeper level, however, the equivalence can be traced to a time at which the contraries are so far undifferentiated, before the concepts have been sorted out, and so the experience is itself undifferentiated. Indeed, the separate concepts are not yet available for associative or any other purposes. High/low is a dimension of experience, and joy/sorrow and love/hate are dimensions of experience; and confronted with either extreme along the dimensions we are confronted with both. They are thus, in a sense, "the same." This provides yet another way of thinking about the persisting presence and influence of love's history referred to earlier. Freud traces aspects of that history in the following passage:

> Preliminary stages of love emerge as provisional sexual aims while the sexual instincts are passing through their complicated development. As the first of these aims we recognize the phase of incorporating or devouring—a type of love which is consis-tent with abolishing the object's separate existence and which may therefore be described as ambivalent. At the higher stage of the pregenital sadistic-anal organization, the striving for the ob-ject appears in the form of an urge for mastery, to which injury or annihilation of the object is a matter of indifference. Love in this form and at this preliminary stage is hardly to be distin-guished from hate in its attitude towards the object. Not until the genital organization is established does love become the opposite of hate.[34]

Ambivalence and the equivalence of love and hate should also be seen in the context of more general issues and complexities concerning con-flict, in particular the fact that denial can function as affirmation. This is the central point in Freud's essay "Negation."[35] While the particular point has everything to do with the functioning of repression and the important psychological mechanism of splitting (which is especially significant in relation to ambivalence),[36] the thing to remember here is that emotional ambivalence itself is really but one of many manifestations of psychological conflict. The naturalness of ambivalent love and hate may thus connect not just with the problems of the self at its boundaries, and with the history and nature of love, but also with the inherent dividedness of the self itself and the nature of inner conflict.

Returning to our immediate theme, while love and hate may in some accounts be the models of emotional opposition, the underlying standard has not yet emerged. If they are opposite, then opposition does not entail incompatibility. If they are opposite, then opposition does not entail uniform concomitant pleasure or pain. If they are opposite, then opposition does not entail uniform attraction or aversion—on one level at least.[37]

So let us ask once more: What do we mean when we call one emotion the "opposite" of another? If emotions were simple sensations, like flavors, they might be grouped, though it would become difficult to see what gave them a direction, a vector, as well as an intensity or strength. At any rate, there is nothing in the nature of sensations that makes the simultaneous having of a diverse variety of them difficult to imagine or problematical. But emotions are not simply sensations. Since emotions are essentially constituted by certain relevant thoughts,[38] perhaps we can give emotional opposition a sense in terms of the relation of the constituent beliefs and other thoughts.

Pride is often said to be the opposite of humility. But opposition, insofar as it suggests incompatibility, does not seem to capture their relation. Certainly one can be proud of one thing and humble about another, but even focusing on a single feature or aspect of oneself, one may be proud yet also humble about it (proud of one's cooking, yet humbly recognizing that there are many whose cooking is better). Shame seems a stronger candidate for the opposite of pride, at least so far as incompatibility is the issue. Again, of course, one can be proud of one thing yet ashamed of another, or proud of a given object in one respect yet ashamed in another. But to be both proud and ashamed of the same thing in the same way simultaneously does seem impossible. The underlying beliefs seem to conflict. Pride is characterized by the belief that something related to oneself is valuable or reflects well on oneself, while shame is characterized by the belief that something related to oneself is bad or inferior and discredits or lessens one. The conflict of beliefs readily amounts to contradiction.

But perhaps the most familiar set of emotional opposites are love and hate. Let us recall and elaborate some of what we have seen so far about their opposition. What do we mean when we describe them as opposite? Certainly not that they cannot occur simultaneously, or even that they cannot occur simultaneously in relation to the same object. Ambivalence is a familiar feature of the human condition. Is such ambivalence best understood as a tendency to have different, indeed incompatible, beliefs—rather as with self-deception? But it is not obvious that love, in particular, is characterized by an essential belief. There may be certain ideals of love that require certain specific beliefs about the object, but love in general is not thought to require reasons (indeed, the citation of particular reasons can quickly come to seem like the bringing in of ulterior motives, motives that cast doubt on the description of the psychological state as love). Even supposing that particular beliefs essential to love and hate could be specified, does that make their opposition amount to conflict of beliefs, that is, to contradiction and incompatibility? Certainly we can both love and hate the same person. That is a common, if not the normal, condition. Insofar as that is because people are mixed bags, so we love them in one respect and hate them in others, the situation seems wholly unproblematical. (It becomes problematical when one engages in splitting, so that one denies one's feelings are in fact mixed feelings directed toward a single object or person.) One may love someone who is generous (loving them insofar as they are generous), and yet hate them insofar as they are abusive or possessive. Even focusing on a particular characteristic of the beloved, we can make sense of mixed feelings by bringing in external relations or divided interests in ourselves (e.g., we may both hate and love persons for their beauty, because while their beauty is attractive to us it may also be attractive to others and so become the grounds of painful jealousy). The more interesting question, however, as we have seen, is whether we can hate a person for the very reason that we love them, indeed, hate them because we love them?

That love and hate are very close can be seen in the ease with which one is transformed or gives place to the other. In some ways they are more alike than opposite. In one sense of opposite, indifference is the true opposite of both love and hate. They are both types of intense emotional involvement; it is emotional neutrality that is incompatible with each and so both of them. They are alike in intimacy, different in emotional tone. Does that offer a sense of "opposition" that can make intelligible what we mean when we say love is the opposite of hate? One might be tempted to say love is pleasant and hate unpleasant or painful (so people are often advised to overcome their hate because it is bad for them, not just for the object of their hate). This would make the opposition of love and hate derivative from the natural opposition of pleasure and pain. Unfortunately, it is phenomenologically false. While love can be pleasant, it can also be painful. Certainly unrequited love is characteristically painful. But even loves that are returned can be painfully bittersweet. And while hate may sometimes in some ways be unpleasant, many people have been known to revel in and enjoy their enmities. Perhaps again it is the feeling of deep emotional involvement that it shares with love that gives it its pleasurable taste, but whatever the explanation of the pleasure in hate, the opposition of hate and love cannot be simply reduced to the natural opposition of pleasure and pain.

Returning to the question raised a moment ago, Can we hate a person because we love them? we have seen in our earlier discussion that the answer seems to be yes. If, for example, love brings dependence and dependence is hateful, a kind of bondage, or even just fearful, creating risk and danger, then love may well bring hate naturally in its train. This was an argument pursued by Hegel and by Sartre. What sense does it leave to the opposition of love and hate? Unlike the opposition of pride and shame, it cannot be a matter of a conflict between the relevant beliefs, at least not if such conflict amounts to contradiction. For even were the beliefs specifiable, the conflict would not amount to contradiction. One cannot simultaneously and with full awareness maintain contradictory beliefs. But one can (as Catullus assures us) maintain love and hate toward a single object at the same time. Perhaps the opposition is not in the beliefs, but in the constituent desires. When Hume analyzes love and hate along with the other emotions as peculiar and distinctive sensations ("impressions of reflection") he explicitly denies that their characteristic desires are essential. "If nature had so pleas'd, love might have had the same effect as hatred, and hatred as love. I see no contradiction in supposing a desire of producing misery annex'd to love, and of happiness to hatred."[39] But in fact an apparent love would be rejected as love if we discovered that at the center of the passion was a wish for harm to the putative beloved. We would say the feeling was ambivalent or redescribe the situation in terms of the subject's beliefs (e.g., that the "harm" was not harm in his eyes). While particular beliefs may not be essential to love and hate, particular types of desires may well be. And if that is so, it is in terms of their relation that we can understand what we mean when we describe the love and hate as opposites. And it is important to see that opposition understood in terms of desire is rather different from opposition in terms of belief. While incompatible beliefs may be contradictory, so that they cannot be simultaneously and self-consciously maintained, incompatible desires need not "contradict" each other and can be simultaneously and self-consciously maintained.[40] That is, incompatibility of desires typically amounts to the fact that they cannot be mutually satisfied. But that is rather different from the situation in which two beliefs cannot both be true. I may have many desires that cannot be simultaneously satisfied (I may wish both to eat and to sleep, or to buy both of two objects when I only have money enough for one); that is the typical position for most people most of the time. It does not follow that one of the conflicting desires, like one of two conflicting beliefs, must yield. It can persist, be maintained, even if it cannot be satisfied. This difference in the nature of conflicting beliefs and desires has important consequences in psychoanalysis. Freud indicated to his patients early on that "much will be gained if we succeed in transforming your hysterical misery into common unhappiness."[41] When a desire is unacknowledged, its unconscious functioning can produce neurotic symptoms. Making the unconscious desires conscious does not guarantee their satisfaction: there may in fact be good reason not to act on them or circumstances may not allow it or, as in the normal condition, they may conflict with other desires. But at least once made conscious one should be freed from the additional suffering produced by the emergence of unconscious desires in symptomatic form. Once desires are conscious, one is in a position to deal with them as one does with any conflicting desires, weighing alternatives and seeking opportunities for appropriate satisfaction, though one remains subject to the ordinary unhappiness that conflicting desires may bring. Thus, while there is hope, overcoming emotional ambivalence is not so simple as pointing out an intellectual conflict of beliefs and insisting that (as reason demands) one be abandoned.

While love and hate are doubtless opposites, there is no reason to think their opposition or emotional opposition in general has a single sense, any more than that psychological conflict in general has a single explanation.

LOVING: COUNTING THE WAYS

While considering what we mean by saying two emotions are "opposite," by direction in emotions, I have too often been oversimplifying by speaking as though love and hate are not internally complex, and as though we all agree in ascribing a single clear meaning to each. While we use a single word in English, we nonetheless distinguish different types of love in terms of their objects and aims (e.g. family love, erotic love, love in friendship), and other languages employ different words for some of these.[42] And, as noted, the literature of love reveals no end to the different conceptions of the concept.[43] There have, however, been significant efforts at unification. Plato unified some of the forms of love in terms of a broad notion of desire (*eros*) and a narrow notion of egotistic motives. While Freud distinguished a separate affectionate current in love relations, he attributed great importance to what he called the sensual current (*libido*), and found it widely present—in particular, in infantile development, family relations, and the sublimated forms of higher cultural activity (from science to art to making and hoarding money). But whatever the persuasiveness of the efforts at unification, erotic desire is itself internally divided. This is especially clear if one follows Plato in thinking of desire in terms of lack. So far as the desirability of the love object derives from its lack, so far as it reveals the insufficiency and limits of the self, and so far as the history of displacement leading to the current object in turn leads to dissatisfaction, the tension and pain of erotic desire are part of its nature.

I have said it is simply not the case that love is uniformly pleasant and hate uniformly painful. I think that is true. But perhaps it is not *simply* true. Emotions are not simple sensations. Really, when we are ascribing an emotion to ourselves, we are giving an interpretation of complexes of sensation, desire, behavior, thought, and much else. To ascribe love or hate is not to describe a sensation; it is to summarize many inner and outer perceptions, their context, and our individual and social understandings. As a consequence, the "directions" or relations of emotions as apparently simple as love and hate are also complex.[44] As a further consequence, trying to draw sharp lines between these and other emotions on the basis of linguistic usage is not likely to get us very far in understanding their relationship. For example: We tend to spend more time with those we love, providing more occasions for possible irritation, and so anger. Anger can be distinguished from hatred (it tends to be more focused on particular wrongs or slights, rather than on the whole person; the desires involved are more typically for retribution or revenge than for destruction; and anger generally does not require or generate the sort of intimacy hatred seems to—though these differences, like differences of intensity, may be matters of degree); nonetheless occasions for anger can aggregate into sources of hatred. But we should not put too much weight on this

point. First, because any distinctions we make between anger and hatred can be no more firm than the best psychological theory available
to us. Linguistic habits do not alone suffice; after all, as often as not,
"hate" is used as equivalent to "dislike," as in "I hate eggplant." And,
second, because it overcivilizes our attitudes. As Freud says, "When . . .
hostility is directed against people who are otherwise loved we describe it as ambivalence of feeling; and we explain the fact, in what is
probably far too rational a manner, by means of the numerous occasions for conflicts of interest which arise precisely in such intimate
relations."[45]

Love and hate are not social equals. We readily accept that we love; we
do not so readily accept that we hate. Thus hate is more often suppressed and repressed. Love has all the time in the world. Hate, we think,
must give way. When in love, we desire to keep on desiring. We do not
want our state to change. We have no standard way to think our way
from love to hate. Religion makes it its business to think a way from hate
to love, to offer a path through atonement, forgiveness, and mercy.[46] But,
as we have seen, love and hate come already mixed in the nature of
erotic desire. Erotic love is not selfless; it desires its own satisfaction. It
disturbs equanimity, lifting and troubling the spirit at the same time.
Eros, in our imagination and experience, is "bittersweet." And this may
have its value; as Blake insisted: "Without contraries is no progression.
Attraction and repulsion, reason and energy, love and hate, are necessary
to human existence."[47]

To retrace some of our steps briefly: That we should hate people we
love because they abuse or betray us presents no mystery. After all,
people are mixed bags and so there is no problem about loving them in
some respects while hating them in others. The interesting question is
why we should hate people precisely because we love them (presuming
even that they love us back, that it is not unrequited love). Part of the
answer, I think, is that love brings with it dependence, and so vulnerability and risk; we naturally come to resent those we love *because* we love
them, because it makes us dependent. The next, deeper, question is why
or whether dependence should be thought of as hateful (rather than
merely risky). So far as our identities are at stake in love, death enters the
picture and helps make extreme fear (which so often functions as a
source of hate) intelligible. The naturalness of ambivalent love and hate
may thus connect with problems of self-identity. Added to this the dividedness of the self itself (including instinctual dualism and other forms of
mixed desire) and the inherent dividedness of love and other primal
emotions (which may have its origins in the history of loving but persists

in later development and gets complicated as other features are added by experience and varying ideals of love) make emotional ambivalence a natural manifestation of inner conflict.

What might have seemed a puzzle in our emotional lives, that we also hate those we love, is no accident; indeed—frightening thought—it may be inevitable. When it comes to love, as Freud teaches, the normal is pathological. The logic of emotional identification explored by Spinoza, the dialectic of the rivalrous desires to be free and to be loved explored by Sartre, as well as the history and dynamics of our conflictual life at our boundaries explored by Freud, lead to the ambivalence of love and hate. But then the other side of Freud's insight, that the normal is pathological, is that the pathological is normal. This should be some comfort.[48]

NOTES

1. *The Poems of Gaius Valerius Catullus,* trans. F. W. Cornish, Loeb Classical Library (Cambridge: Harvard University Press, 1962), 162–63, poem 85:

> Odi et amo. quare id faciam, fortasse requiris.
> nescio, sed fieri sentio et excrucior.

Louis Zukofsky, *Catullus fragmenta* (London: Turret Books, 1969) offers a modern English play on the Latin:

> O th'hate I move love. Quarry it fact I am, for that's so re queries.
> Nescience, say th' fiery scent I owe whets crookeder.

2. Spinoza, *Ethics* (1677), part 3, proposition 27. See, for example, "He who imagines one he loves to be affected with hate toward him will be tormented by Love and Hate together. For insofar as he imagines that [the one he loves] hates him, he is determined to hate [that person] in return (by P40). But (by hypothesis) he nevertheless loves him. So he will be tormented by Love and Hate together." *Ethics,* part 3, proposition 40, Cor. 1—*The Collected Works of Spinoza,* ed. and trans. Edwin Curley (Princeton: Princeton University Press, 1985).

3. Cf. Spinoza, *Ethics,* part 3, props. 38 and 44.

4. See Freud, *Psycho-Analytic Notes on an Autobiographical Account of a Case of Paranoia* (1911), in *Standard Edition* [*SE*] 12:part III; and "Some Neurotic Mechanisms in Jealousy, Paranoia and Homosexuality" (1922), *SE* 18:223–32.

5. See Anna Freud, *The Ego and the Mechanisms of Defence* (London: Hogarth Press, [1936] 1966), chap. 9, "Identification with the Aggressor."

6. See Neu, *Emotion, Thought, and Therapy* (Routledge and Kegan Paul and University of California Press, 1977), 32–34.

7. "How We Cry and Laugh for the Same Thing," *The Complete Works of Montaigne* (1588), trans. Donald M. Frame (Stanford: Stanford University Press, 1958), 173.

8. Again Spinoza sees clearly. He writes of cases of "vacillation of mind" in which "two contrary affects" occur "at the same time," noting "we can easily conceive that one and the same object can be the cause of many and contrary affects" (*Ethics,* part 3, prop. 17 and Schol.).

Emotions in general should not be confused with fleeting sensations. Emotions, like beliefs, are typically dispositional states that occur over time. As Patricia Greenspan puts it, "we may be said to have or exhibit a particular emotion (and indeed, I might add, to exhibit it consciously) over a span of time which includes, but is not limited to, the times (supposing there are some) when we are actually experiencing it" ("A Case of Mixed Feelings: Ambivalence and the Logic of Emotion," in *Explaining Emotions,* ed. Amelie Rorty [Berkeley and Los Angeles: University of California Press, 1980], 229). But the possibilities of ambivalence, of conflicting feelings toward a single object, do not depend on the feelings involved being extended over time. Philip J. Koch nicely brings out how the complexity of emotions, emotional components, and the self itself makes for the various common forms of ambivalence in "Emotional Ambivalence," *Philosophy and Phenomenological Research* 48 (1987): esp. 264–65.

9. Freud, *New Introductory Lectures on Psycho-Analysis* (1933), *SE* 22:73.

10. Plato, *Phaedrus* 243C, trans. Hackforth.

11. Jean-Paul Sartre, *Being and Nothingness,* trans. Hazel E. Barnes (New York: Philosophical Library, 1956), part 3, chap. 3, "Concrete Relations with Others." The quotations that follow in the text are, respectively, from 394, 377, 411.

12. "Why does the lover want to be *loved?*" and "to love is to wish to be loved" (*Being and Nothingness,* 366, 377). If not the essence of love, as in Sartre, Spinoza makes the desire to be loved part of the logic of love: "When we love a thing like ourselves, we strive, as far as we can, to bring it about that it loves us in return" (*Ethics,* part 3, prop. 33; the proof, via prop. 29, involving as it does a reversal from active to passive, is obscure. It might be clearer if it went through props. 21 and 25).

13. Carol Gilligan, *In a Different Voice* (Cambridge: Harvard University Press, 1982), 8. See also Nancy Chodorow, *The Reproduction of Mothering* (Berkeley and Los Angeles: University of California Press, 1978). The Hegelian dialectic of recognition, domination, and submission is most fruitfully explored in relation to psychological theory by Jessica Benjamin, *The Bonds of Love* (New York: Pantheon Books, 1988).

14. See Norman O. Brown, *Love's Body* (New York: Vintage Books, 1966), chap. 8, "Boundary."

15. Freud, *Civilization and Its Discontents* (1930 [1929]), *SE* 21:part I. Plato, *Symposium* 189–92.

16. Freud, *Three Essays on the Theory of Sexuality* (1905), *SE* 7:222.

17. Freud, "On the Universal Tendency to Debasement in the Sphere of Love (1912), *SE* 11:188–89.

18. Rivalry with those we love (and identify with) is a natural source of ambivalence. "If something like ourselves (another person, with whom we identify) causes us pain *by* gaining pleasure for itself—by getting something we would like to have ourselves, for instance—then according to Spinoza, it ought to cause us *both* pain and pleasure, and hence be an object of *both* hatred and love" (Patricia Greenspan, "A Case of Mixed Feelings," 226).

Catullus's personal problems with rivalry are considered in Anne Vannan Rankin, "Odi et Amo: Gaius Valerius Catullus and Freud's Essay on 'A Special Type of Choice of Object Made by Men,' " *American Imago* 19 (1962): 437–48.

The special intensity of infantile ambivalence is discussed by Freud in his lecture on "Femininity," *New Introductory Lectures on Psycho-Analysis* (1933 [1932]), in *SE* 22: "A powerful tendency to aggressiveness is always present beside a powerful love, and the more passionately a child loves its object the more sensitive does it become to disappointments and frustrations from that object" (124); he speaks also of the child's "insatiable" needs (122) and points out its "demands for love are immoderate, they make exclusive claims and tolerate no sharing" (123).

19. Norman O. Brown, *Love's Body,* 142. "At the very beginning, it seems, the external world, objects, and what is hated are identical. If later on an object turns out to be a source of pleasure, it is loved, but it is also incorporated into the ego" (Freud, "Instincts and their Vicissitudes" [1915], in *SE* 14:136).

20. Freud, *Beyond the Pleasure Principle* (1920), in *SE* 18:53–54; *The Ego and the Id* (1923), in *SE* 19:part 4; *Civilization and Its Discontents* (1930 [1929]), in *SE* 21:part 6.

21. Freud, *Civilization and Its Discontents* (1930 [1929]), in *SE* 21:113.

22. Freud, "Instincts and their Vicissitudes" (1915), in *SE* 14:139.

23. See Edward Bibring, "The Development and Problems of the Theory of the Instincts," *International Journal of Psychoanalysis* 21 (1941): 102–31; "Editor's Note" to "Instincts and their Vicissitudes," *SE* 14:111–16.

24. Freud, "Notes Upon a Case of Obsessional Neurosis" (1909), in *SE* 10:190.

25. Ibid., 241. Freud elsewhere connects doubt, as the repudiation of instincts for knowledge and mastery, with sadism ("The Disposition to Obsessional Neurosis" [1913], in *SE* 12.

26. See Freud, "Mourning and Melancholia" (1917 [1915]), in *SE* 14: esp. 250–52, 256–58; "Taboo and Emotional Ambivalence", chap. 2 of *Totem and Taboo* (1913 [1912–13]), in *SE* 13. See also Neu, "Getting Behind the Demons," *Humanities in Society* 4 (1981): 171–96.

27. Freud, *Group Psychology and the Analysis of the Ego* (1921), *SE* 18:101.

28. Freud, *Three Essays on the Theory of Sexuality* (1905), in *SE* 7:160–61. See "Freud and Perversion," in *The Cambridge Companion to Freud,* ed. J. Neu (Cambridge: Cambridge University Press, 1992).

29. Freud, "Observations on Transference-Love" (1915 [1914]), in *SE* 12:169.

30. *Ethics,* part 3, Definitions of the Affects 6 and 7.

31. The paradoxes of erotic desire emerge as dilemmas of sensation, action, and value that are elegantly discussed in connection with ancient poetry by Anne Carson, *Eros the Bittersweet* (Princeton: Princeton University Press, 1986). See also, Jon Elster, *Ulysses and the Sirens* (Cambridge: Cambridge University Press, 1979), chap. 4, "Irrationality: Contradictions of the Mind."

32. As Freud helpfully points out: "Loving admits not merely of one, but of three opposites. In addition to the antithesis 'loving-hating', there is the other one of 'loving–being loved'; and, in addition to these, loving and hating taken together are the opposite of the condition of unconcern or indifference" ("Instincts and their Vicissitudes" [1915], in *SE* 14:133). The Bible speaks of such neutrality: "So then because thou art lukewarm, and neither cold nor hot, I will spew thee out of my mouth" (Rev. 3:16). Literature is full of talk of "nearest and dearest" enemies. Hume notes "The connexion is in many respects closer betwixt any two passions, than betwixt any passion and indifference" (*A Treatise of Human Nature* [1739], ed. L. A. Selby-Bigge [Oxford, 1888], 420). Freud writes of himself in *The Interpretation of Dreams:* "My emotional life has always insisted that I should have an intimate friend and a hated enemy. I have always been able to provide myself afresh with both, and it has not infrequently happened that the ideal situation of childhood has been so completely reproduced that friend and enemy have come together in a single individual—though not, of course, both at once or with constant oscillations, as may have been the case in my early childhood" (*SE* 5:483).

33. "The Antithetical Meaning of Primal Words" (1910), *SE* 11:155–61. See Neu, "A Tear Is an Intellectual Thing," *Representations* 19 (1987): 35–61.

34. Freud, "Instincts and their Vicissitudes" (1915), *SE* 14:138–39.

35. "Negation" (1925), *SE* 19:235–39.

36. The importance of splitting (and projection) in the psychology of ambivalence is emphasized by Melanie Klein and her followers. See Hanna Segal, "The Achievement of Ambivalence," *Common Knowledge* (1992), 1:92–103.

37. This does not make them indistinguishable or the same. Love and hate remain at least as distinguishable as the life and death instincts for which Freud has them do duty (*The Ego and the Id* [1923], in *SE* 19:42–43).

38. See Neu, *Emotion, Thought, and Therapy.*

39. Hume, *A Treatise of Human Nature,* 2:368.

40. See Bernard Williams, "Ethical Consistency," in his *Problems of the Self* (Cambridge: Cambridge University Press, 1973).

41. Freud, *Studies in Hysteria* (1895), in *SE* 2:305.

42. We distinguish different kinds of love, but not different kinds of hate. Why not? Some might think because the objects of hatred are more uniform. This was Descartes's view though it is rather implausible; see *The Passions of the Soul* (1649), trans. Robert Stoothoff, in *The Philosophical Writings of Descartes* (Cambridge: Cambridge University Press, 1985), 1:358, sect. 84.

43. See such surveys as Irving Singer's three-volume *The Nature of Love* (Chicago: University of Chicago Press, 1966–88); Denis de Rougemont, *Love in the Western World,* trans. M. Belgion, rev. ed. (Princeton: Princeton University Press, 1983); and C. S. Lewis, *The Allegory of Love* (Oxford: Oxford University Press, 1936).

Even in our brief discussion of Sartre, one can discern two different conceptions of love. The first—taking its essence as the desire for the full possession of a free being—is what for him makes satisfactory love impossible. But while that definition relies on dubious notions of freedom and possession, he has a second definition—according to which love is equated with the desire to be loved—which seems to me to contain important psychological truth.

44. Given the vast literature on love, it should perhaps be emphasized that hatred too is not to be understood as an isolated sensation. Its ascription similarly involves the summary of much. Even a Cartesian such as Sartre allows for error in relation to certain "states," notably including hatred, that extend over time; see *The Transcendence of the Ego,* trans. Williams and Kirkpatrick (originally published in French 1936–37; New York: NoonDay Press, 1957), 61–68; and *Being and Nothingness,* 162.

45. *Group Psychology and the Analysis of the Ego* (1921), in *SE* 18:102.

46. There are helpful thoughts on this in Jeffrie G. Murphy and Jean Hampton, *Forgiveness and Mercy* (Cambridge: Cambridge University Press, 1988). They start with hatred and ask how it *should* be modified by compassion: tempering justice with mercy, anger and resentment with forgiveness, hate with love. In this discussion I have been starting with love and asking how it *is* (in fact) modified by hatred, anger, and resentment.

47. William Blake, "The Marriage of Heaven and Hell," 7–9.

48. I was invited to participate in an American Philosophical Association symposium, "Hatred," in March 1989. I was also invited to participate in an American Academy of Psychoanalysis symposium, "Love," in May 1989. It seemed appropriate to present the same paper to both.

I express (unambivalent) thanks to Norman O. Brown and Lynn Luria-Sukenick.

4

Anger . . . and Anger: From Freud to Feminism

KATHLEEN WOODWARD

I had early discovered . . . that passions often lead to sorrows.
—Freud, *The Interpretation of Dreams*

The streets of London have their map; but our passions are uncharted.
—Virginia Woolf, *Jacob's Room*

Ⓘn this essay I plot a line of development in Freud's thought about the strong emotions, with anger as my focal point. By "strong emotions" I mean those such as fear, hate, triumph, jealousy, horror, greed, and *l'amour fou,* most of which could also be referred to as the "passions" but not all (disgust and shame are examples of strong emotions that we would not term passions). In their intensity, duration, and focus, the strong emotions differ from what I call the quiet emotions (nostalgia, sadness, and tranquillity, for example), the chafing emotions (annoyance, irritation), and the expansive emotions (oceanic feeling, amusement, sympathy).[1]

The passages I've chosen with the strong emotion of anger in view are drawn from *Studies on Hysteria* (1893), *The Interpretation of Dreams* (1900), "The Moses of Michelangelo" (1914), and *Civilization and Its Discontents* (1930). I've selected them in great part because, with the exception of *Civilization and Its Discontents,* they focus on what could be termed "professional" relations between people rather than on erotic wishes, for so long now familiar to us in Freud. The path traced through these four texts leads from feminized hysterical anger to grandiose annihilating anger, from frozen wrath to guilt. It defines a trajectory of emotional development in Freud's work culminating in the containment of the drive of aggressivity (and anger, its emotional representative) by guilt, the quintessential Freudian emotion.

I hope I shall not be understood as suggesting that Freud did not value the emotions. On the contrary, as he asserted clearly in "Delusions and Dreams in Jensen's *Gradiva*" (1907), the emotions are the only valuable things in psychic life.[2] But in general for Freud, the strong emotions are explosive, volatile, dangerous (or perhaps it would be more accurate to say that Freud was ambivalent about the strong emotions; certainly it would be more "Freudian" to phrase it this way). Thus at every one of these four points we shall see that one of Freud's major themes is the mechanism that *inhibits* the expression of the strong emotions. In each case it is different: in the first three texts I discuss, Freud considers in turn the inhibition of anger by repression, suppression (the dreamwork), and self-control. Ultimately Freud will conclude in *Civilization and Its Discontents* that fire must be fought with fire, emotion with emotion. In the final analysis, then, the controlling emotion—Freud's passion for guilt—is a chilling and paralyzing one.

I am drawn to this subject by my general interest in theories and discourses of the emotions, but more specifically by what may seem at first to bear a rather far-flung relation to Freud: the value placed on the emotion of anger in recent feminist writing in the United States. Anger is the contemporary feminist emotion of choice. I am fascinated by this discursive emphasis on anger. It is indisputably one of the prime examples of the general redistribution of the emotions in terms of gender taking place in contemporary culture. Anger, long associated with men, is being appropriated by women. (Another prime example is grief, an emotion historically linked predominately with women, now being put passionately into discourse by men.)[3] What is entailed by this feminist valorization of anger? At whom or what should it be directed? What tone or shape should it take? What assumptions about anger are contained in this work? What are the limits of anger? I shall take the opportunity to address at least some of these questions at the end of this essay. By returning to Freud I intend to provide a contrasting perspective from which to do so. My project in this essay, then, is to understand more clearly the bases of both discourses of anger—Freudian and feminist—through their differences, and ultimately to test the limitations of each of them through the other.

So, what, I wondered, did Freud have to say about anger? I turned to the index of the *Standard Edition.* Under "anger" I was startled to find virtually no entries. The index did refer me to *Studies on Hysteria* but all of the references were to sections authored by Breuer with the single exception of one attributed to the two of them. This short passage from the "Preliminary Communication" I shall consider in a moment. First, however, I insist on a distinction between anger and aggressivity, a distinction signaled by the Index itself: under "aggressiveness" there are many entries (this may be in part a result of scholars traditionally not being interested in the emotions). Anger is an *emotion,* what in Western culture we understand as an interiorized affective state (other cultures, as anthropologists point out, conceive of emotion as something that exists *between* people, not as something *in* individuals).[4] Aggressivity is a *drive:* to action, to behavior. In his work as a whole Freud placed much more emphasis on a theory of the drives than he did on the emotions. In fact he devoted remarkably little attention to the emotions in comparison, say, with Melanie Klein, whose work is a veritable theoretical atlas of the strong emotions of psychoanalysis. What, then, is the relationship between emotion and aggressivity? Certainly the two are linked but not indissolubly so. We can imagine aggression that does not proceed from feelings of anger or rage or hate. Likewise we can imagine angry feelings that do not eventuate in aggressive behavior toward others; indeed Freud astutely theorized the conversion of aggressivity toward others into self-aggressivity—in the form of an emotion. With these brief observations in mind I turn to *Studies on Hysteria.*

FEMINIZED HYSTERICAL ANGER

Hysteria is associated of course overwhelmingly with women and with the repression of sexual desire, which I understand more precisely as a drive than as an emotion. But in *Studies on Hysteria* Freud does report one case that deals explicitly with the repression of the emotion of anger. I call it the case of the hysterical employee. It is, as we shall see, a case with a distinctly contemporary flavor. Given the traditional understanding of anger as a male emotion, it should not surprise us that this hysterical patient is not a woman but a man. He is furious at his employer who has mistreated him physically and at the legal justice system that has accorded him no redress. What is the outcome of his repression of anger? It erupts hysterically in the guise of "a frenzy of rage" as if its repression had compressed it into a denser, more volatile force. I quote the entire passage devoted to the scenario:

> an employee who had become a hysteric as a result of being ill-treated by his superior, suffered from attacks in which he collapsed and fell into a frenzy of rage, but without uttering a word or giving any sign of a hallucination. It was possible to provoke an attack under hypnosis, and the patient then revealed that he was living through the scene in which his employer had abused him in the street and hit him with a stick. A few days later the patient came back and complained of having had another attack of the same kind. On this occasion it turned out under hypnosis that he had been re-living the scene to which the actual onset of the illness was related: the scene in the law-court when he failed to obtain satisfaction for his maltreatment. (*SE* 2:14)

For Freud and Breuer this case is an illustration of a hysterical attack that consists only of "motor phenomena" (that is, it does not exhibit a hallucinatory phase). Like other forms of hysteria, the root or precipitating cause is a memory of a psychical trauma, a memory that has been repressed. But of what is the memory? An event? An emotion? A desire?

Although Freud does not say anything more about this case (certainly he does not pretend to adjudicate it), we can assume that he understands it as he does other cases of hysteria: the person afflicted with hysteria must remember and rehearse either his desire or affect (to repeat: I am here associating desire with a drive, affect with an emotion). The psychical trauma, signaled by the symptom of hysterical rage, must be "disposed of by abreaction or by associative thought-activity" (*SE* 2:15).

But on second thought, is there not a significant difference between this case of hysterical anger and a case of hysterical erotic desire? In the latter instance, Freud counsels the assumption and acceptance of sexual desire, which is the manifestation of what he will later understand as the libidinal drive. In effect he approves it. In the case of the hysterical employee, on the other hand, it appears to be the emotion itself—his anger at the legal justice system and at his employer—that is the precipitating factor of the illness. Repressed anger, in other words, may not be a mere symptom of the illness but its very root. Thus it is the anger itself that should be "abreacted," released as it were into the air.

In his essay "The Unconscious" (1915), Freud explains the relation between memory, representation, and emotion this way: "affects and emotions correspond to processes of discharge, the final manifestations of which are perceived as feelings," while "ideas are cathexes—basically of memory-traces" (178). James Hillman, glossing this passage in *Emotion*, offers the following analogy, which captures perfectly Freud's view of anger as a violent and destructive emotion: "let us conceive of these 'cathexes—ultimately of memory-traces' as bombs. The bombs 'exist' in the unconscious, but the affect as the quantitative explosive potential of the bombs" (53).

Hysteria in this altogether unusual case is not associated with the private sphere (the familiar Freudian bedroom). Rather, it is set in the public sphere (the workplace, courts of law), which in the nineteenth century was the confirmed province of men. Furthermore its unexpected scenario underscores the unequal power relations of men: in this situation, of employer-employee. Freud of course does not address the issue of power. He does not politicize the emotion of anger. But if in general men have the cultural "right" to express their anger, this particular man—an employee—evidently did not. He did not experience "satisfaction" in his anger. Instead his hysterical anger feminizes him.[5]

Today we would likely consider this case in terms of harassment, which turns precisely on the analyzing pivot of unequal power relations with a "superior" or "dominant" taking advantage of a "subordinate." *Acting* on the emotion would be part of the therapy. We would look to the courts for "satisfaction," for redress that was not forthcoming in the nineteenth century. But therapy, not legal action, was Freud's then innovative answer, therapy to exorcise the anger. Psychic repression was the mechanism that Freud theorized had concealed this anger in the first place; as he wrote in "The Unconscious," "to suppress the development of affect is the true aim of repression and . . . its work is incomplete if this aim is not achieved" (178). Therapy in the form of hypnosis would release it. The patient would be purged of the anger that was, in effect, attacking him. Thus in this context anger is understood as a debilitating emotion. In *Studies on Hysteria* both the psychic mechanism of repression and the corresponding treatment of hypnosis have as their goal the effacement or catharsis of the self-destructive emotion of anger. As we know, Freud was soon to reject hypnosis as ineffective.

GRANDIOSE ANNIHILATING ANGER

In *The Interpretation of Dreams* Freud explores another psychic mechanism which inhibits the emotions: the dream-work. It serves to *suppress* and *dilute* the emotions, thereby allowing them to be staged in the dream. If in the case of the hysterical employee the diagnostic complement of repression is hypnosis, here the diagnostic complement of the dream-work is the analysis of the dream mass into its dream-thoughts. But within the context of my emphasis on anger, the term "dream-passions" would seem a far more appropriate term than "dream-thoughts." Freud's conviction is that analysis will ultimately allow the strong emotions to present themselves and that, as a result, they will be resolved into a calming order.

One dream in particular is relevant here. In the important section on "Affects in Dreams" Freud analyzes at quite some length the "emotional storm" released by what we have come to refer to as the "Non Vixit" dream. I quote it in full:

> *I had gone to Brücke's laboratory at night, and, in response to a gentle knock on the door, I opened it to* (the late) *Professor Fleischl, who came in with a number of strangers and, after exchanging a few words, sat down at his table. . . . My friend Fl.* [Fliess] *had come to Vienna unobtrusively in July. I met him in the street in conversation with my* (deceased) *friend P., and went with them to some place where they sat opposite each other as though they were at a small table. I sat in front at its narrow end. Fl. spoke about his sister and said that in three quarters of an hour she was dead, and added some such words as "that was the threshold." As P. failed to understand him, Fl. turned to me and asked me how much I had told P. about his affairs. Whereupon, overcome by strange emotions, I tried to explain to Fl. that P. (could not understand anything at all, of course, because he) was not alive. But what I actually said— and I myself noticed the mistake—was, "NON VIXIT." I then gave P. a piercing look. Under my gaze he turned pale; his form grew indistinct and his eyes a sickly blue—and finally he melted away. I was highly delighted at this and I now realized that Ernst Fleischl, too, had been no more than an apparition, a "revenant"; and it seemed to me quite possible that people of that kind only existed as long as one liked and could be got rid of if someone else wished it. (SE 5:421)*

About this angry dream I want to make three points. First, Freud's fantasy in the "Non Vixit" dream—it is surely grandiose—is that his anger is itself a lethal weapon. Related to this is his implication that the dream-work, which serves to suppress (not repress) affect in the first place, may ultimately work to magnify it.

To me the most memorable aspect of the "Non Vixit" dream is the "scene of annihilation" (520) where Freud "acts" on his anger, exterminating his friend with a wounding glance, causing him as if in some bizarre science fiction film to liquefy and finally to evaporate into nothing, leaving no bodily trace. This Freud analyzes as a reversal of the very same treatment he had once received from his employer-teacher Brücke who had chastised him for his renowned tardiness as an assistant in his lab.[6] Here, then, the anger of the professor provokes the anger of the student. Elsewhere in *The Interpretation of Dreams* Freud vividly describes this event, which so clearly had a mortifying effect on his self-esteem:

> One morning he turned up punctually at the hour of opening and awaited my arrival. His words were brief and to the point. But it was not they that mattered. What overwhelmed me were the terrible blue eyes with which he looked at me and by which I was reduced to nothing. . . . No one who can remember the great man's eyes, which retained their striking beauty even in his old age, and who has ever seen him in anger, will find it difficult to picture the young sinner's emotions. (422)

In the case of the hysterical employee, the anger of his employer (who, as we recall, beat his subordinate with a stick) provoked the employee's anger. The employee took his grievance to the courts where, however, he found no "satisfaction" (*SE* 2:14). The result is that the employee turned the anger against himself, making himself physically sick. In the case of the "Non Vixit" dream, anger also calls forth anger. But here the comparison ends. The anger is wildly out of proportion. Freud *was* late. Moreover, anger is vented in fantasy that does result in satisfaction and delight. What an amazing phenomenon is the dream!

Indeed the grandiose fantasy of the dream is that anger is itself a firearm, that Freud's anger is so powerful the mere expression of it constitutes murderous aggression. An emotion is converted into a physical force in fantasy. Freud succeeds in destroying his friend with a laserlike look of piercing anger. To his shame. And to his anxiety. For might he not expect retaliation in an endless escalation of anger and action?

In his discussion of the "Non Vixit" dream Freud repeatedly refers to the "raging" of the emotions that accompany it. To my mind the high degree of its emotional intensity is its most striking feature, especially given Freud's argument in this section of *The Interpretation of Dreams* that the dream-work serves to weaken or dilute the emotions, to bring "about a suppression of affects" (467). As he puts it elsewhere in *The Interpretation of Dreams,* "the purpose for which the censorship exercises its office and brings about the distortion of dreams" is "*in order to prevent the generation of anxieties and other forms of distressing affect*" (267). The dream-work itself must therefore possess great power, as is underscored in Freud's vivid description of it: "the whole mass of these dream-thoughts is brought under the pressure of the dream-work, and its elements are turned about, broken into fragments and jammed together—almost like pack-ice" (312). Freud pictures the resulting dream as a dense, cold mass of different elements that have been fused together. When I read this passage I think of the dream-work in terms of my high school atomic physics, of fission and fusion, the particles of the dream-thoughts being smashed together with a force inconceivable in terms of the weights and measures, the pulleys and levers, of everyday life. Imagine, then, the force in turn required to separate these elements, a force equivalent to that of an atom smasher. More, imagine the emotional storm that would then be released.

Second, given that the emotional world of the "Non Vixit" dream is far more complicated than that of the case of the hysterical employee (which revolves around the single emotion of anger), how does Freud explain his anger (which was, he tells us, "strange")? What accounts for his overwhelming sense of emotional strangeness? In part it may be due to the eerie feeling arising from the altogether peculiar situation of addressing a person who is in fact dead. But more fundamentally, I think, what struck Freud as "strange" was the complex of *contradictory* strong emotions released by the dream.

In his analysis of the dream-mass, Freud focuses on the different categories of emotions—what he calls the "various qualities" of affect—that accompanied it at two nodal points: "hostile and distressing" feelings when he "annihilated" his friend and enemy with two words and a piercing look, and feelings of "delight" and "satisfaction" at the end of the dream when he realized not only that such people could be eliminated whenever one (he) wanted but even more pleasurably, that such aggressivity was justified (480). Thus what may have been particularly troubling to Freud was the presence of contradictory emotions with regard to the same person. As we know, this emotional knot would come to be one of Freud's decisive contributions to a theory of strong attachments: that they are characterized by binary emotions, with love and hate being the primary pair.

We should not be surprised to learn, therefore, that later in his analysis of the "Non Vixit" dream Freud traces the roots of the pattern of his present-day intense emotional relationships to his colleagues and friends back to the *emotional world* of his early childhood, to his relationship with his nephew John who was a year older than he was, his "senior" and "superior" (483). As Freud observes earlier in *The Interpretation of Dreams,* "Until the end of my third year we had been inseparable. We had loved and fought with each other; and this childhood relationship . . . had a determining influence on all my subsequent relations with contemporaries" (424). In relation to the "Non Vixit" dream one childhood memory (or fantasy) in particular of his nephew returns to Freud: when Freud, not yet even two years old, is interrogated by his father for hitting his playmate. Freud's defense? "I hit him 'cos he hit me" (484). Notice that retaliation against a "superior" is at issue, one of Freud's dominant fantasies. In his discussion of the "Non Vixit" dream Freud concluded, "My emotional life has always insisted that I should have an intimate friend and a hated enemy" (483). Thus in adulthood the personal intersects (or perhaps more accurately, infects) the professional, upping the ante of emotional engagement. We should not fail to note that the site of the first part of the dream is Brücke's laboratory where Freud had worked and that all of the major figures in the dream are men. Here again anger is gendered male.

Third, given Freud's emphasis on the intensity of the emotions (in particular his annihilating anger), it is peculiar to me that nowhere in his analysis does he name the emotion of guilt, which will become so central to his thought later on. Instead he repeatedly uses the word "reproach" (the reproach of others and self-reproach). With reproach we seem to find ourselves in a novel of manners rather than in a tragedy or a romance of passion. Reproach is one of the chafing emotions, not one of the strong or quiet emotions. Reproach implies disapproval, rebuke, reproval. Thus it is primarily a social emotion. And as a social emotion, it is altogether in keeping with Freud's emphasis on shame in his analysis of the "Non Vixit" dream.[7] Shame implies an external, observing other as opposed to guilt, which implies an internalized, observing other (although Freud does mention self-reproach, he does not identify it as guilt, which, as we will see, he will ultimately come to associate with an action that is *not* taken, only fantasized). Thus in the short history of the emotions that I am sketching here, guilt seems to emerge later than shame in the development of Freud's thought. Or, we might speculate that the emotion of guilt was too distressing for Freud at this point in his life, that in the "Non Vixit" dream it could only escape the censorship of the dream-work under the guise of shame.

"FROZEN WRATH"

In *Studies on Hysteria* we encounter a hysterical man whose frenzied attacks of rage physically mimic his anger, reducing him to a feminized position. His rage and his body are out of control. Repression is ultimately an ineffective mechanism for containing anger. In the "Non Vixit" dream, the dream-work (which is, like repression, an unconscious process) serves both to suppress and stage that anger. If the anger is out of proportion to the event that prompted the dream, nonetheless the phenomenon of the dream allows the safe and satisfying expression of aggressive fantasies entailed by anger. Furthermore, the phenomenon of analysis puts those emotions into perspective. In my third text, "The Moses of Michelangelo," Freud considers an altogether different mechanism for the control of anger, one that is conscious, indeed self-conscious.

The relay between the affect of anger and destructive action is Freud's subject in "The Moses of Michelangelo." As his analytic point of departure he takes his own powerful reaction of "intellectual bewilderment" (also a preferred Freudian emotion) on repeated viewings of Michelangelo's sculpture of Moses. Freud comes to the conclusion that Michelangelo brilliantly rewrote the scriptural history of anger embodied by Moses. Similarly, we may read Freud's essay as a rewriting of his own evolving thought on the emotion of anger, in particular, its containment.

It is a question of reading for the plot, of the timing of action and emotion. As Freud remarks, the seated figure of Moses is traditionally understood to be represented in a state of anger incipient to ruinous behavior, that he is on the verge of bounding up and hurling down the Tables of the Law, demolishing them in a single furious gesture. Freud, however, reads the plot differently. He advances Moses and his audience in time. He concludes that Moses has already half-risen in his rage, only to stop his angry action and return to a state of wrathful immobility, or "frozen wrath" (*SE* 13:229). The heat of passion is chilled to the sculptural bone. Moses resists the temptation to act on "rage and indignation," which would have been "an indulgence of his feelings" and would have entailed the annihilation of the Law. He "controlled his anger," "he kept his passion in check" (229–30).

For Freud the statue expresses "the passage of a violent gust of passion visible in the signs left behind it in the ensuing calm" (236). It is precisely this tension between the quietude of Moses's exterior aspect and the interior storm of his rage that arrested Freud's eye. How does Freud explain the ability of Moses to contain his anger? For Freud it is a matter of character, of the attachment of Moses to a higher cause to which he has consciously pledged himself. It is, in other words, a matter of self-discipline. Thus for Freud, Moses is a figure of heroic restraint, all the more noble for his wrath and the powerful self-control that countervails it. The implication is that Moses's control of his anger, rather than his indulgence of it, allows him to fulfill his responsibilities as a leader to his religious community. At this point I suspect I hardly need draw attention to the fact that the nobility of frozen wrath is gendered male.

GUILT

In his dedication to a higher cause and in his prodigious self-control, Freud's Moses is larger than human, an incarnation of a mental and moral ideal, a figure who upholds the law of the land. Few could be expected to succeed in following his example. I turn, then, to my fourth and final Freudian text, *Civilization and Its Discontents,* in which Freud theorizes a different mechanism to counter aggressivity. Here, to be sure, Freud does not directly address anger as an emotion. Instead he deals with the drive of aggressivity to which he believed all human beings are subject and which he regarded as the greatest impediment to civilization. (As I read human history and today's papers filled with the fighting in Bosnia and hate crimes in Germany, nothing seems so indisputable.)

That there is a clear connection between anger and aggressivity is suggested by the infamous prehistorical fable of the primal origin of guilt that Freud offers in *Totem and Taboo* (1913) and to which he returns in *Civilization and Its Discontents.* It is a scenario of power, sexual desire, and the strong, indeed primal emotions. Freud, as we recall, hypothesizes that civilization began when the sons of the despotic father (he had denied them sexual access to women) banded together in hatred and killed him—and ate his body.

What can restrain the drive to aggressivity, particularly when it is inflamed by the strong, divisive emotions? *In Civilization and Its Discontents* Freud argues that so powerful is the drive to aggressivity that the sense of guilt emerges to counter its force. Indeed the drive to aggressivity, when introjected, becomes guilt; there is a kind of mathematical principle of conversion between drives and emotions at work. Guilt is thus for Freud arguably the most important achievement of civilization.

Much of *Civilization and Its Discontents* is devoted to a consideration of the etiology and origin of guilt on the levels of the individual and of the group. I shall not rehearse the complex trajectory of Freud's argument, which is in any case well known. Here I shall instead confine myself to three points, hoping to gain in clarity what I may lose in simplification. First, in Freud's world the emotion of guilt is not understood as a technology of control or a disciplinary technique in the Foucauldian sense, imposed by a historically specific set of discourses and institutions. Rather for Freud the regulating emotion of guilt emerges inevitably from a primal psychology of the emotions, from the tension or ambivalence between hate and love, the emotional representatives of the two basic drives: the drive to aggressivity (power) and the libidinal drive (sexual desire). In Freud's view guilt is both genetic and structural to the human psyche from the moment of the constitution of civilization (that is, the founding moment of the sons revolting against the father). If love and hate are the two primary emotions, guilt is a secondary emotion, entailing self-consciousness. Guilt is the third term, unsettling and oppressive yet paradoxically also stabilizing. Like a point on a nuclear thermostat, guilt works homeostatically to maintain a fluctuating equilibrium between love and hate, to regulate the temperature, to keep things cool.

Second, we should note that the prehistorical paradigm on which Freud bases his theory of the constitution of civilization (out of hatred) and the emergence of guilt (out of love) is gendered male. The sons, who fiercely love the father as much as they hate him, internalize the father as their superego, turning aggressivity—and anger— against themselves.

Third, for Freud the sense of guilt is produced from hostile feelings that are *not* acted upon (Freud ultimately reserves the term "remorse" for the emotion one experiences after one *has* committed an act of aggression). Concomitantly the sense of guilt is, startlingly, often unconscious. It is what I call a disabling emotion. Guilt is simultaneously an inhibition of aggressivity and an exacting, gnawing punishment for aggression in fantasy. I find this a stunning conclusion: an emotion is itself a self-punishment for what has *not* taken place. Guilt inhibits the development of anger—before it even exists. Thus if for Freud the sense of guilt is "the most important problem in the development of civilization, " in the final analysis it may also represent a crippling, enervating limit to it

(*SE* 21:134). In Freud's etiology of guilt, we find implicit a catastrophe theory of the emotions—and of civilization. If the sense of guilt is at first stabilizing, at a certain limit it may become radically destabilizing. This is because Freud theorizes that the larger the group or community, the more intense the guilt, the greater its quotient.[8] We are presented with a dismaying future, one in which the burden of guilt (which inhibits the expression of anger) grows heavier and heavier, a future we may have come close to realizing today as transnational corporate structures and communication networks circle the globe, drawing everyone more tightly together. The sense of guilt may become so onerous, Freud suggests, as to be intolerable, not only for the individual but for civilization as a whole, rendering culture neurotic, crippled. As he writes in *Civilization and Its Discontents,* "the price we pay for our advance in civilization is a loss of happiness through the heightening of the sense of guilt" (134). But if Freud theorizes the "fatal inevitability" of guilt (132), we may conclude that at its limit condition guilt carries with it an inevitable fatality, manifesting itself as "a tormenting uneasiness, a kind of anxiety" on the level of the individual and a "malaise" on the level of society or civilization as a whole (135).

At its limit condition then, guilt, the emotion that makes possible the survival and development of civilization, may devolve into anxiety, which is, according to Freud, perhaps the most fundamental and primitive of all the emotions.[9] As he points out, "the sense of guilt is at bottom nothing else but a topographical variety of anxiety" (*SE* 21:135). Thus if Freud is ambivalent about the strong emotions, he is equally ambivalent about guilt.

The trajectory I have traced in Freud's thought about anger finds its endpoint in guilt, an emotion that, as I read Freud, is highly individualizing and isolating. Guilt turns us back on ourselves. Guilt separates us from one another. Guilt inhibits us from anger and aggressive action— and in the final analysis not just from action but also from pleasure. (I am thinking here in particular of Freud's somber text "A Disturbance of Memory on the Acropolis" which he published six years after *Civilization and Its Discontents* in 1936 when he was eighty years old. In it Freud broods on guilt as a paralyzing impediment to a past pleasure. He also presents guilt as casting a long shadow into the dubious future as a fateful emotion: in Freud's view of the emotions they "belong" not just to the past, but also to the future.)[10]

If Freudian guilt is isolating and individualizing, feminist anger is conceived in precisely the opposite terms. It is presented as an emotion that will not only be the basis for a group but will also politicize the group, as an emotion furthermore that is created in a group, as an emotion that is enabling of action, not inhibiting of it. In Freud anger is gendered as male but Freud does not unambiguously approve it. The weight of his work is on containing and regulating violent anger, on de-authorizing male anger. Conversely the work of feminists appropriates male anger, using it to establish the authority with which to challenge patriarchal culture. Thus in this discursive circulation of anger in Freud and feminism, we find anger being redistributed in terms of gender. In the rest of this essay I turn to anger as the quintessential contemporary feminist emotion, drawing on a selection of essays that have been published in the last fifteen years in the United States by feminist literary critics and philosophers. The essays by literary critics Jane Marcus, Carolyn Heilbrun, and Brenda Silver all focus on Virginia Woolf. The three by philosophers Naomi Scheman, Elizabeth Spelman, and Alison Jagger revolve in great part around the relation of emotion to epistemology, and make the case for the cognitive dimension of the emotions.

Woolf's *A Room of One's Own* (1928) is the founding text of feminist literary criticism in the United States. It was published just two years before *Civilization and Its Discontents,* when Woolf was forty-six. One of its most remarkable passages is a scene that dramatizes and analyzes feminist anger. The setting is the British Museum where the author has gone one afternoon to do research for her upcoming lecture "Women and Fiction" (which is, of course, the subject of *A Room*). While reading the hypothetical *Mental, Moral, and Physical Inferiority of the Female Sex* by Professor Von X, she finds herself, like an unruly student, absent-mindedly, "unconsciously," drawing a picture of him, a picture that reveals to her both his anger *and* hers:

> A very elementary exercise in psychology, not to be dignified by the name of psycho-analysis, showed me, on looking at my notebook, that the sketch of the angry professor had been made in anger. Anger had snatched my pencil while I dreamt. But what was anger doing there? Interest, confusion, amusement, boredom—all these emotions I could trace and name as they succeeded each other throughout the morning. Had anger, the black snake, been lurking among them? Yes, said the sketch, anger had. It referred me unmistakably to the one book, to the one phrase, which had roused the demon; it was the professor's statement about the mental, moral and physical inferiority of women. My heart had leapt. My cheeks had burnt. I had flushed with anger. There was nothing

specially remarkable, however foolish, in that. One does not like to
be told that one is naturally the inferior of a little man. . . . One has
certain foolish vanities. It is only human nature, I reflected, and
began drawing cartwheels and circles over the angry professor's
face till he looked like a burning bush or a flaming comet—
anyhow, an apparition without human semblance or significance.
The professor was nothing now but a faggot burning on the top of
Hampstead Heath. Soon my own anger was explained and done
with; but curiosity remained. How explain the anger of the professors? (40–41)

Woolf astutely concludes that the anger of the professors is a self-
offensive mechanism (the phrase is mine) adopted by those in power
(men); anger is used as a weapon to fortify their position, to create
others as inferior. In a chain reaction her anger is provoked by his: "I had
been angry because he was angry."

I am reminded here of the "Non Vixit" dream: Freud's anger at his
angry professor results in his wishful dream of annihilating his friend and
colleague with a lethal glance of anger. As we saw, Freud traces his
aggressive impulses back to his early childhood. Similarly, Woolf defaces
"her" professor in daydreaming fantasy, doodling, doodling, until he goes
up in flames. Her analysis of anger, however, is not psychological but
political. What Freud did not take into account in the case of the hysterical employee—abusive, unequal relations of power—Woolf places at
the center of her analysis of gender relations; at the root of the matter is
the injustice at the heart of patriarchy. We can understand her anger as
an instance of what Jagger calls "outlaw" emotions, emotions experienced by those who are oppressed and who thus have what Jagger
argues is an "epistemological privilege" with regard to the authority or
appropriateness of their emotions. I cannot take up the argument for
"epistemological privilege" in this essay. I turn instead to the tone of
Woolf's anger, which is in fact the subject of Silver's essay.

Woolf presents her anger as light, even charming. She writes in ironic
tones leavened with a deft touch of melodramatic self-humor. Her anger
is altogether palatable. "Had anger, the black snake, been lurking among
them?" she writes. "Soon my own anger was explained and done; but
curiosity remained." Woolf leaves her anger behind, she tells us (although I do not completely believe her). She casts it off to pursue
thought "dispassionately."

Actually I have exaggerated. Woolf's anger is not so easily swallowed
by everyone. The three literary critics I've mentioned strongly disap-

prove of what they take to be this "feminine" expression of anger. They prefer the flatout anger of Woolf's *Three Guineas* (1938), a political tract on the economic and social position of women and war. For Marcus, the Woolf of *Three Guineas* is, wonderfully, in "a towering rage"; she relishes the image of Woolf as "an angry old woman," a "witch, making war, not love, untying the knots of social convention, encouraging the open expression of hostilities" (123, 135). (Old? Woolf was only fifty-nine at the time, but that is another subject). For Heilbrun, her own early preference for *A Room of One's Own* over *Three Guineas* is a cause for shame. She revels in Woolf's "unladylike" tone in *Three Guineas,* the text where finally Woolf "was able to indulge the glorious release of letting her anger rip" (241). Heilbrun sees this as an achievement all the more impressive because "like all women," she says, Woolf "had to fight a deep fear of anger in herself" (241). For both Heilbrun and Marcus, the Woolf of *Three Guineas* finally allows anger to drive her art, her writing. Marcus especially is impassioned on this point. Although she acknowledges that thought must accompany anger in the making of art, her own rhetoric belies her preference for anger. Marcus: "we must finally acknowledge that it was anger that impelled her art, and intellect that combed out the snarls, dissolved the blood clots, and unclogged the great sewer of the imagination, anger" (138).

Silver shows how the issue of the authority of feminist anger has driven the reception of *Three Guineas* ever since it was published, for many years impeding the serious consideration of its ideas (Woolf is *too* angry, many readers concluded). But with the emergence of essays by Marcus, Heilbrun, and others, Silver argues, anger, *expressed angrily,* has been recuperated. Flat-out anger has been established as "righteous" and "prophetic"; in short, as unambiguously and purely political. Woolf's anger is no longer heard as "neurotic, morbid, or shrill" (need I add "hysterical"?), but as the expression of "an ethical or moral stance" (361). Silver accepts Scheman's argument that from this perspective the expression of anger itself is a political act. Scheman: from a feminist point of view, anger is "moved away from guilt, neurosis, or depression, and into the purview of cognition, external behavior, social relations, and politics. To become angry, to recognize that one has been angry, to change what counts as being angry becomes a political act" (362).

It would be inaccurate to say that Freud regarded the strong emotions as "irrational," although as we have seen, he did view anger and aggressivity as disruptive to the fragile ties binding civilization together. He firmly believed, as he wrote in *Civilization and Its Discontents,* that "instinctual passions are stronger than reasonable interests" (112). Feminist philosophers reject the view of anger as "irrational." They argue for the cognitive dimension of the emotions in general, using anger as their prime example and the relation between oppressor and oppressed as their paradigm. As Spelman puts it, "there is a politics of emotion: the systematic denial of anger can be seen in a mechanism of subordination, and the existence and expression of anger as an act of insubordination" (270). For Spelman, anger—as opposed to rage, which is anger in excess—has "clarity of vision" (271).

In contradistinction to Freud's emphasis on anger and aggressivity as disruptive to social bonds, here anger is the basis for a political (action) group (however vaguely defined). On this point Scheman's reflections are especially challenging, persuasively so, to the Freudian discourse of the emotions. She argues that in the social context of, for example, a consciousness-raising group, the "discovery of anger can often occur not from focussing on one's feeling but from a political redescription of one's situation" (77). Thus from a feminist perspective, it is not the Freudian case that emotions are located inside us, repressed, as if they were highly idiosyncratic personal property only waiting to be discovered. Rather, they are created in the group. Moreover, they can be created *retrospectively,* as it were. A woman may, for example, retroactively identify as anger her emotional state in the past even though she did not feel anger then. In this view it is not the Freudian case that she had *repressed* her anger and it is only now coming to the surface. Rather, the emotion is being projected from the present into the past. Emotions from a feminist perspective are thus *conscious* social constructions.

One of the most thought-provoking questions posed by Freud about the emotions is, How are they transmitted? (In *Totem and Taboo* he assumes that guilt is an "emotional heritage" that is experienced long after the primal act of parricide has been committed. But how?) One of the answers I would give to this question today is that emotions are transmitted through discourse. The feminist essays to which I've referred constitute a significant case in point. They are intended to create a politicized community out of their readers. They are the scholarly equivalent of the consciousness-raising group. Anger is generated, sustained, and strengthened through discourse—or at least that is the goal. But on further thought, I suspect that really is *not* the goal; the commitment to feminist principles of analysis is. After all, can emotion be located *in* discourse? Nothing would seem more impossible. Thus it is the word "anger" and not necessarily the emotion to which it refers that in fact constellates the group. Scholarly feminist "anger" is a discursive site around which persons cluster who have similar if not the same objectives. Thus feminist literary criticism looks back through its mothers and constructs its own discursive tradition: a literature of anger. Marcus is explicit on this point: in her essay she moves from the anger of Virginia Woolf when she was older, to the anger of the middle-aged Adrienne Rich in her poem "The Phenomenology of Anger" to—this is Marcus's challenge—the anger of the young ("Why wait until old age...? Out with it. No more burying our wrath" [153]). What is the relation of writing to feminist "anger"? Often writing is itself the action.

In *Civilization and Its Discontents* Freud perceptively observes that "a feeling can only be a source of energy if it is itself the expression of a strong need" (72). Women have so long been identified with the emotions, albeit *not* with anger, that I find it fascinating an emotion should be the basis for a rallying cry for solidarity, even if—or more accurately precisely because—that emotion has long been identified as the forbidden fruit (or snake, to allude to Woolf). In the case of women it is clear that there is a strong need to resist patriarchal injustice. To do so we have needed to assert our cultural right to anger. But what are the consequences of flat-out anger? This is the question to which Freud in great part devoted himself and which he answered with great wisdom in *Civilization and Its Discontents*. This is also the very question that (to my knowledge at least) is not entertained at any length in this feminist work. To my mind this is the question to which we need to turn today, especially since certain styles of anger are being advised as *better.* Silver too concludes that today "feminist criticism stands in a problematic relationship to the authority of anger that infused its early rhetoric and vision" (367). She ends by saying that "there is no one feminist anger, and no one appropriate to its end," that "all these angers, all these voices are necessary to feminist critique today" (370). After her astute inquiry into anger and her careful scholarship from a historical perspective, this conclusion strikes me as too cautious. What does Silver give as examples of problematic effects of feminist anger? That the convention of scholarly discourse inhibits it. That male literary critics are still critical of it. That feminists of color critique white middle-class feminists for it. I would rather call these effects, not serious consequences. Interestingly enough, they are confined largely to discourse.

I have two major objections to the advocacy of anger, particularly as it assumes the form of the angry expression of anger. One objection is primarily theoretical, the other primarily practical and historical. If Freud's theory of the emotions is limited in his insistence on the psychological interiorization of the emotions, if he does not recognize the cognitive or political value of emotions, nonetheless his work provides

us with ways in which to understand the limits we have reached today in
theorizing the emotion of anger from a feminist perspective.

As we recall, in his analysis of the "Non Vixit" dream Freud was concerned with dissecting the complex of "strange emotions" that accompanied it, separating out the different emotions from one another, isolating
them, identifying them, as if they were precipitants in a chemical experi-
ment. What he discovered was not only the diverse emotions of anger
and shame, triumph and anxiety, but also that in life, as opposed to
analysis, the emotions are bound indissolubly together, that they exist in
compound form. For Freud, ultimately there is no such thing as pure
anger or pure shame. In his homeostatic view of the strong emotions, a
(strong) hostile emotion will be accompanied by its antidote. The con-
verse also holds: a (strong) positive emotion, like love, will be accompanied by its opposite. For Freud our strong emotions are ambivalent, our
motives mixed.

That we should interrogate our wishes for their unconscious components is so fundamental to Freud as to be unnecessary to relearn it here. I
need hardly add that this is a perspective that is lacking in the feminist
work I have been surveying.[11] I consider this a significant shortcoming
but that is not my point. My point is that anger as a "political" emotion
does not exist in a pure form. Emotions come in clusters.[12]

Scheman uses the word "confused" to describe something similar but
in the final analysis quite different. "If we are confused about our emotions," she writes, "those emotions themselves are confused" (179). Her
argument here is that the confusion is a sign of a pre-political state, that
we must identify these emotions, *name* them, as a way of understanding
our position. With this I agree. Her implication if not explicitly drawn
conclusion, however, is that in resolving the confusion, one emotion—
anger—will ultimately emerge with the clarity of clearly drawn lines.
The scenario she offers is that of a nonfeminist becoming politicized in a
consciousness-raising group. Thus in this scenario, out of confusion the
emotion of guilt appears first; guilt is then interpreted as a "cover for
those other feelings, notably feelings of anger" (177). In this scenario,
pre-politicized guilt must disappear to allow a politicized anger to appear. I do not disagree with the pragmatic value of this strategy (for that
is what it is). But I am insisting that a pure and righteous politicized
anger will be accompanied by other emotions as well, precisely because
the emotion of anger will no doubt be an "action."

This brings me to my second objection. In the essays to which I have
been referring the paradigm of oppressor-oppressed is key. It is argued
that oppression can be identified by anger, and that it should be re-

sponded to by anger. But what happens then? We need to advance the scenario in time, interrogating the consequences of letting one's anger rip (Heilbrun). We must focus on the longer view, on the "plot" of anger, looking ahead in time as did Freud in "The Moses of Michelangelo." Anger as an "outlaw" emotion (Jagger) is appropriate when associated with the position of the oppressed. But as we grow older, relations of authority almost inevitably shift. For feminists in the academy, power relations have undergone an indisputable sea change in the last fifteen years. Many women who entered the academy under the banner of the politics of anger find themselves today in positions of authority, responsible to many others. The title of a recent talk by Scheman, "On Waking Up One Morning and Finding That We Are Them," gestures toward this phenomenon. For this generation, which is my generation, "righteous," habit-forming anger, once understood as a "right," can take on the shape of abusive arrogance. "Anger" may be appropriate as a tool of politicization but after this inaugurated point in time flat-out anger is a blunt instrument. Expressions of anger in public discourse (in essays, in debate) can have very different consequences from expressions of anger in the close quarters of the classroom, for example, where flat-out anger can produce a flashpoint, escalating personal conflict. Thus we need a historical perspective on the uses of anger. If the assertion of the authority of anger in the academic community (the humanities in particular) has had enabling consequences at a certain point in time, that time has largely passed. The paradigm of oppressor-oppressed, once so useful to feminism, is producing serious consequences of its own in terms of generational politics within feminism. With this paradigm in hand, younger women in the academy, for example, analyze their position in relation to older women "in power" as that of the oppressed, their anger authorized by their "epistemological privilege" of being a student or an assistant professor. Never mind that the general paradigm of oppressor-oppressed is inappropriate in this case. Certainly from this perspective "anger" senselessly divides women from one another, creating smaller, oppositional groups. This is indeed a serious consequence of the politics of the authority of anger.

I end with a question that has been recurring for several months. It is a question I cannot answer but can only pose. We speak approvingly of self-reflexive thought, of thought that turns back on itself, interrogating its foundations, its principles, its implications, its consequences. Is there an analogy to self-reflexive thought in the domain of the strong emotions? For Freud anger is inhibited, or regulated, by guilt; in *Civilization and Its Discontents* he offers a homeostatic view of the strong emotions. In Freud's view, passions lead often to sorrows. But this system operates unconsciously. It is not consciously self-reflexive. One of the important contributions of feminist thought is the theorization of the cognitive dimension of the emotions. Here we come close, I think, to considering the emotions in a self-reflexive way. But the long-term consequences of the feminist passion for anger, to allude to the epigraph from Virginia Woolf with which I opened this essay, remain "uncharted."

NOTES

1. I borrow the term the "expansive emotions" from Edith Wharton's *The House of Mirth.*

2. As Freud states it in "Delusions and Dreams," "We remain on the surface so long as we are dealing only with the memories and ideas. What is alone of value in mental life is rather the feelings. No mental forces are significant unless they possess the characteristic of arousing feelings" (48–49).

3. I discuss this phenomenon in the context of psychoanalytic theories of mourning in "Grief-Work in Contemporary Cultural Criticism."

4. Recent work in anthropology also takes anger as its focal point. See Michelle Z. Rosaldo who, with Renato Rosaldo, studied the Ilongots of the Philippines. The Ilongots conceptualize anger in altogether different ways from Freud: although anger could be hidden, it was not a disturbing energy that could be repressed, buried in the unconscious. In addition, the Ilongots can be "paid" for "anger" and can simply "forget" an anger (144).

5. As Elizabeth Spelman observes, in women "anything resembling anger is likely to be redescribed as hysteria or rage instead" (264).

6. I take a dream Freud reports earlier in *The Interpretation of Dreams* as an elementary version of the "Non Vixit" dream. The text of the dream runs as follows: "*His father was scolding him for coming home so late.*" What the dream conceals through the reversal of affect is that the son is angry at the father. The dynamic of the Oedipus complex is at its familiar work: "the original wording must have been that *he* was angry with his *father,* and that in his view his father always came home too *early* (i.e. too soon). He would have preferred it if his father had not come home *at all,* and this was the same thing as a death-wish against his father" (*SE* 4:328).

7. Here is Freud in *Totem and Taboo* on the "social emotions": "We may describe as 'social' the emotions which are determined by showing consideration for another person without taking him as a sexual object" (*SE* 13:72). In *Violent Emotions* Suzanne Retzinger, a communications scholar, argues that shame is the primary social emotion. By this she means that shame is concerned above all with the survival of a relationship. In her study of quarrels of married couples, she concludes that it is in fact *shame* that incites anger rather than anger responding *tout court* to anger.

8. Freud in *Civilization and Its Discontents:* "What began in relation to the father is completed in relation to the group. If civilization is a necessary course of development from the family to humanity as a whole, then—as a result of the inborn conflict arising from ambivalence, of the eternal struggle between the trends of love and death—there is inextricably

bound up with it an increase in the sense of guilt, which will perhaps reach heights that the individual finds hard to tolerate" (*SE* 21:133).

9. As Freud argues in "The Uncanny" (1919), "every affect belonging to an emotional impulse, whatever its kind, is transformed, if it is repressed, into anxiety" (*SE* 17:241).

10. See the chapter on "Reading Freud" in my *Aging and Its Discontents* for a discussion of "Acropolis," aging, and guilt.

11. I borrow the term "clusters" from Carol Tavris.

12. It is present in other feminist work. In much feminist pedagogy, anger has also been the emotion of choice. In *Gendered Subjects: The Dynamics of Feminist Teaching,* edited by Margo Culley and Catherine Portuges, we are brought back to a fundamentally psychoanalytic view of the strong emotions. Cully, in her chapter in the volume "Anger and Authority in the Introductory Women's Studies Classroom," asserts that "anger is a challenging and necessary part of life in the feminist classroom" (216). And in their introduction, the editors of the volume note that the model of the psychoanalytic family helps them to understand why in the feminist classroom there are "outbreaks of temper, tears, denunciation and divisiveness, notions that courses must offer total salvation or else fail, strong feelings of vulnerability, awareness that students/teacher love or hate student/teachers, that students/teachers see or reject themselves/their sisters/ mothers/fathers in the course of content or interactions in the classroom" (15). But if the model helped clarify a certain aspect of a pedagogical situation, it also worked to produce this volatile, adversarial pedagogical world. The model constricts us to a hothouse vision of a two-generational family when the academy houses many and far-flung generations, which is to say that it itself embodies or is witness to a multilayered historicity. Moreover, in its emphasis on the strong emotions, the psychoanalytic model implicitly restricts us to certain forms of feeling—ambivalent and ultimately oppositional emotions. Taken to its extreme, the psychoanalytic model produces the concept of a "poisonous pedagogy" (I am here using the phrase coined by the psychoanalyst Alice Miller) or of "pedagogic violence" (here I am referring to a provocative essay by Lynn Worsham), with anger as the privileged emotion: emotion is linked to the domain of the personal, to woman, and through feminism to the political, with the classroom being the space for the drama.

REFERENCES

Culley, Margo, and Catherine Portuges, eds. *Gendered Subjects: The Dynamics of Feminist Teaching.* Boston: Routledge and Kegan Paul, 1985.

Freud, Sigmund. *The Standard Edition of the Complete Psychological Works of Sigmund Freud.* Trans. and ed. James Strachey. 24 vols. London: Hogarth and Institute of Psycho-Analysis, 1953–74.

———. *Civilization and Its Discontents.* 1930. *SE* 21:64–145.

———. "Delusions and Dreams in Jensen's *Gradiva.*" 1907. *SE* 9:7–93.

———. *The Interpretation of Dreams.* 1900. *SE* 4–5:xi–338, 339–627.

———. *Leonardo da Vinci and a Memory of His Childhood.* 1910. *SE* 11:63–137.

———. "The Moses of Michelangelo." 1914. *SE* 13:211–36.

———, with Joseph Breuer. *Studies on Hysteria.* 1893. *SE* 2:1–309.

———. *Totem and Taboo.* 1913. *SE* 17:1–161.

———. "The 'Uncanny.'" 1919. *SE* 17:218–56.

Heilbrun, Carolyn G. "Virginia Woolf in Her Fifties." In *Virginia Woolf: A Feminist Slant,* edited by Jane Marcus, 236–53. Lincoln: University of Nebraska Press, 1983.

Hillman, James. *Emotion: A Comprehensive Phenomenology of Theories and Their Meanings for Therapy*. 1960. Evanston: Northwestern University Press, 1992.

Jagger, Alison M. "Love and Knowledge: Emotion in Feminist Philosophy." *Gender/Body/Knowledge: Feminist Reconstructions of Being and Knowing*, edited by Alison M. Jagger and Susan R. Bordo, 145–71. New Brunswick: Rutgers University Press, 1989.

Marcus, Jane. "Art and Anger: Elizabeth Robins and Virginia Woolf." 1978. In *Art and Anger: Reading Like a Woman*, 122–54. Columbus, Ohio: Ohio State University Press, 1988.

Miller, Alice. *For Your Own Good: Hidden Cruelty in Child-Rearing and the Roots of Violence*. 1980. Translated by Hildegarde and Hunter Hannum. London: Virago, 1987.

Retzinger, Suzanne R. *Violent Emotions: Shame and Rage in Marital Quarrels*. Newbury Park, Calif.: Sage, 1991.

Rosaldo, Michelle Z. "Toward an Anthropology of Self and Feeling." In *Cultural Theory*, edited by Richard A. Shweder and Robert A. Levine, New York: Cambridge University Press, 1984.

Rosaldo, Renato. *Culture and Truth: The Remaking of Social Analysis*. Boston: Beacon, 1989.

Scheman, Naomi. "Anger and the Politics of Naming." In *Women and Language in Literature and Society*, edited by Sally McConnell-Ginet, Ruth Borker, and Nelly Furman, 174–87. New York: Praeger, 1980.

———. "On Waking Up One Morning and Discovering That We Are They." In *Pedagogy: The Question of Impersonation*, edited by Jane Gallop, 106–16 (Bloomington: Indiana University Press, 1995).

Spelman, Elizabeth V. "Anger and Insubordination." In *Women, Knowledge, and Reality: Explorations in Feminist Philosophy*, edited by Ann Garry and Marilyn Pearsall, 263–73. Boston: Unwin Hyman, 1989.

Silver, Brenda R. "The Authority of Anger: *Three Guineas* as a Case Study." *Signs* 16, no. 2 (1991): 340–70.

Tavris, Carol. *Anger: The Misunderstood Emotion*. Rev. ed. New York: Simon and Schuster, 1989.

Wharton, Edith. *The House of Mirth*. 1905. New York: NAL, 1964.

Woodward, Kathleen. *Aging and Its Discontents: Freud and Other Fictions*. Bloomington: Indiana University Press, 1991.

———. "Grief-Work in Contemporary American Cultural Criticism." *Discourse* 15, no. 2 (winter 1992–93): 94–112.

Woolf, Virginia. *A Room of One's Own*. Oxford: Oxford University Press, 1992.

Worsham, Lynn. "Emotion and Pedagogic Violence." *Discourse* 15, no. 2 (1992): 119–48.

5

Freud and the Passions of the Voice

CLAIRE KAHANE

> Hearing is a physiological phenomenon; listening is a psychological act.
>
> —Roland Barthes

To speak of "the passions" in relation to psychoanalysis is somehow to articulate an anachronism; "the passions" seems very much a pre-Freudian term, having more of an affinity with religion in its exaltation of suffering or romance and its homage to obsessional desire than with the "science" that Freud conceived in his attempt to formulate principles of mental functioning in the service of the cure. Yet as this collection attests, the passions are not alien to psychoanalysis. Derived etymologically from *passus,* to suffer, and thus the antonym of action, passion is defined as "the capacity to be acted upon by an external force," as well as "to be subject to, to suffer intense and violent emotions" (*Webster's New Collegiate Dictionary*). It is primarily in the latter sense, denoting the subject's passive relation to influences primarily from within, but also including the external insofar as it is internalized, that the passions are the primary interest of psychoanalysis. Although Freud, in his quest for scientific status, attempted to give *dispassionate* accounts of his patient's histories, intending them to serve as the ground for his metaphysical speculations, it was Freud who empowered us to hear the passions in the very act of enunciation, to theorize enunciation itself as a form of passion, an erotically compelling oral/aural exchange between voice and ear, speaker and listener. Indeed, Freud's talking cure specifically elicits and utilizes the passions of that exchange in and through the discursive connection between analyst and analysand.

André Green has called passion a derangement of the senses; the phrase itself alludes to a prior organization of the sensorium, an ordered, proper, lawful regimen of the body, presumably undone—de-ranged—by what Green calls an "erotic madness" (1986, 223). The primary passion that Freud identified in himself and in his patients, the original passion of psychoanalysis, was that erotic madness called hysteria, a derangement of heterosexual imperatives manifest in a corporeal derangement—a consequence of the hysteric's conversion of symbol into symptom. For Freud the content of the conversion was an unconscious scene of sexual seduction in which the hysterical subject performed both the masculine and feminine parts. The hysteric thus articulated a conflictual split of sexual positioning across the body rather than in language, a displacement that allowed a dissociation of the subject from what it knew.[1]

Certainly neither Freud nor Breuer—his colleague in the early pursuit of passion called *Studies on Hysteria* (1893–95) (*SE* 2)—were comfortable with its vicissitudes. Recall that Breuer ran from Anna O. when he could no longer ignore her passion for him, when her body dramatically enacted a fulfillment of her desire as a hysterical pregnancy. But Anna O.'s case also revealed that the symptom was embodied in language as well. By cutting up her mother tongue into disjunctive fragments, forgetting the grammar and syntax of German and replacing it with a grotesque synthesis of foreign languages, Anna O. symptomatically announced her self-alienation through speech (Hunter 1985). Indeed, in a voice fissured by "absences," Anna O. explicitly performed a dissociation of the subject from action, from the verb, substituting infinitives for the normal syntax of subject and verb. If, as Julia Kristeva suggests in "Women's Time" (1981), the enunciation of noun plus verb places the subject in linear time, Anna O.'s enunciation through the infinitive refused both agency and the temporality of history.

Breuer ran from this derangement of the body and language, but Freud remained with his hysterics, finding a way to restrain, retrain, their passion and his, by containing and homeopathically deploying it in language. Through what Anna O. had named the talking cure, Freud provoked the repetition of a prior passion, a transference mediated by and worked through in speech, compelling his hysterics for the sake of the cure, but even more for his stake in his new science, to enter a conversation about the erotic body and its secrets. What Freud discovered was that conversation about sexual matters itself evoked sexuality: that especially the embodied dialogue between a masterful doctor and a vulnerable patient provoked erotic effects through and in the circulation of the voice.

As articulated sound, the voice circulates between two interiorities, constituting the intersubjective dialogue of analysis. Uncanny in its ability to transgress bodily boundaries, the speaking voice evokes both the mother's unlocalized voice in all its ambivalent resonance, a voice that is the subject's first link to its environment, and the cultural laws that constitute language.[2] Indeed, the speaking voice is the site of a division in language itself, conveying the traces of maternal presence through its materiality: tone, timbre, rhythm, what Barthes calls the "grain of the voice," (1977) or Kristeva (1986b) the semiotic register, while its semantic register signifies a patriarchal system of representation subtended by maternal absence. Through manipulations of this double register of the voice, of absence and presence, the analyst as doctor-healer, functions as a combined parent figure, an imaginary ideal Other, father-mother, who has it, knows it, all.[3]

Freud and his hysterics both spoke; both listened; but in that room where women come and go, the dialogic position of analyst and analysand was neither symmetrical nor fixed. The effects of that intersubjective dialogue depended in large part on who had the voice, who the ear. Although the hysteric was the ostensible speaking subject enunciating her history, she told a piecemeal story to a privileged ear, to a custodian of meanings whose very silence functioned as ideal Other. Moreover, while her voice issued from a body that was under the analyst's scrutiny, controlled by the gaze and read for its symptomatic acts, she spoke to an unseen interlocutor, whose disembodied vocal intervention could too easily be experienced as an internal demand. As Kaja Silverman (1988) points out, by destabilizing the configuration of body/speaker, dissociating the voice from a particular body, psychoanalysis allows the analyst's speech to be attached to the analysand's interior objects. The analyst's voice thus privileged could serve as the bridge to a passionately desired identification with an ideal Other—fantasmatic source of the law that Kristeva terms the imaginary Father—or could be experienced as an intrusive and undesirable violation of boundaries.

But if Freud as bearer of this transgressive voice and privileged ear seemed especially empowered to influence the internal script of the hysteric, he was himself subject to the voice: his primary task was to listen to the hysteric's story with the third ear. What does it mean to listen with the third ear? Where is this third ear situated? What can it hear? One can think of that ear as similar to the ear of the poet or musician, as in "he has a good ear"; that is to say, a sensitivity for catching the semantic and phonemic play of speech. Freud had a good ear for pursuing the disguises and dispersions of the subject in language. Reading his case histories, one can observe him on the track of those switchwords that led toward the hysteric's secret center. Yet his position as analyst-listener, pursuer of truth was not only the position of a mastery he initially claimed for analysis, but also the position of a submission to the story of the other. For the third ear is a fantasmatic ear located in the domain of the Other. To listen to his patient's stories with that ear, Freud had to be literally receptive; to be open; to allow an empathic identification with the speaking subject of a narrative; to assume, that is to say, the passion of the speaker's narrative voice as his own. In the analytic dialogue, the permeable boundaries of the ear became the zone of exchange for the introjection of mobile fantasies carried by the voice of the speaker and the tale it told. For this reason, as Lacan remarked, Freud could not avoid participating in what the hysteric was telling him.

If the very act of listening to the hysteric's voice and probing its secrets destabilizes the analyst's subject-position, Freud complicated the effects of listening by theorizing that listening had an inevitable history. Doubling the temporality of the listening act, Freud linked listening in the present to a prior fantasy of listening, a primal scene in which a hapless passive subject "discovers" sexuality by overhearing sounds in the night. Freud theorized that these sounds are narrativized into a drama of parental intercourse by the listener who assumes the various parts of that drama through identifications. Listening thus acquires the value of mapping one's way into a subject position through an enigma. What is going on? Who is doing what to whom? These are the questions of the primal scene listener; these are the questions that Freud pursues in the case histories. Just as the subject in a dream is dispersed across the dreamscape, so Freud's case histories suggest that he as analyst listener is caught up in the analysand's secret sexual scenario at different points.

The mystery is also deepened by the demand for interpretation that language itself presents. Language is urged into existence by a double itch: to "communicate"; that is, to heal the breach between self and other, and to express the drives, as anxiety or as desire. Verbalization is, however, a rupture of being, a re-presentation of an absence as well as a move toward union. The resounding question behind interpretation, "What is the meaning?" confirms the gap between subject and object that language would bridge. Thus the formal quality of any text is fraught with intimations of unknown possibilities (a menace? a promise?) contained within words themselves. Listening to the voice is thus for analyst and analysand an experience of anxious potentiality and self-dispersion.

In short, the passions of the voice in analysis emerge from a scenario in which the intersubjective dimension is multiplied; the speaking voice of the analysand narrating a story of identification, desire, and transgression acts as a medium for the identifications and desires of the analyst. This countertransference is especially provoked by the demands of narrativization in Freud's case histories. Narrative depends for its power upon transgressive identifications that are not provoked in Freud's more theoretical constructions. Thus in writing the case histories Freud himself complained that this new scientific genre sounded more like fiction than fact.

If in the psychoanalytic dialogue, identification with the other through the voice is a condition of interpretation, what did it mean for Freud to assume the passions of the voice when it belonged to Dora, an eighteen-year-old hysterical girl, and the only female subject of a major case history? Several critics have played out a number of the implications of Freud's identification with Dora, showing how Freud's written narrative voice performs as well as analyzes the passions of a subject compelled by an internal demand.[4] Listening with the third ear to Dora meant taking on the part of a hysterical daughter caught in a series of transgressive erotic triangles, while at the same time, attempting to preserve his own discrete boundary as analyst-father.[5] It meant supplementing a fractured verbal narration (her story) with meanings he read into her physical symptoms (his story), joining them together as a single story. And especially because the Dora case, originally to be called "Dreams and Hysteria," was meant to substantiate *The Interpretation of Dreams,* it signified grounding his metaphysics in her physics. But in Dora's case, one story led to another; the ground kept shifting, so that even as writing, Freud's narrative structure helplessly mimed the symptomatic narrative he was analyzing. Thus the text gives us the continual erosion of Freud's attempts to narrativize the auditory fragments of an a priori hysterical narrative, as father and daughter exchange places in a dance around an absent center. The excessive digressions, the reversals and displacements of Freud's voice that mark it as hysterical have been amply elucidated by contemporary critics (Bernheimer and Kahane 1985). In what follows I add to that body of interpretation by focusing on the significance of certain switchwords and phrases that function as metonymic displacements, directing Freud's narrative voice toward stories other than the one he wants to tell.

We know the story he wants to tell: a nineteenth-century Oedipal narrative of heterosexual romance, of the exchange of a daughter from

one family to another, ending in an appropriate marriage that will resolve all the contradictory tensions let loose in the course of that exchange. But Dora's position in that story refuses to hold. To recall the
principal elements of the plot: Dora's father, engaged in an affair with
Frau K., had handed Dora over to Herr K. in return for his complicity, and
Dora herself had raised no objections to this arrangement, even suppressing information about a sexual advance by Herr K., a kiss he had forcibly
impressed upon her when she was fourteen. Although Dora refuses to
continue her role in this sordid melodrama, she develops symptoms—
loss of voice, fainting fits, a mysterious limp, a nervous cough—that, in
the logic of the psychoanalytic symptom, mark her own conflict and
complicity. Dora must have a secret desire as well as an overt demand, a
desire that Freud names; Dora unconsciously desires the virile—and in
Freud's eyes entirely "prepossessing"—Herr K. Voicing his own attraction to the object he desires *for* her, through a series of perversely
compelling interpretations, he presses Dora to recognize his desire as
hers. Indeed, in a neurotic confusion of fantasy and reality, he asks her to
consider *marrying* Herr K. as the perfect resolution of this domestic
romance.

This is the situation that contemporary readers have defined, noting
the various textual signs that mark Freud's voice in the text as hysterical:
the excessive defensive digressions, reversals, and displacements of the
narration (Bernheimer and Kahane 1985). But equally significant to the
hysterical structure of the narration is the fact that Freud's tale of erotically ambiguous family relations is plotted in the oral register. If Dora
displaces sexuality upward, so does Freud's narrative: it constitutes
Dora's history as a series of seductive oral exchanges, ranging from
eroticized conversations that have actually occurred—Herr K. and Dora,
Frau K. and Dora, the governess and Dora, among others—to the primal
fantasy of the case, an imaginary act of fellatio, a sexual exchange that
reverberates with the dynamics of the talking cure in which Freud and
Dora were engaged.

Freud isolates as the crucial scene that provokes Dora's most recent
hysterical attack a conversation with Herr K., at a resort. Herr K. has
propositioned her in words that repeat a phrase that Dora had heard
before: "I get nothing out of my wife"—the very phrase she knew Herr
K. used to seduce a governess before her (*SE* 7:98, 106). It is this
repetition that triggers her slap in his face and her flight. Significantly,
Freud writes virtually this same phrase as a direct quotation of Dora's
father: "I get nothing out of my own wife." (The differential modifier,
"own," constitutes an admission of adultery lacking in Herr K.'s use of

the phrase to seduce.) In assigning both Dora's father and Herr K. virtually the same sentence, Freud makes both the linguistic subject of a complaint that is also a justification of paternal seduction, and inserts both into a chain of fathers that includes himself. For as we know by now, Freud also wants something out of Dora that he doesn't get at home, wants her to open herself to his collection of picklocks, wants Dora to satisfy his theoretical desire to know. Indeed, the phrase "I get nothing out of my wife" is a nodal point in Freud's narration, an overdetermined phrase of oral desire, deprivation, and impotence that resonates with ambiguity about who can get and who has it to give, who is allowed to get and who to give. Reappearing in Freud's text at significant junctures, this paternal complaint also resonates with the fellatio fantasy that Freud constructs for Dora, an imagined scene of sexual relations between "a man without means" (*SE* 7:47) who can get nothing out of his wife, Dora's impotent father, and Frau K., the idealized sexual mother of Dora's family romance who gives him the means.

Moreover, in constructing a scene of paternal sexuality as fellatio, Freud reifies a metaphor that informs his own transgressive exchange, his pressing Dora to accept his "interpretations." Luce Irigaray has addressed the orality of this metaphor:

> So the enigma of the feminine seems, largely, to come down to that of the lips and to what she keeps hidden. This would explain the reaction of Dora—and many of her sisters—to Herr K.'s kiss. . . . The lips as such represent an important enough place of investment for the imposition of a kiss to be an almost unbearable sort of violation. To take a woman's lips would be like taking the fort-da away from a man. . . . [T]he lips are the woman herself, the threshold of the woman, undistanciated by some object or other. To take a kiss from her is to take what is most virginal in her, what is closest to her feminine identity. To make her pregnant, is possibly, another violation, crossing another threshold. To force a woman to speak, what is more, to force a woman lying down to open her lips, to come out of herself, may represent an analytic violation. (1989, 136)

Yet Dora must open herself for Freud's fragmentary theorization to be completed, made whole. Freud's fellatio fantasy can thus be read as an overdetermined linguistic reversal, moving from lack to fulfillment, and a trope of his narrative desire for closure as well.

Lacan (1952) was the first to point out that when confronted with

Dora's claim that she knew sexual satisfaction could be achieved by means other than genital intercourse, Freud assumed she was referring to fellatio rather than cunnilingus. That Freud imagines fellatio as the answer to the question, "Who does what to whom when the male is impotent?" suggests that female desire and jouissance are an absence to him—the sign of a repression. Yet if Freud forecloses female genital sexuality in constructing the fellatio fantasy—he literally remarks that the "sexual organ proper" is the penis[6]—as Madelon Sprengnether (1985) pointed out, at the same time he displaces the male organ by interpreting fellatio as a repetition of the erotics of sucking at the breast. By thus transforming the impotent father into the nursing phallic mother, Freud reconstitutes the primal scene of hysteria and virtually eliminates the "true" male from the scene.

Indeed, at the climax of Freud's discussion of fellatio is an image of the sexual indeterminacy of *the phallus itself* that is characteristic of hysterical representation and its anxious question, Who has "it" to give? Thus he writes: "It is a new version of what may be described as a prehistoric impression of sucking at the mother's or nurse's breast—an impression which has usually been revived by contact with children who are being nursed. In most instances the udder of a cow has aptly played the part of an image intermediate between a nipple and a penis" (*SE* 7:52). This sexual ambiguity at the very site of Freud's primal scene is covered over by an insistent plotting of heterosexual cause and effect that, as Sprengnether (1985) convincingly argues, defends against Freud's own orality, passive desire, and femininity—a hysterical triad animated by the conjunction of Freud's and Dora's voice.[7]

If the sympathetic intersections of Dora's and Freud's voices generates a symptomatic discourse in "The Clinical Picture"—those digressions, shifts into French, reversals and omissions already catalogued (Bernheimer and Kahane 1985)—the difference in narrative voice between "The First Dream," and "The Second Dream," both of which constitute the double structural center of Freud's text, point to another symptomatic aspect of Freud's narration: the appropriation of dialogue by monologue. While on the one hand, in the "Prefatory Remarks," Freud claimed for purposes of simplification to have omitted the technique of psychoanalysis—the analysand's associations and the analyst's interpretations—he nevertheless does include it in these two sections of dream interpretation, presumably to invoke precisely the dialogic construction of meaning that is psychoanalysis. But in "The First Dream," Freud uses direct discourse and textually embodies as dialogue the exchange between him and Dora. As in the novelistic use of direct quotation, which implies a reality external to the narrator's voice, here Freud allows Dora's voice to be heard, even though he pursues it and directs its story. In "The Second Dream," however, after the presentation of Dora's dream, direct discourse is eclipsed; there is no dialogue, no representation of his technique, nor of Dora's voice, which is withheld from the reader. Instead, Freud narrates both his interventions and Dora's associations using indirect discourse to maintain his monological mastery. Here Freud's narration functions to obscure technique and to bind Dora and her dream to his own purpose, and to confirm his more overarching text, *The Interpretation of Dreams.* Why the difference in narrative voice?

Let me suggest that in elaborating the first dream, Freud allows Dora as the other to speak because what he hears represented is Dora's desire for the father, for Herr K., for him. Recall, for example, his interpretation of Dora's longing for a kiss from a smoker, Herr K.:

> The thing which I had to go upon was the fact that the smell of smoke had only come up as an addendum to the dream, and must therefore have had to overcome a particularly strong effort on the part of repression ... that is, concerned with the temptation to show herself willing to yield to the man ... the addendum to the dream could scarcely mean anything else than the longing for a kiss, which, with a smoker, would necessarily smell of smoke. (*SE* 7:73)

After connecting this to Herr K.'s kiss, Freud continues:

> Taking into consideration ... the indication which seemed to point to there having been a transference on to me—since I am a smoker too—I came to the conclusion that the idea had probably occurred to her one day during a sitting that she would like to have a kiss from me. (*SE* 7:74)

Dora's first dream, in which her father saves her from danger, confirms Freud as the good and powerful father-analyst as well as the erotic object of desire, the figure upholding Oedipal law and sexual difference.

But the second dream is more problematic; it presents a maternal letter that announces the death of the father; it is, as he points out, a dream of rage rather than love, of Dora's desire for revenge rather than submission. More significant, Dora's associations to this dream lead to women: to the governess, to an aunt, to the adored Madonna, to Frau K.,

with her "adorable white body"—all maternal figures of desire and identification. Rather than trace these displacements by means of which Dora
attempts to recuperate a denigrated maternal object, Freud instead asks
Dora and the reader to follow a different track, his associations to the
material of analysis, which he presents, as he writes, "in the somewhat
haphazard order in which it recurs to my mind" (*SE* 7:95). His associations lead to a medical discourse that as he himself points out "is known
to physicians though not to laymen" (*SE* 7:99). With such phrases as
"There could be no doubt," "it was easy to guess" (*SE* 7:96), "a certain
suspicion of mine became a certainty" (*SE* 7:99), Freud's text authorizes
the attribution of his knowledge and his desire to Dora. Insisting on
Dora's active desires to enter a woman's body, he marks her subject
position as masculine and defines her fantasy as a "defloration."

But Freud does not stay with this narrative of homoerotic desire; he
switches the tracks of narrative reconstruction to Dora's heterosexual
feminine desire for Herr K., and for the child that would be its consequence. Indeed in his retrospective footnote, Freud inserts a question
into her dream as logically necessary to its meaning: "Which way to Herr
K's house?" (*SE* 7:104 n. 2). The question shifts the narrative quest from
mother to father, from the body of a woman to the house of a man and
reasserts the heterosexual paternal figure as object of desire.[8] If Freud's
narration of "The Second Dream" increasingly reveals his own desire as
well as Dora's, whether Dora's subject position is defined as masculine
or feminine, desire as the passion *for* an object (that is to say, Oedipal
desire) is foregrounded, and identification (the passion to be the object
that psychoanalysis names pre-Oedipal desire) is virtually foreclosed.

But Dora's dream has been heard by a number of feminist critics to
articulate the problematics of that pre-Oedipal desire, which is conflated
with identification, even more than Oedipal desire. Indeed, Dora's
dream literally questions the very relation between identification and
desire. A question mark is the primary figure of the second dream, a
literal diacritical mark disrupting the normal syntax of a sentence, in the
phrase "if you like?" that appears both in her mother's dream-letter, and
in her association to a letter from Frau K. inviting her to the lake. Although Freud questions the appearance of the question mark, he does
not question it as a signifier. But it is precisely the question of Dora's
desire that is at issue. The dream's question—if you like?—is the question of the hysteric, of the relation between desire and identity. How is
sexual identity assumed? How represented? Is "gynecophilic" (Freud's
initial term for Dora's desire) the same as "masculine"? Freud's interpretation that underlying Dora's dream is a fantasy of a *man* seeking to force

entrance into a woman not only erases the question mark of the dream, but also compounds hysterical conflict by constituting heterosexuality as a forced entrance of an active man into a passive woman, fixing passivity as the position of femininity and thus obliterating the active female subject.

It also injects into the text itself the fantasy of rape underlying Freud's own interpretative position. Insistently trying to open Dora up, Freud both hears a fantasy of defloration in Dora's description of wandering with an obscure goal and enacts it by appropriating Dora's voice in his use of indirect discourse, and appropriating her dream as his own, giving her his question, his goal. As he points out, his goal is to further his understanding of "Dreams and Hysteria," to supplement *The Interpretation of Dreams.* Interestingly, Freud used an analogous metaphor for the structure of his dream book: an imaginary walk into a dark wood "where there is no clear view and it is very easy to go astray. There, there is a cavernous defile through which I lead my readers . . . and then, all at once, the high ground and the prospect and the question: Which way do you want to go?" (*SE* 4:122 n. 1). Representing his quest for knowledge through an image that he identifies in the Dora case as the body of a woman, Freud implicates himself in the fantasmatic probing of the woman's body and raises the same question that informs the hysteric's dream: Which way to go? For theorist and hysteric, the crossroads loom as a site of anxious and unknown possibility.

Dora seems indeed to be searching for a way to go, but just as important, for a goal: for an image of woman different from the unacceptable representations offered her. But Freud inserts his own question into Dora's dream, answers it, and then says: "I informed her of my conclusions. The impression upon her mind must have been forcible" (*SE* 7:100). Freud's own diction, with its linguistic associations to force, resonates with the implications of mind-rape. Dora's immediate response to this forcible impression is to yield a little, to open another part of the dream to Freud's picklock: "she went calmly to her room and began reading a big book that lay on her writing table" (*SE* 7:100). As Freud points out, Dora's odd words here are "calmly" and "big"; their emphatic presence as markers suggests that both are to be interrogated. Freud notes that "calmly," suggests a linguistic cover-up of perturbation; and that Dora later added "not sadly" to clarify the meaning of "calmly." But he neither questions the negation ("not") nor indicates whether this negation is also a cover-up for a profound sadness bespeaking a loss relevant to her dream quest. As for the other term to be questioned, the "big" book, Freud immediately understands it as a confirmation of his speculation that an encyclopedia was the source of Dora's sexual knowledge. But could this *big* book on *her* writing table be a trope of her situation, her "calm" reading a denial of the agitation that her symptoms spoke? Could the big book be Freud's own big book, *The Interpretation of Dreams,* the authoritative cultural inscription of the Father to which her case was a "little" addendum?

These questions, suggested by the dream's scenario of Dora reading indicate also the anxious underlying trope of sexual violation that inhered more generally in the daughter's cultural situation in fin-de-siècle Europe. Too often compelled to experience the forcible imposition of the paternal word as a violation through the voice of her integrity and will, while at the same time identifying with and loving the father, the daughter reflected in her ambivalent resistance that trauma to which Freud's original seduction theory had attributed hysteria.

But as the Dora case revealed, if analytic mastery is supported by and supports the fantasy of the virile father, it is at the expense of the devalued mother. The father's voice occludes the potentiality of the maternal letter. Recall that Freud tells us that Dora hides a letter from her grandmother when he enters the waiting-room of his office, but its contents remain negligible: "I believe that Dora only wanted to play secrets with me, and to hint that she was on the point of allowing her secret to be torn from her by the physician" (*SE* 7:96). Perhaps. Certainly the violence of the metaphor, which occurs elsewhere in the text, indicates Freud's sense of his role in that game of heterosexual pursuit called "playing doctor." But his sadomasochistically toned representation of the doctor-patient relation, a representation that governs his descriptions of heterosexual relations throughout his writings, suggests more than a perversion on his part: it suggests that sadomasochism defines the erotic power-politics of heterosexuality, that it is ineluctably linked to the cultural positionalities of masculine and feminine.

Irigaray has suggested that "the enactment of sadomasochistic fantasies is governed by man's relation to his mother: the desire to force entry, to penetrate, to appropriate for himself the mystery of this womb where he has been conceived, the secret of his begetting, of his origin" (1985, 164). Irigaray's remark illuminates Freud's obsession with the source of Dora's knowledge—Was it oral or written? Did it come from the mother's voice or the father's text?—as well as his motivation for turning away from the maternal letter to the big book. Yet to his credit, Freud did not exclude the maternal letter from his story or eliminate its effects from the psychoanalytic exchange. The corporeal remainder of the voice continued to assert the body's presence in the utterance and (especially when a woman was speaking her secrets) to remind Freud of the mother, to lead him as the receptive ear through evocative articulations into an unconscious where the line between his and hers was obscured. Through what Garrett Stewart calls "the verbal stream in which otherness mutters to us" (1990, 33)—mutters, mutter, matter, mother—the vocative, provocative and evocative, of the analytic dialogue repeatedly opened into a radical otherness, a feminine alterity that required a filling in, a covering up, lest one fall in. Thus Freud writes of his narrative, "Part of this material I was able to obtain directly from the analysis, but the rest required supplementing." Narrativization enacted that supplementation. If his narrative constructed the "true sexual object" as "the penis," the semiotic resonance of his text suggests that hysteria takes a more indeterminate object as its truth. "Passion modifies the subject's relation to reality, alters it so that the passionate object is center," Green remarks in his analysis of passion (1986, 222–23). Freud's narrative unveiled the voice itself as the passionate object of the hysteric and of psychoanalysis. Who has the voice? Who does what with it? To whom does it belong?

NOTES

1. The relation between the hysteric's inability to hold a fixed subject position and her/his inability to assume a masculine or feminine positional identity made manifest the inevitable link between subject and gender position.

2. In *The Acoustic Mirror,* Silverman (1988) surveys the psychoanalytic literature that describes the mother as the primal voice for the child.

3. This is the figure Kristeva (1986a) names "the imaginary father of prehistory."

4. See especially Gallop, Gearhardt, Sprengnether, and Hertz in Bernheimer and Kahane (1985).

5. Only Neil Hertz had dealt with this particular aspect of the Dora case, focusing on the way in which Freud's position as listener effeminizes him. Hertz reads Freud's self-representation of his relation to the medical elders of his profession, through a critical scene of overhearing the secrets of the alcove like the woman, from the margins. Hertz convincingly argues that Freud represents himself as ingenue, marginal to the phallic authority of those who know; "Dora's Secrets, Freud's Technique," in Bernheimer and Kahane (1985).

6. *SE* 7:52. In the Collier paperback, this is translated as "true sexual organ" (69).

7. Of course, in attributing to Dora a fellatio fantasy, Freud may be right; Freud is extrapolating a causality from her infantile thumb-sucking, making the connection between the gratifications of sucking the nipple, sucking the thumb, and sucking the penis. Yet he arrives at his conclusion by following the track of his own associations. If he inserts himself into her fantasy in order to know her secrets, he nevertheless also uncovers his own.

8. Although Freud singles out "with a view to subsequent investigation the theme of the virgin mother" (96), and mentions it in a later footnote, he has virtually nothing to say about it.

At this point, it is buried in his abrupt transition to a reading of Dora's identification with a young man.

REFERENCES

Barthes, Roland. 1977. "The Grain of the Voice." In *Image—Music—Text,* translated by Stephen Heath. New York: Noonday.

Bernheimer, Charles, and Claire Kahane, eds. 1985. *In Dora's Case: Freud—Hysteria—Feminism.* New York: Columbia University Press.

Freud, Sigmund. 1953–74. *The Standard Edition of the Complete Psychological Works of Sigmund Freud.* Translated and edited by James Strachey. 24 vols. London: Hogarth.

Green, André. 1986. *On Private Madness.* New York: International Universities Press.

Hunter, Dianne. 1985. "Hysteria, Psychoanalysis, and Feminism: The Case of Anna O." In *The M/Other Tongue: Essays in Feminist Psychoanalytic Criticism,* edited by Shirley Garner, Claire Kahane, and Madelon Sprengnether. Ithaca: Cornell University Press.

Irigaray, Luce. 1985. *This Sex Which Is Not One,* translated by Catherine Porter and Carolyn Burke. Ithaca: Cornell University Press.

———. 1989. "The Gesture in Psychoanalysis," In *Between Feminism and Psychoanalysis,* edited by Teresa Brennan, 127–38. London: Routledge.

Kristeva, Julia. 1980. *Desire in Language.* Edited by Leon S. Roudiez. New York: Columbia University Press.

———. 1981. "Women's Time." *Signs* 7, no. 1 (Autumn): 13–35. Repr. *The Kristeva Reader,* edited by Toril Moi, 187–213. New York: Columbia University Press, 1986.

———. 1986a. "Freud and Love: Treatment and Its Discontents." In *The Kristeva Reader,* edited by Toril Moi. New York: Columbia University Press.

———. 1986b. "Revolution in Poetic Language." In *The Kristeva Reader,* edited by Toril Moi. New York: Columbia University Press.

Lacan, Jacques. 1952/1966. "Intervention on Transference." Translated by Jacqueline Rose and reprinted in *Feminine Sexuality: Jacques Lacan and L'Ecole Freudienne,* edited by Juliet Mitchell and Jacqueline Rose. New York: Norton, 1983.

Silverman, Kaja. 1988. *The Acoustic Mirror: The Female Voice in Psychoanalysis and the Cinema.* Bloomington: Indiana University Press.

Sprengnether, Madelon. 1985. "Enforcing Oedipus: Freud and Dora." In *The M/Other Tongue: Essays in Feminist Psychoanalytic Criticism,* edited by Shirley Garner, Claire Kahane, and Madelon Sprengnether. Ithaca: Cornell University Press.

Stewart, Garrett. 1990. *Reading Voices: Literature and the Phonotext.* Berkeley and Los Angeles: University of California Press.

6

"Russian Tactics": Freud's "Case of Homosexuality in a Woman"

MARY JACOBUS

> The impression one had of her analysis was not unlike that of a hypnotic treatment, where the resistance has in the same way withdrawn to a certain boundary line, beyond which it proves to be unconquerable. The resistance very often pursues similar tactics—Russian tactics, as they might be called—in cases of obsessional neurosis.
>
> —Sigmund Freud, "The Psychogenesis of a Case of Homosexuality in a Woman" (1920)

The "Russian Tactics" of my title are Freud's code-name for the strategies employed by resistance in the face of psychoanalytic enlightenment. As he writes of his "beautiful and clever" eighteen-year-old patient in "The Psychogenesis of a Case of Homosexuality in a Woman" (1920), "the resistance ha[d] . . . withdrawn to a certain boundary line [*Grenze,* or frontier], beyond which it prove[d] to be unconquerable."[1] Freud's Russian analogy has a prehistory. It goes back twenty years to a period when Russia, viewed from the perspective of German enlightenment, would have been the symbol of an unreformed autocracy intent on protecting itself from new and alien ideas (especially German ideas).[2] In *The Interpretation of Dreams* (1900), Freud had written of a "ruthless" censorship that "acts exactly like the censorship of newspapers at the Russian frontier, which allows foreign journals to fall into the hands of the readers whom it is its business to protect only after a quantity of passages have been blacked out" (*SE* 5(II):529). Still earlier, he wrote to Fliess in 1897:" Have you ever seen a foreign newspaper which has passed the Russian censorship at the frontier? Words, whole clauses and sentences are blacked out so that what is left becomes unintelligible. A *Russian censorship* of this kind comes about in psychoses and produces the apparently meaningless deliria" (*SE* 1:273).[3] Freud's prerevolutionary analogy points not only to a similar time-lag in his thinking about female homosexuality but to a blockade of information at the frontier of his own psychoanalytic inquiry—a resistance that equals his patient's.

Poised at the opening of the great debate over the question of female sexuality that occupied both male and female analysts during the 1920s, "A Case of Homosexuality in a Woman" looks back to the precursor text of twenty years before, Freud's "Fragment of an Analysis of a Case of Hysteria" (1901).[4] Another spirited young hysteric handed over to Freud by her exasperated father, Dora notoriously broke off the analysis, confronting Freud himself with his failure to recognize both the nature of the transference and her homosexuality; as he writes in his famous afterthought, "I failed to discover in time . . . that her homosexual (gynaecophilic) love for Frau K. was the strongest unconscious current in her mental life" (*SE* 7:120 n). This time, however, Freud is the one who breaks off the analysis when he discovers "the sweeping repudiation of men" his patient has transferred to him: "As soon . . . as I recognized the girl's attitude to her father, I broke off the treatment and advised her parents that . . . it should be continued by a woman doctor" (*SE* 18:164). In an attempt to explain her decisive turn toward homosexuality, Freud suggests that the girl has "retired in favour of someone else" (*SE* 18:158, 159 n)—her mother. Just as the disappointed girl turns away from her father, Freud himself could be said to "retire in favour" of a female analytic rival.[5] Is it too much to suggest that he too had "withdrawn to a certain boundary line"—a line beyond which a resistant psychoanalysis might also prove to be unconquerable? The identification here would be not so much the obvious one between Freud and the girl's baffled, angry father, as the one between Freud and the girl herself, whose "resistance"—her willed refusal to know—revives the Russian analogy at the contested frontier of female homosexuality.

Freud boasts at the outset of the unbrokenness of his narrative; the case, he says, allows him to trace the origin and development of female homosexuality "with complete certainty and almost without a gap:

(*lückenlos;* SE 18:147), despite suppressions that are "easily to be explained by the medical discretion necessary in discussing a recent case"
(*SE* 18:147). But Freud observes later on that "the information received
by our consciousness about our erotic life is especially liable to be
incomplete, full of gaps [*lückenhaft*], or falsified" (*SE* 18:167). His own
production of psychoanalytic knowledge contains similar gaps and falsifi-
cations in the face of unwelcome information. I shall explore here
Freud's representation of what he calls (mystifyingly) "the mystery of
homosexuality" under three interconnected headings: the "psychogenesis," not of homosexuality, but of passion; the "enigma of suicide"
(the phrase is Freud's); and what he calls the "deliria" of censorship, or
the apparent meaninglessness that he had earlier identified with psychosis. I argue that this unconcealed censorship—the Russian tactics that
Freud associates with the girl's own resistance—becomes especially evident in the delirious finale of "A Case of Homosexuality in a Woman,"
where the operations of the Freudian unconscious and those of the sex-
change operation converge at the imaginary site of the lesbian body.

THE "LADY" AND THE TRAMP

Freud's patient, a young woman of the *haute bourgeoisie* [*aus sozial
hochstehender Familie*]—referred to throughout as "the girl" (*das
Mädchen*)—has aroused her parent's displeasure by her open adoration
of "a certain 'society lady' [*"aus der Gesellschaft"*] about ten years older
than herself." Her parents insist that "in spite of her distinguished name,
this lady was nothing but a *cocotte* [*Kokotte*]." Freud himself calls her a
"*demi-mondaine*" [*Halbweltdame*] placing the term "lady" in quotation
marks, for the lady is also a tramp, whose sexuality belongs in the public
domain. According to the girl's parents, she is well known to be living on
intimate terms with a married woman while carrying on promiscuous
affairs with a number of men. The girl loses no opportunity of displaying
her devotion—hanging about outside the lady's door and sending her
flowers—as well as openly flaunting her attachment by accompanying
her about the streets in the vicinity of her father's workplace ("she did
not scruple to appear in the most frequented streets in the company of
her undesirable friend"; *SE* 18:148). But despite her courtship, the girl
has apparently been unable, in Freud's euphemistic term, to "succeed in
satisfying her passion"—a matter on which he makes his prognosis partly
dependent. Interestingly, the word "passion" (rendered throughout

Freud's text as *Leidenschaft*) is used not only in apposition to the girl's genital sexuality ("her genital chasity, if one may use such a phrase, had remained intact"; *SE* 18:153), but apropos of the fatal attraction—"a consuming passion"—that makes her neglect her studies, social functions, and friends of her own age in pursuit of the "undesirable" lady.

Freud treats the girl's passion as the sign of a masculine identification. Her adoration for the lady is like that of a courtly lover: "the girl had adopted the characteristic masculine type of love," he tells us, "Hoping little and asking for nothing' " ("*che poco spera e nulla chiede*"; the quotation is from Tasso's *Gerusalamme Liberata*).[6] In this it resembles "the first passionate adoration of a youth for a celebrated actress whom he regards as far above him, to whom he scarcely dares lift his bashful eyes" (*SE* 18:160). The quotation from Tasso reminds us that courtly love can be regarded not just as a sign of humility, but as a form of distraction; "devoted" in another sense, for these particular lovers in Tasso's poem risk immolation. Not only that, but the girl's choice of a sexually debased love-object, and her wish to "rescue" her, mimics the one described in Freud's "Special Type of Choice of Object Made by Men" (1910), where "it is a necessary condition that the loved object should be in some way or other 'of bad repute' sexually—someone who really may be called a *cocotte*" (*SE* 18:161; see also *SE* 11:165–75). But when it comes to Freud's discussion of the ways in which the girl resembles her father and his list of the girl's "masculine" intellectual attributes ("her acuteness of comprehension and her lucid objectivity, *in so far as she was not dominated by her passion*"; *SE* 18:154; my emphasis), he tends to associate passion, to the contrary, with an aberration: she is masculine in her passion, but her passion makes her *less* masculine, *less* like her father. Passion turns out to be a form of masquerade (of courtly love, of masculinity) whose meaning is reversed—much as Lacan alleges, apropos of "the phallic mark of desire," that "virile display itself appears as feminine."[7] In Freud's gender scheme, it is masculine to desire the lady, but feminine to make a virile display of phallic desire. Loving a woman as a man might do (Freud's earlier definition of Dora's "gynaecophilia") takes on the paradoxical appearance of femininity.

Freud traces the "special type of choice of object made by men" back to maternal attachment; the mother, not the father, is the original object of passion. The girl may have given up her father and "retired in favour of her mother," but it turns out that her earlier love-objects had all been substitute mothers anyway: schoolteachers or the "women between thirty and thirty-five whom she had met with their children during summer holidays" (*SE* 18:156), and whom she could identify with her own mother. Her present lady-love is just such a substitute for the mother who had recently given birth to a much younger child.[8] Freud describes this current in her feelings ("one that we may unhesitatingly designate as homosexual") as "a direct and unchanged continuation of an infantile fixation on her mother" (*SE* 18:168). Strong maternal attachment leads not only to "a special type of choice of object," but to homosexuality in men (later on in the case, Freud reminds us "that homosexual men have experienced a specially strong fixation on their mother"; *SE* 18:171)—and apparently, in women too. What would it mean for a woman to repudiate the strength of her fixation on her mother, instead of repudiating her father, as this girl does? The answer, presumably, is the normative outcome of the feminine Oedipus complex; namely, the castration anxiety that ensures the girl's repudiation of her first love-object (the mother) in favor of a heterosexual object (the father) and his symbolic substitute (penis = baby). But this particular girl ("a spirited girl, always ready for romping and fighting") has "brought along with her from her childhood a strongly marked 'masculinity complex'" and "a pronounced envy for the penis." As Freud puts it, bluntly, "She was in fact a feminist' (*SE* 18:169). Rebelling against the lot of woman, she has come particularly to dislike the idea of having a baby, which would provide the only cure for penis envy known to Freud; as we've seen, he attributes the decisive homosexual turn and timing of the girl's choice of object to her disappointment when her father gives this precious penis-substitute to her mother instead of her ("it was not *she* who bore the child, but her unconsciously hated rival, the mother"; *SE* 18:157). Whereupon she "foreswears" Freudian womanhood altogether, repudiating, not just her father, but "her wish for a child, her love of men, and the feminine role in general."

As Freud sums up the perverse trajectory of disappointed womanhood, "She changed into a man and took her mother in place of her father as the object of her love" (*SE* 18:158). This is his definition of female homosexuality, insofar as he offers one. But his definition risks collapsing two distinct aspects of psychic life: *identification* and *object-choice*. Has the girl *identified* with her father in choosing her maternal love-object, or has she never really yielded up that prior maternal object in the first place? And what is the relation between this subsequent paternal identification and the earliest emergence of the maternal object-choice that Freud takes as a given? A footnote signals the slippage: "It is by no means rare," Freud writes, "for a love-relation to be broken off through *a process of identification* on the part of the lover with the loved object, a process equivalent to a kind of regression to narcissism"

(*SE* 18:158 n; my emphasis). In identifying with her father, the girl not only "regresses" to her original love-object, the mother, but to an earlier form of identification too. We know that narcissistic object-choice under-lies all others for Freud. Her regression-through-identification serves to confirm what Freud has implied throughout: that all object-choice is narcissistic in origin, and that the prototype for later identifications is the narcissistic form of identification that actually occurs prior to object-choice proper. If the psychogenesis of both sexuality and homosexuality can be traced back to maternal fixation, the wonder is that all men aren't homosexual, and all women too—indeed, as Freud himself acknowl-edges, they may well be: "a very considerable measure of latent or unconscious homosexuality can be detected in all normal people" (*SE* 18:171).[9] On this deconstructive note, Freud lets his case rest: "It is not for psycho-analysis to solve the problem of homosexuality" (*SE* 18:171).

Before leaving the "lady," however, I want to note what amounts to an implicit "feminine identification" on Freud's own part. Determined to combat his daughter's homosexuality "with all the means in his power," the girl's father turns to psychoanalysis despite (in Freud's words) "the low estimation in which [it] is so generally held in Vienna" *(SE* 18:149). Even the girl treats Freud with some hauteur: "Once when I expounded to her a specially important part of the theory, one touch-ing her nearly, she replied in an inimitable tone, 'How very interesting,' as though she were a *grande dame* being taken over a museum and glancing through her lorgnon at objects to which she was completely indifferent" (*SE* 18:163). This indifference to the "objects" in Freud's psychoanalytic *galerie*—and above all to the tour-guide himself—suggests Freud's sensitivity to the social standing of his Viennese profes-sion; however veiled by "medical discretion," he too, like the lady, threatens to bring sexuality out of the home into the public domain. Readers of Dora's case history will recall Freud's preoccupation with the sources of Dora's sexual knowledge, which he traces not only to her undercover reading but to an oral source: Frau K., her father's mistress, and Dora's homosexual love-object.[10] She knows very well, she tells Freud, "that there was more than one way of obtaining sexual gratification" (*SE* 7:47). In "A Case of Homosexuality in a Woman," the girl similarly tells Freud that "she meant to marry 'in order to escape her father's tyranny and to follow her true inclinations undisturbed.' As for the husband, she remarked rather contemptuously, she would easily deal with him, and besides, one could have sexual relations with a man and a woman at one and the same time" (*SE* 18:165). The source of her knowledge is none other than "the example of the adored lady." Even more than the woman doctor in whose favor Freud "retires," the lady turns out to be a rival authority on lesbian and bisexual matters. What's more, there is no "indifference" with regard to *this* object. The most telling aspect of Freud's emphasis on the girl's "passion" for the lady is her contrasting dis-passion for psychoanalysis, her indifference to Freud himself. Freud's story of a woman spurned—a girl made vengeful by "the disappointment she had suffered from her father" (*SE* 18:164)—looks uncomfortably like a displaced inversion of his own. Hell hath no fury like a father spurned. But an obscure "something" remains to be explained in the depth of her father's bitter reaction ("There was something about his daughter's homosexuality that aroused the deepest bitterness in him"; *SE* 18:149). This mysterious "something," I suggest, is the father's own "feminine" identification, aroused and implicated by the daughter's homosexuality—the troubling "feminine" identification that characterizes both Freud's countertransference and his resistance.

THE "ENIGMA" OF SUICIDE

According to Freud the "lady" only begins to treat the girl "in a more friendly manner" when she provides "unmistakable proof of serious passion" by attempting suicide. As the girl obviously intends, her father eventually encounters her and her beloved in the street, passing them "with an angry glance which boded no good," whereupon "the girl rushed off and flung herself over a wall down the side of a cutting onto the suburban railway line which ran close by" (*SE* 18:148). Freud remarks that the girl's suicide attempt improves her position with both the lady and her parents, who are all forced to take her passion seriously. Later he rehearses the episode, this time offering a fresh explanation—first hers, then his:

> She went for a walk with [the lady] one day in a part of the town and at an hour at which she was not unlikely to meet her father on his way from his office. So it turned out. Her father passed them in the street and cast a furious look at her and her companion, about whom he had by that time come to know. A few moments later she flung herself into the railway cutting. The explanation she gave of the immediate reasons determining her decision sounded quite plausible. She had confessed to the lady that the man who had given them such an irate glance was her

father, and that he had absolutely forbidden their friendship. The lady became incensed at this and ordered the girl to leave her then and there, and never again to wait for her or to address her—the affair must now come to an end. In her despair at having thus lost her loved one for ever, she wanted to put an end to herself. (*SE* 18:161–62)

Uncovering "another and deeper explanation," Freud calls the attempted suicide both "the fulfillment of a punishment (self-punishment) and the fulfillment of a wish." The wish fulfilled by this "fall" is "the wish to have a child by her father, for now she 'fell' through her father's fault" (*SE* 18:162; Freud's reading turns on the word *niederkommen,* meaning both "to fall" and "to be delivered of a child"; see also *SE* 18:162 n). But the girl's suicide also reveals her unconscious, vengeful death wishes against both her father (for impeding her love) and her mother (for becoming pregnant with her little brother). The connecting link, according to Freud, is the double prohibition uttered by the irate father and the incensed lady: "the affair must now come to an end."

It is in this connection that Freud invokes "the enigma of suicide." Absorbing "all that is enigmatic" in the girl's homosexuality (*SE* 18:161), suicide stands in for "the mystery of homosexuality" while again bringing the matter of narcissistic identification and object-choice to the fore. Freud explains suicide as an attempt to kill an object with whom the subject has identified herself ("turning against [oneself] a deathwish which had been directed at someone else"; *SE* 18:162). In "Mourning and Melancholia" (1917), written three years before the "Case of Homosexuality in a Woman," Freud has a similar solution to "the riddle of the tendency to suicide" (*SE* 14:252). The melancholic ego, he says, can only kill itself by treating itself as an object. But the violence directed against itself is a manifestation of the hostility representing the ego's original reaction to objects—a reaction that is strictly speaking pre-objectal. Freud had originally offered this explanation of suicide in "Instincts and their Vicissitudes" (1915). Here he says that when the object first makes its appearance, during the stage of primary narcissism, "indifference" to the external world coincides with "unpleasure"; only at this stage does the opposite to loving (i.e., hating) emerge. But as Freud points out, "loving" has not one but *three* opposites: hating, being loved, and indifference; or rather, rearranged in a developmental sequence: (1) indifference, (2) hating, and (3) being loved.[11] Indifference is a special case of hate, having first appeared as its forerunner (much as homosexuality is a special case of object-choice, having first appeared as maternal attachment). Put differently, as ego is to the external world, so love is to indifference; and as pleasure is to unpleasure, so love (the quest for pleasure) is to hate (self-preservation; see *SE* 14:136). Love and hate only become opposites at the point of genital organization. The upshot, in Freud's account, is that "hate, as a relation to objects, is older than love" (*SE* 14:139). The "enigma of suicide" turns out to be the enigma of passion, whose regressive form is hate, and earlier still, indifference.

The girl's suicide (the act of violence she directs against herself and her father) therefore tells the story of passion's origins in a prior "indifference." Posing as grande dame, the girl at once masks hatred as indifference and regresses to hate's forerunner, the unpleasure with which all external stimuli were originally regarded. The play of glances in Freud's narrative—the grande dame's indifferent glance through her lorgnon, the father's "angry glance" [*Blick*] as he passes his daughter in the street—stages a narcissistic drama. In "Mourning and Melancholia," Freud had written that frustrated object-choice regresses to narcissism, enshrining "a preliminary stage of object-choice" (*SE* 14:249) characterized by narcissistic identification. This substitution of narcissistic identification for object-love—the transformation of object-loss into ego-loss—is the key to melancholia (as he puts it epigramatically, "the shadow of the object [falls] upon the ego"; *SE* 14:249). Being in love and attempting suicide represent two alternate ways in which the ego may be overwhelmed by the object. In *Black Sun: Depression and Melancholia* (1987), Kristeva argues that the affective and aesthetic elaborations of melancholia preserve the pre- of object relations. Prior to the Oedipus complex and its resolution (prior, that is, to both the splitting and the prohibition that constitutes subjectivity and gender) melancholia implicates the in-difference of un- or dis-passion.[12] The subject of melancholia is an improper subject, an "abject" insufficiently differentiated from its not-yet-object—what Kristeva calls the maternal "Thing" that will be (but is not yet) the mother. The interest (and the difficulty) of Kristeva's account of melancholia lies in the specificity of its implications for women. I pursue these implications briefly in connection with the "Case of Homosexuality in a Woman."

Kristeva suggests that women's "specular identification with the mother" and their "introjection of the maternal body and self" are more immediate, and hence more problematic, than men's. Because of this primary narcissistic identification, she asserts, it is more difficult for women to turn matricidal drive into saving representation; more difficult, in other words, for women to symbolize (i.e., to mourn a lost object). This failure at the level of symbolization tends to trap the feminine subject in the incorporatory psychosis of melancholia, addicted as she is to the maternal, pre-objectal Thing. Hence the destructive drive that women, more than men, turn against themselves ("the melancholy woman is the dead one that has always been abandoned within herself").[13] Depression and even suicide take the place of mourning. Only by an act of symbolic matricide can the maternal object be lost and found again, "transposed," as Kristeva puts it, "by means of an unbelievable symbolic effort" (28). The extra symbolic effort demanded of women becomes for Kristeva the defining asymmetry between the sexes. While heterosexual men and homosexual women can recover the lost maternal object as erotic object, finding an erotic object other than the primary maternal object (i.e., a heterosexual object) involves *for heterosexual women* "a gigantic elaboration"—a symbolic elaboration—far greater than men are called upon to undertake in the interests of their own heterosexuality. Freud implies that femininity is a high-risk condition for neurosis, given women's difficulties in negotiating the Oedipus complex: Kristeva implies that women are similarly at risk for melancholia given their primary maternal identification. If female homosexuality looks like the path of least resistance in the face of the disproportionate difficulty of this symbolic undertaking, the "enigma of suicide" represents the psychotic outcome when that path is blocked, and incorporation has to take the place of erotic cathexis.

In Freud's narrative, the girl identifies with her father, turning his angry and punitive glance on herself. A Kristevan narrative points instead to the melancholy that *Black Sun* defines as "*impossible mourning for the maternal object*" (9). The girl is overwhelmed by the Thing. But there is a difficulty here for feminism. Freud claims that her suicide attempt signals "her attitude of defiance and revenge against her father," much as in "Mourning and Melancholia" he detects "a mental constellation of revolt" in his melancholy patients' complaints and self-reproaches (*SE* 14:248). One obvious objection to the Kristevan reading is that it leaves no scope for the girl's defiance ("She was in fact a feminist") to exert political leverage on the symbolic realm embodied by her heterosexist father and Freudian theory.[14] Where Freud equates the "mystery" of female homosexuality with the "enigma" of suicide, Kristeva seems to make female homosexuality a flight from female psychosis. But this may be to misread Kristeva, for whom the symbolic is always accompanied and disrupted by its failures, and for whom psychosis is as much a mode of signification as a pathology. If the performance of homosexuality unsettles the masquerade of heterosexuality, psychosis (defined as the failure to symbolize) points to the precariousness of the symbolic realm while providing a permanent record within the subject of the immense price paid for admission. This is not to romanticize female homosexuality as a spanner in the symbolic works (much as hysteria was romanticized by earlier feminist psychoanalytic criticism). Rather, Freud's text of female homosexuality can be read as uncovering this prehistory of the (failed) institution of (heterosexual) boundaries—boundaries that are constantly being breached in the time-present of the subject's psychic narrative. I turn, finally, to this narrative; or rather, to the cut (at once a literal trace and a trace of the literal) that disrupts Freud's own story with a form of signification it is tempting to call "psychotic" in this specialized Kristevan sense.

THE UNKINDEST CUT

According to Freud's Russian analogy, censorship (i.e., resistance) produces "apparently meaningless deliria" (*Delirien,* elsewhere defined as delusional structures of thought).[15] In *The Interpretation of Dreams,* "deliria" are "the work of a censorship which no longer takes the trouble to conceal its operation." Just as the girl in "A Case of Homosexuality in a Woman" is at once "too open" and "full of deceitfulness" (*SE* 18:148), the censored (resistant) text is characterized by its blatantly unconcealed deception: "instead of collaborating in producing a new version that shall be unobjectionable, it ruthlessly deletes whatever it disapproves of, so that what remains becomes quite disconnected" (*SE* 5:529). Its cuts are brutally visible. Freud's textual analogy is striking, not least in associating the disruption of meaning with psychosis (as he had written in the letter to Fliess, "A Russian censorship of this kind comes about in psychoses"; *SE* 1:273). The psychotic text contains the disconnected traces of impossible meanings. At the end of Freud's "Case of Homosexuality in a Woman," the unconcealed operations of the censor are preserved in the very objectionableness of its representation of female homosexuality. Disconnection—the sign of "deliria" or psychosis—openly defeats Freud's boasted attempt to trace a coherent "psychogenesis" of female homosexuality ("almost without a gap," *lückenlos*). The cut that we glimpse in the girl's enigmatic suicide attempt surfaces in Freud's closing discussion of Steinach's sex-change operations, where the operations of the Freudian unconscious and those of castration converge on the phantasmatic lesbian body.

Confronted with the double prohibition uttered by both father and lady ("the affair must now come to an end"; *SE* 18:162), the girl flings herself into a railway cutting (in German, *Einschnitt [der Stadtbahn]*).

Freud discusses the meaning of her "fall" (her imaginary pregnancy) in terms of her simultaneous wish for fulfillment and punishment. But the meaning of the "cutting" remains unexplored. The "enigma" of her suicide implies both what it covers and what the girl herself does not recover from: the literalness of the cut into which she flings herself when her father "cuts" her in the street with his furious glance. Metaphorically speaking, such a cut is equivalent to castration—the castration that the girl is forced to recognize in both herself and her mother, according to Freud's account of the feminine Oedipus complex, thereby setting in motion the girl's repudiation of the castrated mother (as opposed to the boy, for whom castration anxiety, by contrast, brings about a resolution of the Oedipus complex). Flinging herself into the breach, you might say, the girl identifies herself in a literal sense (a psychotic sense) with both cutting and cut. Contrary to Freud's assertion, she identifies with what she hasn't got (rather than with what the father has). Her refusal to be the phallus for the man (the symbol of his desire) identifies her in a literal fashion with the psychoanalytically prescribed lack that is enjoined on her. By improperly literalizing the symbolic castration that assigns her to her proper place within a heterosexualized Oedipal structure, the girl makes visible the hideous literalness of the Oedipal narrative. Freud and her father tell her: "you just don't get it [i.e., the phallus], and you never will." To which the girl makes her suicidal reply, aiming it at both her father and the lady who ventriloquizes his prohibition: "*you* just don't get it [i.e., understand], and you never will." Freud misrecognizes the disconnected meaning (lessness) of her reply, just as he had once failed to recognize Dora's homosexuality, in his preoccupation with what, for him, would compensate the girl for her castration—her imaginary pregnancy. But Freud also tells us that the girl is "always reserved in what she said about her mother" (*SE* 18:149). What is this "reserve" in the relations between mother and daughter, and how does it bear on the matter of castration?

According to Freud, while her father is chagrined by his daughter's homosexuality, her mother's "attitude towards the girl was not so easy to grasp" (*SE* 18:149). Far from being incensed, she even "enjoyed her daughter's confidence concerning her passion." This is the more surprising because she treats her daughter harshly in contrast to her sons and sees her as a rival ("still youthful herself, [she] saw in her rapidly developing daughter an inconvenient competitor"; *SE* 18:157). Freud's cynical implication is that the mother acquiesces in her daughter's homosexual object-choice because it leaves all the men to her ("The mother herself still attached great value to the attentions and the admiration of men"; *SE* 18:158). But if we take a leaf out of Melanie Klein's book, there may be another way to view the mother's acquiescence. In "The Effects of Early Anxiety-Situations on the Sexual Development of the Girl" (1932), Klein follows Freud in viewing female homosexuality as a form of masculine identification.[16] The specifically Kleinian turn consists in viewing castration anxiety in terms of the girl's sadistic fantasies, for instance, of the destruction of her mother by her father's dangerous penis. The result may be the wish to "restore her mother by means of a penis with healing powers," reinforcing her homosexuality—especially if she believes herself to have been successful in castrating her father (like the girl in Freud's "Case," who "realized how she could wound her father and take revenge on him"; *SE* 18:159). In a footnote, Klein goes on: "If her homosexuality emerges in sublimated ways only, she will . . . protect and take care of other women (i.e., her mother), adopting in these respects a husband's attitude towards them."[17] What is the girl's devotion to the "lady" if not just such a sublimated form of caretaking? No wonder, then, that when the lady echoes her father's thunderous prohibition ("the affair must now come to an end"), the girl experiences her rejection as the unkindest cut of all. Where else can she go but over the wall?

Freud's "Case of Female Homosexuality in a Woman" closes with a deliberate aporia. "It is not for psycho-analysis," he says, "to solve the problem of homosexuality" (*SE* 18:171). Now the "enigma" is not suicide, but the "mystery" of the homosexuality whose psychogenesis Freud had initially claimed to trace "with complete certainty." Freud dismisses the popular stereotype of female homosexuality (as he parodically represents it, " 'a masculine mind, irresistibly attracted by women, but, alas! imprisoned in a feminine body' "). For him there is no freakish "third sex." All that psychoanalysis can do is to throw light on the choice of object; it cannot even elucidate "what in conventional . . . phraseology is termed 'masculine' and 'feminine' " (*SE* 18:171); this is the domain of biology. Yet Freud's text takes a disconcerting turn at this point, alluding to "the remarkable transformations that Steinach has effected in some cases by his operations" (*SE* 18:171). Freud seems to take his distance from the drastic intervention of surgical sex-change, noting that Steinach has operated on "the condition . . . of a very patent physical 'hermaphroditism' " (*SE* 18:170–71). "Any analogous treatment of female homosexuality," he says, "is at present quite obscure." Indeed, he regards a physical "cure" for female homosexuality that involves the removal of supposedly "hermaphroditic" ovaries as patently impractical (*SE* 18:172). Interestingly, Freud had updated *Three Essays on the Theory of Sexuality* (1905) in 1920, the same year as the "Case of Homosexuality in a Woman," with a long foot-note on Steinach's biological experiments ("Experimental castration and subsequently grafting the sex-glands of the opposite sex").[18] Freud coun-ters Steinach's notion of a "cure" for homosexuality by resurrecting the theory of bisexuality (which he goes out of his way to attribute to Fleiss). "Psycho-analytic research, " he insists, "is most decidedly opposed to any attempt at separating off homosexuals from the rest of mankind as a group of a special character" (*SE* 7:145 n). But his running commentary on Steinach suggests an undisclosed engagement with the experimental field of endocrinology.

In 1923, Freud himself underwent a small operation on his testicles (technically, "a ligature of the vas deferens on both sides," or a vasec-tomy) known as "the Steinach operation," a fashionable procedure identi-fied with the controversial endocrinologist Eugen Steinach.[19] Suppos-edly restorative of fading sexual potency (Freud hoped it might improve "his sexuality, his general condition and his capacity for work"), the operation was also thought to have rejuvenating effects on aging males and possibly to mobilize the body's resources against cancer (at this time Freud was subject to repeated invasive procedures to combat can-cer of the mouth).[20] It is as if, at the end of "A Case of Homosexuality in a Woman," Freud has suddenly caught a glimpse of the surgically modified body—the castrated body—and looked away. In his strangely com-pressed punchline, the "mystery" of female homosexuality, like the "enigma" of suicide, returns to haunt the Freudian text in the form of an inoperable lesbian body. Here is Freud's closing sentence: "A woman who has felt herself to be a man, and has loved in masculine fashion, will hardly let herself be forced into playing the part of a woman, when she must pay for this transformation, which is not in every way advanta-geous, by renouncing all hope of motherhood" (*SE* 18:172). What female homosexual would submit to the knife on these terms? Freud leaves her, caught on the horns of a cruel dilemma: between the rock of hermaphro-ditic ovaries, and the hard place of irremediable penis envy, unalleviated by "all hope of motherhood" (the only known Freudian cure for the neurosis of femininity). In the half-glimpsed, disavowed violence of this Steinach-induced fantasy, Freud allows us to see the sadistic operations of the unconscious. As the girl's act of homosexual resistance breaches the frontiers of Freudian knowledge, "A Case of Homosexuality in a Woman" produces a new domain of unthinkability within the very fron-tiers of psychoanalytic theory—a moment of repudiation (at once of femininity and of homosexuality) inserted by way of Steinach's experi-ments. Who is to say on which side of this contested frontier one would rather be? With the rhetoric of Freud's psychoanalytic aporia (the knowledge he refuses, since "it is not for psycho-analysis to solve the problem of homosexuality")? Or the literalness of the girl's resistance (her defiant refusal to know)?[21]

NOTES

1. *The Standard Edition of the Complete Psychological Works of Sigmund Freud,* ed. James Strachey, 24 vols. (London: Hogarth, 1953–74), 18:163; subsequently cited as *SE,* with volume and page numbers. For the German text of "Über die Psychogenese eines Falles von Weiblicher Homosexualität," see *Gesammelte Werke,* 18 vols. (Frankfurt: S. Fischer, 1960), 12:271–302.

2. See Marianna Tax Choldin, *A Fence around the Empire: Russian Censorship of Western Ideas under the Tzars* (Durham: Duke University Press, 1985). In 1906, a statute granted the Russian press its "freedom;" see Charles A. Rund, *Fighting Words: Imperial Censorship and the Russian Press, 1804–1906* (Toronto: University of Toronto Press, 1982); foreign censorship continued, however, until 1917.

3. For the original (and highly charged) context in which Freud first makes his "Russian analogy," see *The Complete Letters of Sigmund Freud to Wilhelm Fliess,* ed. Jeffrey Moussaieff Masson (Cambridge: Harvard University Press, 1985), 287–89.

4. For an excellent discussion of "A Case of Homosexuality in a Woman" and the Dora connection, see Mandy Merck, "The Train of Thought in Freud's 'Case of Homosexuality in a Woman,' " in *Perversions* (London: Virago, 1993), 13–32; Merck's essay, the earliest feminist attempt to engage with this case, originally appeared in *m/f* 11/12 (1986): 35–46. See also Jacqueline Rose, "Dora—Fragment of an Analysis," in *Sexuality in the Field of Vision* (London: Verso, 1986), 34–35, and, for recent discussions, Judith Roof, *A Lure of Knowledge: Lesbian Sexuality and Theory* (New York: Columbia University Press, 1992), 177, 210–15, Noreen O'Connor and Joanna Ryan, *Wild Desires and Mistaken Identities: Lesbianism and Psychoanalysis* (London: Virago, 1993), 30–46, and Diana Fuss, "Freud's Fallen Women: The Psychogenesis of a Case of Homosexuality in a Woman," in *Identification Papers: Readings in Psychoanalysis, Sexuality, and Culture* (New York: Routledge, in press).

5. As Mandy Merck points out; see "The Train of Thought in Freud's 'Case of Homosexuality in a Woman' " (30).

6. "*Che . . . poco spera e nulla chiede*" (*Gerusalemme Liberata,* canto 2, stanza 16). The line describes Olindo's love for Sophronia; in Fairfax's translation, "he full of bashfulnes and truth, / Lov'd much, hop'd little, and desired nought." The passage continues: "Thus lov'd, thus serv'd he long, but not regarded, / Unseene, unmarkt, unpitied, unrewarded"; see *Godfrey of Bulloigne,* ed. Kathleen M. Lea and T. M. Gang (Oxford: Clarendon Press, 1981), book 2, stanza 16.

7. See "The Meaning of the Phallus," in *Feminine Sexuality: Jacques Lacan and the Ecole freudienne,* ed. Juliet Mitchell and Jacqueline Rose (New York: Norton, 1985), 85. Lacan is discussing Joan Rivière's essay on masquerade in the context of male and female homosexuality. Cf. Judith Butler, "Imitation and Gender Subordination," in *Inside/Out: Lesbian Theories, Gay Theories,* ed. Diana Fuss (New York: Routledge, 1991), 22–33, for homosexuality as an imitation that exposes heterosexuality as "an imitation of an imitation, a copy of a copy."

8. Freud notes that motherhood itself ceases to be a sine qua non for the girl because it is difficult to combine with another precondition—her (heterosexual) feelings for her brother; see *SE* 18:156.

9. Or, as Jacqueline Rose puts it, "either the girl is neurotic (which she clearly is not) or all women are neurotic (which indeed they might be)"; see "Dora—Fragment of an Analysis," 35.

10. Freud identifies "a second and *oral* source of information.... I should not have been surprised to hear that this source had been Frau K. herself" (*SE* 7:105 n); later, he concludes: "I ought to have guessed that the main source of [Dora's] knowledge of sexual matters could have been no one but Frau K." (*SE* 7:120 n).

11. See "Instincts and their Vicissitudes" (*SE* 14:135–36, 135 n).

12. Judith Butler's otherwise interesting account of what she calls "the melancholia of gender" is problematized by her failure to recognize this undifferentiated state (in both the pre-subject and the pre-object); regarding the melancholy of gender as the melancholy of lost gender-identifications leaves out of account the fact that in Freud's (and Kristeva's) account of melancholia, what is preserved is a pre-objectal, that is, pre-Oedipal (hence pre-gender), form of identification; see *Gender Trouble: Feminism and the Subversion of Identity* (New York: Routledge, 1990), 57–65; see also "Imitation and Gender Subordination," 13–31.

13. Julia Kristeva, *Black Sun: Depression and Melancholia* (New York: Columbia University Press, 1989), 28–29, 30; see also the case histories in "Illustrations of Feminine Depression" (*Black Sun,* 69–94).

14. See Butler's critique of Kristeva in *Gender Trouble,* 79–93 passim.

15. See "Notes upon a Case of Obsessional Neurosis" (1909), *SE* 10:164, 222.

16. In doing so, Klein however also associates herself with Karen Horney, Joan Rivière, and Ernest Jones; see *The Psycho-Analysis of Children,* trans. Alix Strachey (London: Virago, 1989), 212 n, 213 n, 214 n, 215 n.

17. Klein, *The Psycho-Analysis of Children,* 216 n.

18. The extensive footnote on homosexuality to which his comments on Steinach belong represents a running commentary of successive editions of *Three Essays on The Theory of Sexuality* dated 1910, 1915, and 1920, see *SE* 7:144–47 nn.

19. See Peter Gay, *Freud: A Life for Our Time* (New York: Norton, 1988), 426. For contemporary claims about the rejuvenating effects of the Steinach operation, and for its scientific status at the time, see Sharon Romm, *The Unwelcome Intruder: Freud's Struggle with Cancer* (New York: Praeger, 1983), 73–85; interest in the operation, which was very new at the time it was performed on Freud, peaked during the 1920s and 1930s. See also Eugen Steinach, *Sex and Life: Forty Years of Biological and Medical Experiments* (New York: Viking, 1940) for an account of Steinach's life and work, and for a brief discussion of "experimental" hermaphrodites and "congenital" homosexuality (83–92).

20. See *A Life for our Time,* 426; the quotation is from Ernest Jones, *The Life and Works of Sigmund Freud,* 3 vols. (New York: Basic Books, 1953–57), 3:98–99. For an account of Freud's cancer surgery, see Max Schur, *Freud: Living and Dying* (New York: International Universities Press, 1972), 347–66.

21. Cf. the closing aporia of Merck's essay: "And who shall we say was more reluctant to make the journey" ("The Train of Thought," 32)—more evidence of the way Freud's scrupulously even-handed text tends to be weighed in the balance and found wanting by feminist readers.

7

Psychoanalysis and the History of the Passions: The Strange Destiny of Envy

JOHN FORRESTER

In chapter 3 of the Book of Kings, two harlots come before King Solomon to ask for his judgment. They have been living together and have both given birth to sons a short time before. In the night, one of the women inadvertently crushed her child while sleeping and secretly exchanged the dead baby for the living one of her friend. On waking, the friend was certain that the dead child lying beside her was not her own son and tried to take the live baby from the other woman. Both women disputed the other's version of the events. To resolve the dispute, Solomon says: "Bring me a sword. . . . Divide the living child in two, and give half to the one, and half to the other." The King James Bible continues:

> Then spake the woman whose the living child was unto the king, for her bowels yearned upon her son, and she said, O my lord, give her the living child, and in no wise slay it. But the other said, Let it be neither mine nor thine, but divide it.
> Then the king answered and said, Give her the living child, and in no wise slay it: she is the mother thereof.

When I was young, I thought the point of the judgment of Solomon was to demonstrate the chutzpah of the king. It was a detective story, demonstrating the skill and acumen of the hero-detective. Solomon's strategy is a case study in how the master dialectician acts, as he ostensibly sets off in precisely the opposite direction to his actual goal, knowing that the other actors will ineluctably carry him back to that goal. He, the king and absolute master, orders the baby to be cut in half precisely so that the baby will not be cut in half. We could also call this the Zen master reading of the parable.

My second reading of the parable, when I was a little older and had decided that such stories were not usually about the intelligence of men but about the tragedy of life, emphasized the selfless and tragic action of the true mother, who gives up her claim on her beloved child and, in order to preserve its life, is prepared never to see it again. Perhaps her child means more to her than her own life; perhaps she would, given the choice, substitute herself for the child and die in its place. In giving up her claim, then, she gives up something more valuable than her own life; she certainly gives up her motherhood in the act of saving the baby's life. Her conscious motive is thus paradoxical in a similar way to Solomon's: she acts in the opposite direction to her ostensible goal. In order to save her child, she abandons it. In this way, the judgment also becomes a parable of the relationship between mother and child: of how the mother gives life to the child, carries it through life, and exchanges her own life for that of the child.

I was entirely blind to a third possible reading until I came across it in Freud's *Group Psychology and the Analysis of the Ego,* in a chapter where he discusses the hypothesis of a primary herd instinct in human beings:

> What appears later on in society in the shape of *Gemeingeist,* *esprit de corps,* "group spirit," etc., does not belie its derivation from what was originally envy. No one must put himself forward, every one must be the same and have the same. Social justice means that we deny ourselves many things so that others may have to do without them as well, or, what is the same thing, may not be able to ask for them. This demand for equality is the root of social conscience and the sense of duty. It reveals itself unexpectedly in the syphilitic's dread of infecting other people, which psycho-analysis has taught us to understand. The dread exhibited by these poor wretches corresponds to their violent struggles against the unconscious wish to spread their infection on to other people; for why should they alone be infected and cut off from so much? why not other people as well? And the same germ is to be found in the apt story of the judgement of Solomon. If one woman's child is dead, the other shall not have a live one either. The bereaved woman is recognized by this wish.[1]

Freud's reading of the judgment of Solomon focuses neither on Solomon nor on the true mother of the baby, who gives up her claim on her own child. Instead, he focuses on the woman who maintains her claim against the other woman. Freud's simple interpretation is something of a shock. Focusing on the third party, the woman who maintains her claim, reveals how it is *we,* and not Solomon or the true mother, who are led away, by the narrative structure of the parable, from her. The parable-work, to coin a term along the lines of the dream-work and more proximately the joke-work, conceals the fact that it is the second woman, the woman who maintains her claim on the child, who is the principal actor.[2] We have been duped by the structure of the parable.

Freud's interpretation has textual support in the Bible. Uncannily repeating the lofty impartiality of King Solomon, the envious mother says: "Let it be neither mine nor thine, but divide it." Freud generalizes this principle in the following rather dry way: "Social justice means that we deny ourselves many things so that others may have to do without them as well." This is the joke-work of political theory. The high ideal of social justice tendentiously cloaks something altogether more individually self-interested: the envious woman is not truly interested in half a baby, as if half a baby were better than none. Her true aim is to ensure that the other woman has no baby, just like her. For her, no baby is better than one. Her idea of justice, then, is not stably redistributive, nor is it entirely impersonal, despite the iron logic of equal shares for equal subjects; its motivations and its manifestations are destructive and personal, aimed not at any general other, but at any specific other who has the thing she does not have.

To highlight the personal and specific aspect here, we can contrast the woman who wishes to see the baby cut in two with the woman who gives up her claim on the baby, rather than see it cut in two. You do not have to be the baby's mother to wish to see its butchery avoided at any cost; it does not take a specifically maternal love to withdraw a claim under such circumstances. Any *ordinary* human being would prefer the child to live rather than see it cut in two. Therefore what requires explanation is why any human being would maintain her claim under such circumstances. Freud's explanation shows that the parable's structure misleads us into thinking that love of the baby is the center of the dispute, whereas it is more fundamentally the envy of one mother for what the other woman has that provides its motor. Do not forget that the mother who wishes to see the baby cut in two is in mourning for her own baby. The dispute is primarily an attack on the other woman, not a desperate expression of love. We are, after all, observers of a dispute; and when it is love that leads to war, we begin to suspect that there are other motives mixed in and not entirely visible. Paris is undoubtedly known as the man who wished to possess Helen, but he does not figure high on the list of the world's great lovers.

Before passing on to discuss the larger issues contained in the relation of envy to justice, we should pause to consider the remarkable fourth interpretation of the judgment of Solomon to be found in Jean Carbonnier's classic, *Flexible droit.* Carbonnier notes a historically contextual motive for the mother of the dead baby claiming the live one as her own: archaic laws may well have required the death of the mother of the dead baby on the grounds of infanticide. "The mothers are not only pleading for their possession, but for their innocence, maybe even for their lives" (366). Note that under these circumstances, both mothers would have the same motive for claiming the child as her own: fear of execution. Solomon's judgment would then be an even more arduous test of maternal love: the woman who cedes her claim on the live child might well have expected that her act would be equivalent to signing her own death warrant. Greater love hath no woman . . .

Brecht offers a parallel displacement of the frame of the judgment in *The Caucasian Chalk Circle.* The biological mother who has come to claim her child from the poor woman who has raised it does so only out of avaricious motives: under changed legal circumstances, the child will bring with it a vast estate. Both Brecht and Carbonnier "normalize" the motivations of the woman who persists in her claim: one by giving her the motivation of greed, the other by imputing to her a fear for her own life. Unlike Freud, they do not see in the structure of the parable a myth of the origin of justice out of envy.

But Carbonnier goes on to suggest a more provocative interpretation of the meaning of the parable: namely, that it does not have a "deep" meaning, does not depict a set of motives to be discovered and subtle strategies for their uncovering. Rather the naive reading of Solomon's judgment, to which the "deep" reading opposes itself, is that the essence of justice is to be found in the verdict: "Divide the living child in two." Solomon wields the sword of justice in order to cut the Gordian knot of all civil conflicts; and he does it with total disinterestedness, blind as justice must be. Carbonnier points to other ancient Hebrew variants of the parable (Josephus) that endorse this conception of what justice requires: Solomon commanded that both the live baby and the dead baby be cut in two (367 n. 25). The judgment of Solomon is thus: justice is simply the blind observance of the principle of equal division of the objects over which the parties are disputing, as in the rabbinical advice that, when two parties dispute over two apples, the apples should both be cut in two and each party receive two halves. The truth contained in the judgment of Solomon is the ruthlessness with which justice pursues its own ends, a ruthlessness that must, in order to be true justice, outstrip the ruthlessness with which the civil parties pursue their own interests. Do not ask what is the justification for this "instinct for authoritative division":

> if it responds to the need for peace, which is itself a need for order, it may also be a means of stimulating conflict and war in the hope of partial recompense through equal division. *Obiter dictum:* bear in mind the illusions brought with them by those who, in our era, wish to found a politics, even a theology, on the idea of equal division, without realizing that, behind this idea which comes from the law, there are demons, not angels, at work. (372)

And we should pause over Carbonnier's reinterpretation of the aim of justice in general:

> Judgements of equity seem to us to be judgement in its pure state, judgement which does not aim at becoming a rule ("sans tirer à conséquence," the Parlements of the Ancien Régime would say). This judgement in no sense creates less law, but not in the form of a general rule, rather as an individual solution. The resolution of litigation, the subsiding of conflict, bringing peace between men: these are the supreme goals of law; and the smoothing of ruffled feathers, the compromises, the accommodations, the deals are just as much law, if not more so, than all those ambitious norms.[3]

Freud's discussion of envy and Solomon's judgment formed part of an attack on the plausibility of a herd instinct. Freud wished to show that, in contradiction of Trotter's theory of the herd instinct, human beings are not by nature social animals.

> for a long time nothing in the nature of herd instinct or group feeling is to be observed in children. Something like it first grows up, in a nursery containing many children, out of the children's relations to their parents, and it does so as a reaction to the initial envy with which the elder child receives the younger one. The

elder child would certainly like to put his successor jealously aside, to keep it away from the parents, and to rob it of all its privileges; but in the face of the fact that this younger child (like all that come later) is loved by the parents as much as he himself is, and in consequence of the impossibility of his maintaining his hostile attitude without damaging himself, he is forced into identifying himself with the other children. So there grows up in the troop of children a communal or group feeling, which is then further developed at school. The first demand made by this reaction-formation is for justice, for equal treatment for all. We all know how loudly and implacably this claim is put forward. . . . If one cannot be the favourite oneself, at all events nobody else shall be the favourite. (*SE* 18:119–20)

For Freud this argument clinches his case against the assumption of a primary, innate social feeling: "Thus social feeling is based upon the reversal of what was first a hostile feeling into a positively-toned tie in the nature of an identification" (*SE* 18:121). At the core of this argument is the demonstration that the call for justice and equality is founded upon the transformation of envy. Without envy, not only would there be no *need* for a judicial apparatus; there would be no *desire* for justice.

It is this conclusion, this link between an emotion and a principle for the organization of society that I now explore further. But before I do so, I make a few digressionary remarks that will show the interest of this inquiry. Envy as a fundamental fact of psychic life is well known in two different psychoanalytic theories, both of which have had rather mixed fortunes. The first is Freud's thesis that a little girl becomes a woman via the transformation of penis envy into the wish for a baby. Aligning his theory of general social envy with the specific theory of penis envy reveals immediately their closeness of fit, if I can put it like that. The primal scene of penis envy is very similar to the primal scene of envy in general: the girl, like the sibling, *sees* the other child with an object that she thinks gives him complete satisfaction, and she falls prey to envy.[4] What is missing when Freud discusses envy of the penis compared with envy in general is the subsequent reaction-formation: the identification with the other child and the clamorous demand for equality (though some of his remarks concerning the motivations for feminism indicate he envisaged such an outcome for penis envy). And, as Teresa Brennan acutely points out,[5] Freud's theory of justice should mean that women have stronger superegos than men, not weaker as he asserted: "The fact that women must be regarded as having little sense of justice is no doubt related to the predominance of envy in their mental life; for the demand for justice is a modification of envy and lays down the condition subject to which justice can be put aside."[6] I don't think I need say more about this theory, since it is very well known, a part of our intellectual mythology. However, I do ask: In the debates that Freud's notorious account started, which element of the concept of penis envy aroused the most passion: the penis or the envy?

The other psychoanalytic theory is contained in Melanie Klein's short book *Envy and Gratitude*. Klein advances the hypothesis "that one of the deepest sources of guilt is always linked with the envy of the feeding breast, and with the feeling of having spoilt its goodness by envious attacks."[7] Beneath the Oedipus complex, which in Klein's view manifests itself principally in the primal scene of the parents making love, enjoying one another endlessly, there is a deeper fantasy: that of the breast endlessly feeding itself on the good things contained in it—including the father's penis.[8] If there is any failure in the relation to the breast, if there is any frustration, then the child's response is envy of the breast and the attempt to spoil what is good. Klein's theory sees envy as a direct derivative of the destructive impulses, the death instinct. The destructive impulse attaches itself immediately to the first object of love, the breast, which is the immediate object of destructive impulses precisely because it is loved. Destroying what you love most: this fundamental response to the world is summarized in the emotion of envy.

Klein's theories have received an uneasy response, in large part because the theory looks very like a psychoanalytic version of the doctrine of original sin. This comparison is appropriate, yet gives the biblical account of the Fall an interesting twist: the breast is an Eden spied from far off, a paradise where there is no lack, from which the human subject is excluded. Curiously enough, Saint Augustine, with whom original sin is always associated, perceived the relation of the child to the breast in exactly the same way as Klein, and made clear that the envy of the child confronted with the feeding breast supports the doctrine of original sin:

> Who can recall to me the sins I committed as a baby? For in your sight no man is free from sin, not even a child who has lived only one day on earth. . . . I have myself seen jealousy in a baby and know what it means. He was not old enough to talk, but whenever he saw his foster-brother at the breast, he would grow pale with envy. This much is common knowledge. Mothers and nurses say that they can work such things out of the system by one means or another, but surely it cannot be called innocence, when the milk

flows in such abundance from its source, to object to a rival desperately in need and depending for his life on this one form of nourishment? Such faults are not small or unimportant, but we are tender-
hearted and bear with them because we know that the child will
grow out of them. It is clear that they are not mere peccadilloes,
because the same faults are intolerable in older persons.[9]

In Lacan's commentary on this passage, he accentuates one feature, only
implicit in Klein. Lacan affirms that the object of envy is not something
useful to the subject; the child no longer has need of the breast as he
watches his brother feeding. The object of envy is not what I desire, but
rather what satisfies the other with whom I compare or identify myself.
It is the image—and it is important for Lacan that envy is a sin of looking,
invidia, of looking outward—of the other's plenitude closed in upon
itself, of another gaining satisfaction through enjoyment of an object,
that is the scene of envy. The object is given as separate from and outside
the subject in the very inception of envy; included in the very idea of
envy is a throwing outward, a projection.[10] It is then the dialectic of
inner and outer that characterizes envy. The very concept of the subject's interiority depends upon the subject's attention being directed
primarily to the other, in the moment of perception of its being satisfied
by the object of envy.

At this point, I turn to Nietzsche's genealogy of morals to explore a
parallel analysis that, in my view, proves to be very similar to Klein's
analysis of the original sin of envy. It is these passages that also form the
starting point for Max Scheler's influential essay of *ressentiment.* Nietzsche's *Genealogy of Morals* sets out to analyze the development of the
concepts of good, bad, and evil. He counterposes two fundamentally
different principles, associated with two different peoples: the aristocrats
and the Jews. The aristocrats' morality consists in a "triumphant self-
affirmation" (though Nietzsche questions whether such a principle of self-
affirmation can ever give rise to what *we* call morality). But the morality of
the Jews—and by Jews Nietzsche obviously means Christians—develops
from their *ressentiment* or rancor, which are derived from their vengeful
feelings for and hatred of the noble aristocrat. Out of their hatred grows
that "deepest and sublimest of loves" as expressed in the "ghastly paradox
of a crucified god." With the universalization of this slave morality, the
people, the slaves, the herd have triumphed over noble values.

> Slave ethics . . . begins by saying *no* to an "outside," an "other," a
> non-self, and that *no* is its creative act. This reversal of direction

of the evaluating look, this invariable looking outward instead of inward, is a fundamental feature of rancour. Slave ethics requires for its inception a sphere different from and hostile to its own. . . . [T]he "enemy" as conceived by the rancorous man . . . is his true creative achievement: he has conceived the "evil enemy," the Evil One, as a fundamental idea, and then as a pendant he has conceived a Good One—himself.[11]

In his commentary on Nietzsche's genealogy of the slave morality, Scheler characterizes the envy that so often leads to the attitude of *ressentiment* toward the world as arising from a sense of impotence.[12] The awareness of the object envied and the awareness of one's own failure, one's own emptiness, go hand in hand; they are inseparable. Envy thus turns out to be the most "sociable" of the passions; it is the one that reveals one's fundamental failure in relation to the world, at the very moment where it reveals the causally linked success of another.

From envy Freud derives the sense of justice: "If one cannot be the favourite oneself, at all events nobody else shall be the favourite." In a more pungent tone, Nietzsche called this attitude "world-destroying": "This man fails in something; finally he exclaims in rage: 'Then let the world perish!' This revolting feeling is the summit of envy, which argues: because there is *something* I cannot have, the whole world shall have *nothing!* the whole world shall *be* nothing!"[13] For Klein, envy's effect is on the one hand to undermine gratitude toward a good object and on the other to encourage indiscriminate spoiling and destroying of the objects in the world. For Nietzsche, the man of *ressentiment* embodies the reactive, negating attitude of the slave, of the common man, of democratic man. As Bertrand Russell put it in an uncharacteristically Nietzschean moment: "Envy is the basis of democracy."[14] Thus Nietzsche, Freud, and Klein each offer a genealogy of the social and moral world as derived from envy.

It is this project of conjoining an affective state to a configuration of the social world that interests me. Nietzsche characterized the foundation of part of the project as follows: "moralities are also merely a *sign language of the affects.*"[15] Freud derives considerably more than a moral stance, or a moral universe, from the affect of envy; he also derives a sociopolitical regime, one that has been severely criticized by modern commentators. To measure the extent to which this is an unwelcome project, I consider now a theory of justice that vigorously rejects Freud's genealogy of justice.

The most influential recent account of justice, that of John Rawls, illustrates a certain unease in relation to the passions.[16] Having elaborated the fiction of an "original position" from which social actors are to choose the fundamental principles of justice—a position characterized by ignorance both of the specific social world the actors will actually have to inhabit and of their individual dispositions and place in that world—Rawls eventually fills in his account by elaborating a moral psychology, in which both moral and natural attitudes must play a part:[17] "a theory of the moral sentiments . . . setting out the principles governing our moral powers, or more specifically, our sense of justice."[18] His account is explicitly teleological, "founding the account of moral learning explicitly upon a particular ethical theory" (496), that of his contract doctrine.

Rawls distinguishes between moral sentiments, such as guilt and resentment, which are dependent upon a background set of principles or ideas of justice, and natural aptitudes, such as anger and rancor, which arise independently of moral principles. He is quick to point out that some forms of envy are not moral: "It is sufficient to say that the better situation of others catches our attention"; "we are downcast by their good fortune and no longer value as highly what we have."[19] Recognizing that such forms of envy, even though not moral in the sense of arising from the prior principles of justice, may be "excusable" (*TJ* 534) and are certainly common, Rawls seeks to determine whether this fact puts into question the principles of justice derived from the original position (which, it should be remembered, had explicitly excluded consideration of such attitudes or passions).

Even while he recognizes that envy is not a product of moral principles, Rawls emphasizes the social derivation of envy: "although it is a psychological state, social institutions are a basic instigating cause" (*TJ* 536). Rawls looks to the well-orderedness of a society based on his (or similar) principles of justice to mitigate the envy-producing effects of disparities of wealth, endowments, and so forth: the well-orderedness will "reduce the *visibility,* or at least the painful visibility, of variations in men's prospects" (*TJ* 536; my emphasis); various features of social organization will mean that these "discrepancies" will not "attract the kind of attention which unsettles the lives of those well placed" (*TJ* 537). "Taken together these features of a well-ordered regime diminish the number of occasions when the less favored are likely to experience their situation as impoverished and humiliating" (*TJ* 537). Rawls concludes that "the problem of general envy anyway does not force us to reconsider the choice of the principles of justice," even though he has not given an argument for this, but rather has pointed to social conditions that will mitigate any possible effects of envy.

Rawls is by no means alone in finding in the *visuality* of envy a crucial element in its potential destructiveness; we have already seen such a focusing on the visual field in Augustine, Lacan, Klein, and in Freud's theory of penis envy. Put walls around the heavens of contentment, set up barriers between the rich and the poor, between the well endowed and the rest and, with luck, envy will not arise. But Rawls's response to the danger of the invading envious gaze—surely a plausible candidate as the original form of the evil eye—is ironic and salutary. The gesture aiming to ward off the envious gaze repeats the founding gesture of his argument: the positing of an original position in which subjects have a veil of ignorance drawn both between them and the outside (the society in which they will have an as yet unknown place) and between them and the inside (those specific and individual desires, dispositions, and aptitudes with which they will in reality be endowed). The original position is "a situation in which everyone is deprived of this sort of information. One excludes the knowledge of those contingencies which set men at odds and allows them to be guided by their prejudices" (*TJ* 19). The final chapters of Rawls's book thus cannot prevent from creeping back into the social arrangements for a harmonious society exactly that element that Rawls built into the hypothetical original position only to discard it once the principles of justice had been firmly established (i.e., agreed to by those who would, in a real world, prove vulnerable to envy, both as subjects and objects). The fiction of the original position excluded *ab origine* the potentially destructive passions of envy, rancor, and spite (*TJ* 538), and this initial exclusion eliminates all primary social sentiments: "Presuming [in the original position envy's] absence amounts to supposing that in the choice of principles men should think of themselves as having their own plan of life which is sufficient for itself" (*TJ* 144). But Rawls hoped to show how his entirely individualistic starting point would allow the emergence of a primary social sentiment: "the combination of mutual disinterest and the veil of ignorance achieves the same purpose as benevolence" (*TJ* 148). In this way, Rawls hoped that the primacy of benevolence would secure the well-ordered society from the destructive effects of envy, spite, and rancor. But at the beginning of his book, in the original position, and at the end, when he finally confronts, like Hercules, the many-headed hydra of rancor, spite, envy, grudgingness, and jealousy, Rawls has one basic strategy to save the principles of justice: place a veil between oneself and the primordial object of envy.

Having asserted that envy does not constitute a threat to his principles of justice, Rawls turns to confront other arguments. The first argument is a skeptical and pessimistic one: it doubts whether any society in which discernible differences of wealth, prestige, and good exist can be proof against envy. Rawls admits that a specific form of envy, that directed at specific, rather than general kinds of, goods, is "endemic to human life; being associated with rivalry, it may be associated with any society" (*TJ* 537). But he maintains that a well-ordered society, one based on secure principles of justice, will manage the problem of envy. The second argument is the stronger: it maintains that the very principles of justice are themselves based on envy. It is here that Rawls recognizes Freud as a principal opponent.[20]

To counter his "conservative" views, Rawls runs a number of different arguments. The first is the strongest, but also the argument that distances Rawls's theory most from getting a grip on a substantive rather than hypothetical account of justice. Rawls asserts that the principles of justice remain untouched even if the actual motivations for all or most people holding to principles of equality are derived from envy. Second, Rawls notes that many arguments that appear to derive justice from envy in fact derive it from resentment; and, since resentment is already a moral feeling founded on a sense of justice and injustice, justice is actually being derived from itself. I shall return to this argument.

The strongest challenge that Rawls sets for the view that envy is the foundation of demands for justice is the following:

> In order to show that the principles of justice are based in part on envy it would have to be established that one or more of the conditions of the original position arise from this propensity. . . . But each of the stipulations of the original position has a justification which makes no mention of envy. For example, one invokes the function of moral principles as being a suitably general and public way of ordering claims. (*TJ* 538)

Rawls is confident that the envy thesis cannot extend into the constitutive elements of the original position. Here I think he underestimates some of the implicit force of Freud's argument. Freud is principally concerned to show how social feeling derives from the identification of children with each other, the motives for which are derived from original hostility and envy. Thus when Freud notes that "the first demand made by this reaction-formation is for justice, for equal treatment for all," he is observing something more than simply a demand for equality.

Freud's account comes close to accounting in addition for the principles that Rawls explicitly holds up as having nothing to do with envy: the formal constraints on the concept of right, among which there are two principal constraints that principles should be general, and that they should be universal in application (*TJ* 130–32). In other words, Freud is claiming that the very concepts of universality and generality are derived from the sequence of defenses against the original envy and hostility: in a quasi-Durkheimian move, what he calls *"Gemeingeist, esprit de corps,* 'group spirit' "* or the "herd instinct" is this predicate of potential universalizability in action. And it stems from the initial defense of "identifying himself with the other children" (*SE* 18:119–20), giving rise to "a positively-toned tie in the nature of an identification" (*SE* 18:121). So Rawls, while recognizing, as we shall see in a moment, the force of Freud's arguments, does not recognize its challenge to his basic assumption that the formal constraints on the concept of right are formulated without reference to envy. Freud would argue that assenting to universalizable and generalizable principles of any sort is already a reaction-formation to the passion of envy, albeit a formal one.

I mention this *formal* aspect because Rawls recognizes the interest of Freud's argument when it comes to describing the motivational *forces* at play in the development from envy to the call for equality. He expounds with great clarity this aspect of Freud's argument: "Freud means to assert more, I believe, than that envy often masquerades as resentment. He wants to say that the energy that motivates the sense of justice is borrowed from that of envy and jealousy, and that without this energy, there would be no (or much less) desire to give justice" (*TJ* 540). Rawls's response to this, which he takes to be the strongest version of the Freudian argument concerning the derivation of justice from envy, is to assert that the argument derives its persuasive force from the conflation of envy and resentment. When Freud describes the elder child as wishing "to put his successor jealously aside, to keep it away from the parents, and to rob it of all its privileges," Rawls maintains that this desire is derived from resentment, not envy; and when "we resent our having less than others, it must be because we think that their being better off is the result of unjust institutions, or wrongful conduct on their part."[21] So resentment, being a moral feeling, requires that a moral principle be cited in its explanation: the principles governing injustice. Rawls thus accuses Freud of a *petitio principii,* of smuggling the principle of justice into his account of "envy" by having falsely renamed "resentment" as envy, and then deriving the demand for justice, for equal treatment for all, from the covert accusation of injustice (which we call resentment).

The difference between Rawls and Freud is now easier to describe. Rawls wishes to affirm that a child's demand on its parents for love and attention at the expense of the other child's are often justified, and are within the boundaries of that which could in principle be justified:

> if children compete for the attention and affection of their parents, *to which one might say that they justly have an equal claim,* one cannot assert that their sense of justice springs from jealousy and envy. Certainly children are often envious and jealous; and no doubt their moral notions are so primitive that the necessary distinctions are not grasped by them. But waiving these difficulties, we could equally well say that their social feeling arises from resentment, from a sense that they are unfairly treated. (*TJ* 540; my emphasis)

One is tempted to quote Augustine to Rawls: "surely it cannot be called innocence, when the milk flows in such abundance from its source, to object to a rival desperately in need and depending for his life on this one form of nourishment?"[22] Rawls wishes to smuggle the moral principles underlying resentment back into the nursery, and accuses Freud of smuggling them back there but claiming he hasn't, by conflating envy and resentment. Freud, on the other hand, wishes to "smuggle" the passion of envy into the "adult" moral principles of justice and fairness. They work in opposite directions, Rawls to eliminate the childish from the adult world of moral principles, Freud to demonstrate the domination of the adult by the forgotten childish. Rawls implicitly will not accept the Freudian assumption that we often, if not always, continue well into adulthood to employ the original template of childhood experience, whose guiding shape and ruling configuration can be perceived in ghostlike form in the adult world. In his discussion of guilt, he is quite explicit about the necessity to eliminate the "childish" form of guilt that derives from disobeying authority from an account of the properly moral guilt-feelings.[23]

But Rawls does goes so far as to admit that principles of justice that do not follow from his own argument based on the fiction of the original position may derive from envy: "To be sure, there may be forms of equality that do spring from envy. Strict egalitarianism, the doctrine which insists upon an equal distribution of all primary goods, conceivably derives from this propensity" (*TJ* 538). Rawls thinks that he has protected the argument by which he derives the principles of justice from the subversive corrosion of envy and the other passions (his "special psychologies"). He thus thinks that he has shown that there *could* be a motivation for justice that is not derived from envy. But he does not show that, in the actual world, there ever has been or is at present a demand for justice that is not based on envy. He himself leaves up in the air this empirical question: "None of these remarks is intended to deny that the appeal to justice is often a mask for envy" (*TJ* 540). And he ends his discussion of envy reflecting, in all fairness: "I believe, though I have not shown, that the principles of justice as fairness pass this test" (*TJ* 541).

Political discourse was not always so reticent about or mistrusting of the passions. One of the founding questions of sociology requires that one pay attention to the development of discourse on the passions: Max Weber, Ernst Simmel, R. H. Tawney and others trace one of the political foundations of modernity to the transformation in the church's attitude to business, commerce, and banking. Put crudely, although not altogether falsely, avarice became transformed from one of the seven deadly sins into the foundation stone and guarantee of stability of the new social order. Alongside the thesis of religion and the rise of capitalism is the thesis of passion and the rise of capitalism.

One long-standing transformation of theology into political philosophy has regarded the passions as effects of external social and political arrangements, rather than as causes of these. As we have seen, Rawls thinks that a well-ordered society can reduce the general level of envy to manageable proportion. Or, to quote a much earlier example, from Winstanley in the 1640s: "I speak now in relation between the Oppressor and the oppressed; the inward bondages I meddle not with in this place, though I am assured that if it be rightly seached into, the inward bondages of minde, as covetousness, pride, hypocrisie, envy, sorrow, fears, desperation and madness, are all occasioned by the outward bondage, that one sort of people lay upon another."[24] The contrasting of inner with outer, of the passions with the social relation of oppression, is the radical twist on a millenarian theme. The passions are themselves the products of man's fall from grace, of his expulsion from Eden. The restoration of that Eden, in the form of equitable social relations, will bring a revolution in the inner world: freedom from the bondages of the passions.

It is also clear that these passions—Winstanley's covetousness, pride, hypocrisie, envy, sorrow, fears, desperation, and madness; Rawls's envy, anger, spite, jealousy, and rancor—overlap considerably with the Christian table of the seven deadly sins.[25] Elaborated gradually from the fourth century on, given some stability by Gregory the Great, the seven sins provided a way of organizing a discourse of the passions that subordinated worldly to eschatological concerns. Christianity always gave the discourse of the sins and thus of the passions an individualistic bent; one can see this in stark evidence in Saint Augustine's conviction that one should never tell a lie, not even one that might save another person's life, since what did another person's earthly life count when put in the balance against the fate of one's own immortal soul?[26] Yet the revival of classical learning and its routinization in the universities allowed what came to be known as morals to fuse the Aristotelian study of practical philosophy—ethics, politics, and household management—with consideration of the passions in human affairs. More concretely, a less formal consideration of the foundations of politics did grow up within the courts of the European states, from Machiavelli onward.[27] And it was in the courts that the new moralism of the seventeenth century analyzed the place of the passions in a secular context.[28] The theory of the state came to depend upon a depiction of man as he really is.

In his stimulating essay *The Passions and the Interests,* Hirschman has traced the development of the discourse of the passions into the theory of the interests from the late seventeenth century to the end of the eighteenth century. As well as being threats to one's state of grace, the passions were threats to political and moral stability. Hirschman outlines three theories within which the necessary controlling and disciplining of the unruly and dangerous passions were envisaged: first, their coercion and repression; second, their being harnessed, moderated, and refined by the action of civilization, of civil society; third, the principle of the countervailing passion, the principle that one of the passions become the principal ally of the social order in disciplining the others. Gradually, the general framework of benign passions being capable of molding and containing the malignant passions was developed. The court and salon societies that gave rise to the merciless dissection of human motivation by La Rochefoucauld, Nicole, and La Bruyère produced the conviction that self-love is the one founding and unshakable passion.[29] Passing out into a more mercantile society, self-love could become transformed into self-interest, which could be assayed as the stable element in the taxonomy of motives for human action. And it was avarice, the love of money, the most constant and dogged of all passions, Dr. Johnson's "uniform and tractable vice,"[30] that could be granted the position of universal and perpetual passion, in contrast with envy and revenge, which, according to Hume, "operate only by intervals, and are directed against particular persons."[31]

Avarice and greed, the "calm desire of wealth"[32] thereby became officially sanctioned, benevolent, and innocuous passions, the master passions with which anger and sloth, envy, and pride could be tamed without recourse to religiously founded precepts. Hirschman dates the decline of the doctrine of the countervailing passion to Adam Smith's *Wealth of Nations,* which established a powerful economic justification for the untrammelled pursuit of individual self-interest, rather than the political and moral account that the story of the passions and the interests previously gave. Yet the search for an underlying master principle that is universal, that is unifying, that is rationalizing, is characteristic of the nineteenth-century sociologies from the utilitarian calculus of pleasure and pain, via Marx to Weber, Durkheim, and the Frankfurt School. Tentatively, I would suggest that the key document here is the chapter on money in Marx's *Capital,* which demonstrates the way in which the specific qualities of things are transformed by the inner logic proper to money into quantity; we find its echoes in the internal logic of rationalization that Weber and Simmel perceive in modern society. What is eliminated—most conspicuously in the eighteenth-century mechanical algebra of utilities,[33] and in the rational decision theoretic calculations of "interests" developed and criticized by Elster[34]—is the specific color and force of the passions. The passions become epiphenomena, mere effects of the underlying shifts of interests, mere signs of conflicts and clashes of interests, particularly of different self-interests; or else they are privatized, and only retain their own character and flavor in the separate world of the family.

And it is in the family that Freud and Klein find them again. The archetypal scene of envy, remember, is of two children, one at the breast, the other looking on. Or, in the Freudian drama of the sexes, there is a girl who looks, sees, and is instantaneously seized by envy. Riviere pushes the logic one step further in a curious passage that, like the return of the repressed, brings us back close to the scene described in the judgment of Solomon:

> It strikes me as probable that the earliest affective triangular situation of all may be the child's relation to the mother's *two* breasts. There is certainly evidence of a later order of phantasies of dividing or sharing the two breasts (e.g. in men, the boy and the father each taking one), which makes it plausible that the earliest ambivalence may find its first positive and negative attachments to each of the two breasts singly, usually, of course, with constant changes.[35]

However, psychoanalysis blithely takes no notice of the logic of money, or even of self-interest, although part of that concept's force is recaptured by psychoanalytic theory in the new principle of universal narcissism (albeit in a form much less easily assimilable to the arithmetic of financial self-interest). And this is why its social theory so often has an archaic tone to it. Quite clearly, psychoanalysis harkens back to the eighteenth-century principle of the countervailing passion. The story of superego, ego, and id is a new morality play, in which one sin is pitted against another, one passion is subverted by another. For analysis, it takes the always passionate and vindictive superego to curb the unruly passions of envy and greed. The narcissistic pride of the ego can only be tempered by the fear of loss, itself akin to the *acedia* or withdrawal from connection to the world of the early Christian Fathers. Anomie might be the best modern translation for the sin of *acedia* (or sloth).[36] So, in the psychoanalytic morality play, it might well be the balance of pride and anomie that determines the true sources of moral action.

To summarize: I have suggested that psychoanalysis includes a discourse of the passions that has some similarities with the moral and political thought associated with the French moralists of the seventeenth century and with certain strands of "establishment" political theory of the Enlightenment, before the legitimation of capitalism and the stability of the social order could be attributed to the invisible hand of the money market. Freud and Nietzsche are on common ground here, seeking in a genealogy of the passions and the principle of the countervailing passion the only possible derivation of so-called higher principles, such as the concept of equal rights, of justice, or of a universalized morality such as "Love thine enemy." In Freud and Nietzsche we find arguments concerning the origins of morality and society that bypass the structures arising out of the inner rationality of money. In particular, the passion of envy is the source of a society founded on the idea of justice and of individual rights.

And finally we must return to the question of penis envy. Given the more general context I have now supplied for thinking about envy within psychoanalytic theory, it is possible that the criticisms of the theory of penis envy are as much directed at Freud's more general project of locating the cement of the social fabric and its institutions (such as the requirement of social justice) on the vicissitudes of the passions, in particular of envy, as they are against the image of the penis as the dominant symbol of the good, the achieved, the fulfilled. I make two final comments about this.

My first comment stems from this image of the full penis, the enviable penis. It is the envying subject who encounters this image of plenitude, who experiences impotence, that impotence that Max Scheler located as the source of envy, in the face of this image. The impotence or lack upon which this image in the other is founded is remarkably similar to the account of desire that we find in Lacan's work: the fundamental lack upon which desire is based, and the axiom that desire is always desire of the other.[37] Isn't this concept of desire remarkably like envy? The linking of envy, *envie,* and desire in Lacan's tests is clear-cut in his early seminars:

> At first, before language, desire exists solely in the single plane of the imaginary relation of the specular stage, projected, alienated in the other. The tension it provokes is then deprived of an outcome. That is to say that it has no other outcome—Hegel teaches us this—than the destruction of the other. The subject's desire can only be confirmed in this relation through a competition, through an absolute rivalry with the other, in view of the object towards which it is directed. And each time we get close, in a given subject, to this primitive alienation, the most radical aggression arises—the desire for the disappearance of the other in so far as he supports the subject's desire.[38]

If this near identity of desire and envy is the case, then penis envy and the general formula of desire are one and the same.

Second, we should ask ourselves why the Freudian account of the derivation of the sense of justice from the passion of envy is regarded with such suspicion. Is the very idea of the countervailing passion, the idea that we are protected from one malignant passion by the force of another an implausible one? I presume we all find plausible the idea that we can be shamed out of acting upon cruel impulses, or restrained by fear from making love to someone we love. Bear in mind the moral of the story, derived from early Teutonic law, of four brothers who take out a suit for recovery of a dowry against their widowed mother on account of her adultery. On hearing from the judge that their mother has agreed to admit to her adultery, and will also make known which of the brothers is the fruit of her adultery, the litigants agree to withdraw their suit.

Or is it, as Klein suspected, that we still hanker for some higher foundation for what we value in ourselves and our social worlds, something more like love than hate, something more like Adam Smith's "sympathy" or John Rawls's benevolence, something more worthy than envy or avarice? La Rochefoucauld noted that we are often proud of even the most criminal of our passions, "but envy is so cowardly and shameful a passion that we can never dare to acknowledge it."[39] To be noble is to be free of envy: "All the conspirators save only he / Did that they did in envy of great Caesar."[40]

There is one additional factor at work here. We may have become prepared to accept a base genealogy for religion and Christian morality; at the very least the Freudian and Nietzschean critiques have habituated us to the idea that humility and brotherly love may be based on fear and resentment. But how relaxed are we about seeing our sense of justice based on envy? It seems we are now accustomed to God being dead, but would be reluctant to admit that social justice is dead.

NOTES

1. Sigmund Freud, *Group Psychology and the Analysis of the Ego*, in *The Standard Edition of the Complete Psychological Works of Sigmund Freud*, under the general editorship of James Strachey in collaboration with Anna Freud, assisted by Alix Strachey and Alan Tyson, 24 vols (London: Hogarth and the Institute of Psycho-Analysis, 1953–74) [hereafter abbreviated to *SE*], *SE* 18:120–21.

2. At one point in his discussion, in *Flexible Droit: Pour une sociologie du droit sans rigueur*, 6th ed. (Paris: Librairie Générale de Droit et de Jurisprudence, 1988 [1st ed., 1969]), Carbonnier notes that "ne pas réclamer l'enfant vivant était reconnaître pour sien l'enfant mort," a formulation that focuses on the same question as Freud's, but eliminates the question central to envy—who has a baby and who doesn't—by substituting the quasi-psychotic imperative: "if I have a baby, it means that I will not have to recognize my loss, my impotence" (361ff.).

3. "Le jugement d'équité nous apparaît comme le jugement à l'état pur qui, lui-même, ne croit pas pouvoir devenir règle ("sans tirer à conséquence," disaient les Parlements de l'Ancien Régime quand ils jugeaient en équité). Ce jugement n'en crée pas moins du droit, non pas une règle générale, mais une solution individuelle. Solution d'un litige, apaisement d'un conflit: faire régner la paix entre les hommes est la fin suprême du droit, et les pacifications, les accommodements, les transactions sont du droit, bien plus certainement que tant de normes ambitieuses." Jean Carbonnier, cited as general epigraph in Théodore Ivainer, *L'Interprétation des Faits en Droit: Essai de mise en perspective cybernétique des "lumières du magistrat"* (Paris: Libraire générale de droit et de jurisprudence, 1988).

4. For a provocative discussion of the importance of this seeing, see Stephen Heath, "Difference," *Screen* 19 (1978). 51–112; and Luce Irigaray, *Speculum* (Paris: Editions de Minuit, 1974; trans. Ithaca: Cornell University Press, 1985).

5. Teresa Brennan, *The Interpretation of the Flesh: Freud's Theory of Femininity* (London: Routledge, 1992), 103ff.

6. Freud, "Femininity," in: *New Introductory Lectures on Psycho-analysis* (*SE* 22:134).

7. Klein, *Envy and Gratitude*, in Melanie Klein, *The Writings of Melanie Klein*, under the general editorship of Roger Money-Kyrle, in collaboration with Betty Joseph, Edna O'Shaughnessy, and Hanna Segal, 4 vols. (London: Hogarth and the Institute of Psycho-Analysis, 1975), 195.

8. As Juliet Mitchell has pointed out to me, Klein's views in this respect draw considerably

on Joan Riviere's classic paper, "Jealousy as a Mechanism of Defence" (1932), reprinted in *The Inner World and Joan Riviere: Collected Papers, 1920–1958*, ed. with a biographical chapter by Athol Hughes, foreward by Hanna Segal (London: Karnac Books, 1991), esp. 111.

9. Saint Augustine, *Confessions*, trans. R. S. Pine-Coffin (Harmondsworth: Penguin, 1961), 27–28, bk. 1, chap. 7.

10. Jacques Lacan, *Le Séminaire: Livre XI, Les Quatre Concepts Fondamentaux de la Psychanalyse, 1964* (Paris: Seuil, 1973), 105–6; *The Four Fundamental Concepts of Psychoanalysis*, trans. Alan Sheridan (Tavistock, 1977; repr. Penguin, 1986), 116.

11. Friedrich Nietzsche, *The Genealogy of Morals*, Essay 1, sects. 8–10, in Nietzsche, *The Birth of Tragedy and The Genealogy of Morals*, trans. Frances Golffing (New York: Doubleday Anchor, 1956), 168–73.

12. Max Scheler, *Ressentiment* (1912), trans. William W. Holdheim, ed. Lewis A. Coser (New York: Free Press, 1961), 52.

13. Friederich Nietzsche, *Daybreak: Thoughts on the Prejudices of Morality*, trans R. J. Hollingdale, intro. Michael Tanner (Cambridge: Cambridge University Press, 1982), para 304, pp. 155–56.

14. Bertrand Russell, *The Conquest of Happiness*, 1930, chap. 6.

15. Friedrich Nietzsche, *Beyond Good and Evil*, trans. with commentary by Walter Kaufmann (New York: Vintage, 1966), no. 187, p. 100.

16. I thank José Brunner for pointing out the extent to which Rawls's account of justice is sometimes implicitly, sometimes explicitly, geared to avoiding the problems raised by "the problem of envy" (530), the most pressing of what Rawls calls "the special psychologies," that "in some way must be reckoned with."

17. For an account that underlines the centrality of Rawls's moral psychology, see Ronald Dworkin, "The original position," in Norman Daniels, ed., *Reading Rawls: Critical Studies of A Theory of Justice* (New York: Basic, 1974), 25ff.

18. John Rawls, *A Theory of Justice* (Oxford: Oxford University Press, 1972), 51; hereafter cited as *TJ*.

19. Rawls, *TJ* 533. The faint allusion to Shakespeare's famous sonnet is no doubt intentional; the consequences of the allusion are worth reflecting upon:

> When in disgrace with Fortune and men's eyes,
> I all alone beweep my outcast state,
> And trouble deaf heaven with my bootless cries,
> And look upon my self and curse my fate,
> Wishing me like to one more rich in hope,
> Featured like him, with friends possessed,
> Desiring this man's art, and that man's scope,
> With what I most enjoy contented least,
> Yet in these thoughts my self almost despising,
> Haply I think on thee, and then my state,
> (Like to the lark at break of day arising
> From sullen earth) sings hymns at heaven's gate,
> > For thy sweet love remembered such wealth brings,
> > That then I scorn to change my state with kings.

Shakespeare melds together a range of sentiments and attitudes to the world that Rawls is keen to distinguish: emulative envy, itself close, as I point out below, to the Lacanian notion of desire; moral resentment; loss of self-respect; self-disgust. The continuity and contiguity of these sentiments, so successfully evoked in Shakespeare's poem, puts into doubt the validity of Rawls's distinctions. At the very least, it highlights their contrived quality.

20. Rawls, *TJ*, 539–41. Rawls first lumps Freud in with those "conservative writers" who "have contended that the tendency to equality in modern social movements is the expression

of envy" (538). See Helmut Schoeck, *Envy—A Theory of Social Behavior,* trans. Michael Glenny and Betty Ross (New York: Harcourt, Brace and World, 1970).

21. Rawls, *TJ,* 533. In passing let us note that Rawls makes this redescription easier for himself by redescribing Freud's vision of the scene in the nursery in the following, subtly altered light: "if children compete for the attention and affection of their parents, to which one might say that they justly have an equal claim, one cannot assert that their sense of justice springs from jealousy and envy. Certainly children are often envious and jealous; and no doubt their moral notions are so primitive that the necessary distinctions are not grasped by them. But waiving these difficulties, we could equally well say that their social feeling arises from resentment, from a sense that they are unfairly treated" (540). The key shift in the redescription is that Rawls adopts the parent's-eye view of the competition for love and attention, whereas Freud adopts the child's-eye view, whose starting point is a desire to eliminate the other.

22. Though it should be noted that Rawls had addressed the question invoked by Augustine's vision of the abundant breast when he discussed the supposed pervasiveness of envy in peasant societies, noting that such envy is based on the probably erroneous economic theory that "the aggregate of social wealth is more or less fixed, so that one person's gain is another's loss" (539).

23. Rawls, *TJ,* 481ff. But Rawls does implicitly admit the correctness of Freud's view of the superego: "our existing moral feelings may be in many respects irrational and injurious to our good. Freud is right in his view that these attitudes are often punitive and blind, incorporating many of the harsher aspects of the authority situation in which they were first acquired. Resentment and indignation, feelings of guilt and remorse, a sense of duty and the censure of others, often take perverse and destructive forms, and blunt without reason human spontaneity and enjoyment" (489).

24. Gerrard Winstanley, "The law of freedom in a platform; or, True Magistracy Restored" (1652), in *The Works of Gerrard Winstaneley,* ed. George H. Sabine (Ithaca: Cornell University Press, 1941), quoted as epigraph, in Carolyn Steedman, *Landscape for a Good Woman. A Story of Two Lives* (London: Virago, 1986).

25. Stanford M. Lyman, *The Seven Deadly Sins,* rev. and expanded ed. (Dix Hills, N.Y.: General Hall, 1989).

26. Saint Augustine, *De mendacio* (Lying) (395) and *Contra mendacium* (Against lying) (420), in *Treatise on Various Subjects,* ed. R. J. Deferrari, Fathers of the Church 16 (New York: Fathers of the Church, 1952), 51–110 and 121–79. See also, in Shakespeare's *Measure for Measure,* Isabella's willingness to sacrifice her brother's life for her chastity.

27. See Johan Heilbron, "The Tripartite Division of French Social Science: A Long Term Perspective," in *Discourses on Society: The Shaping of the Social Disciplines,* ed. P. Wagner, B. Wittrock, and R. Whitley (Dordrecht: Kluwer, 1990), 15:73–92.

28. A. Levi, *French Moralists: The Theory of the Passions, 1585 to 1649* (Oxford: Clarendon Press, 1964). See also P. Janet, *Histoire de la science politique dans ses rapports avec la morale* (1858) (Paris: Alcan, 1913).

29. Louis Hippeau, *Essai sur la morale de la Rochefoucauld* (Paris: Nizet, 1978).

30. Johnson, *Rasselas,* chap. 39, quoted in A. O. Hirschman, *The Passions and the Interests* (Princeton: Princeton University Press, 1977), 55.

31. Hume, *Treatise,* book 3, part 2, sect. 2, quoted in Hirschman, *Passions,* 54.

32. Hutcheson, *A system of moral philosophy,* 1755, vol. V, p. 12, quoted in Hirschman, *Passions,* 65.

33. See for instance Frances Hutcheson, *Inquiry into the Original of our Ideas of Beauty and Virtue* (1725), 2d ed., 1726, 182–84; and the commentary in Louis I. Bredvold, "The invention of the ethical calculus," in R. F. Jones et al., *The Seventeenth Century* (London: Oxford University Press, 1951), 165–80.

34. Jon Elster, *Sour Grapes. Studies in the Subversion of Rationality* (Cambridge: Cambridge University Press, 1983).

35. Riviere, "Jealousy as a mechanism of defence," in *Collected papers,* 111.

36. See Mark D. Altschule, "Acedia: Its Evolution from Deadly Sin to Psychiatric Syndrome," *British Journal of Psychiatry* 3 (1965): 117–19; Morton Bloomfield, *The Seven Deadly Sins: An Introduction to the History of a Religious Concept, with Special Reference to Medieval English Literature* (East Lansing: Michigan State University Press, 1967).

37. For example, Jacques Lacan, *Ecrits: A Selection,* trans. Alan Sheridan (London: Tavistock, 1977), 264; Jacques Lacan, *Le Séminaire. Livre IV. La relation d'objet* (1955–56) (Paris: Seuil, 1994).

38. Jacques Lacan, *Le Séminaire. Livre I. Les écrits techniques de Freud* (1953–54) (Paris: Seuil, 1975), 193; *The Seminar. Book I. Freud's Papers on Techinque, 1953–1954* (1975), trans. with notes by John Forrester (Cambridge: Cambridge University Press; New York: Norton, 1988), 170.

39. La Rochefoucauld, *Réflexions ou Sentences et Maximes morales, suivi de Réflexions diverses et des Maximes de Madame de Sablé,* ed. Jean Lafond (Paris: Gallimard, 1976), no. 27, p. 48: "On fait souvent vanité des passions même les plus criminelles; mais l'envie est une passion timide et honteuse que l'on n'ose jamais avouer."

40. William Shakespeare, *Julius Caesar* 5. 5. 69–70.

8

The Passion of Ignorance in the Transference

ELLIE RAGLAND

Jacques Lacan considered ignorance to be the fundamental passion in human relations. As such, it is inseparable from the transference—that is, the transfer of feelings from one person to another—that is usually thought of in terms of the passions of love or hate. By pulling together various textual threads of Lacan's teaching, I shall try to explicate his theory that ignorance is a passion. But why call ignorance a passion? Why would it play a central role in transference relations?

We know that in treating Dora, Freud discovered transference as the psychic operation that allows analysis to function (*SE* 7). Dora mistook Freud, alternately for her father or for Herr K. Out of this error, Freud realized that Dora's reactions to him were carried over (*überbeträgt*) from somewhere else. Out of this discovery, psychoanalytic transference developed around the knowledge that substitutions of one person for another—or transferences—allow the analysand to rework childhood identifications because the analyst is taken as a parental figure.

I shall conclude this essay by suggesting that Freud's particular passion—*his* ignorance of the cause of Dora's hysteria—blinded him to the deeper meaning of the transference. Only by going *beyond* the love (and hate) directed toward the analyst, can the analysand begin to constitute the passion that truly enslaves him or her in a bond of love (or hate) with another: the ignorance or refusal to know what was done to one in the name of family love. A major difference between the

Lacanian clinic and today's ego, object, or "self" clinical theories and
methods, is to be found in what one might label Freud's mistakes
regarding the transference.

IGNORANCE AS A PASSION

When one first encounters Lacan's idea that ignorance is a passion, the
claim seems self-evident: People hold on to their prejudices and misun-
derstandings, misrecognizing the subjective nature of this material. And
at one level, Lacan meant this. But to grasp the radical aspect of his
theory—the idea that ignorance marks all ordinary language and human
interchange with lies and illusions—one must acknowledge that the ego
by which we negotiate a position in the world is not to be trusted. Lacan
quotes from Freud's *Outline of Psycho-Analysis* (1940/1938) from a
section entitled "The Technique of Psychoanalysis" where Freud says
that the point of entry into the analytic situation requires the ratification
of a pact:

> The sick ego promises us the most complete candour—promises,
> that is, to put at our disposal all the material which its self-
> perception yields it; we assure the patient of the strictest discre-
> tion and place at his service our experience in interpreting mate-
> rial that has been influenced by the unconscious. Our knowledge
> is to make up for his ignorance and to give his ego back its
> mastery over lost provinces of his mental life. This pact consti-
> tutes the analytic situation. (*SE* 23:173; Lacan 1988a, 65)

But what does the ego misrecognize? Lacan answers Freud: the ego
ignores the fact that the identifications and signifiers that constitute it
are idealizations, fantasies, and false hopes. Yet the ego holds on to these
illusions that constitute the power of ignorance precisely because transference works by repeating familiar scenes. One speaks, for example, for
a purpose other than merely to provide information or to communicate.
One speaks to teach others who one *imaginarizes* oneself to be. That is,
one tries to verify one's ideal picture of oneself in the eyes of others. Yet,
since the imaginary order of transference relations is commanded by the
desire *not* to know why one speaks or thinks as one does, individuals
must narrow their circle of intimates to those who share a similar image
of who one idealizes oneself to be. As a consequence, individuals project

an image of being, while ignoring this truth: one desires to *be* one way, rather than another because one's desire for being is already structured in the field of the Other.

Moreover, certain patternings structure desire as normative, neurotic, perverse, or psychotic. Each structure of desire implies a certain relation to law that is taken for granted. That the place of law—superego or paternal metaphor—was constituted in the wake of Oedipal identifications remains unconscious. One *ignores* the fact that being is constituted, and not natural. Commanding the other to love him, the obsessional (identified with his mother) indirectly asks to be left untouched by the messiness of desire. The hysteric (identified with her father and lacking a signifier to represent herself as a woman in the symbolic order) implicitly asks for a place in the Other. The pervert speaks in order to teach the other the law that is the law of *jouissance,* while the paranoid psychotic relies on appearance. Lacking an internalized law with which to identify, the psychotic's ego IDEAL serves as the unquestioned principle of being that other people consign to fantasy, seeking to reify the ideal in transference relations.

Perhaps we can grasp the novelty of Lacan's theory of ignorance if we consider his idea that we cannot see the evidence of truth underlying ignorance. We do not "have" our ignorance at our disposal to get rid of, or to change at will. Lacan did not use ignorance in the positivistic sense, then, of being ignorant of something; having (or not having) knowledge. Indeed, Lacan points ironically to university professors as those who never see themselves as ignorant, as *lacking* through ignorance. Thus, he distinguishes between a false teaching and a genuine one, arguing that university professors speak an academic discourse whose basis of certainty equates mastery with knowledge. Yet, not only the professor, but anyone who speaks, filling up time and space with language, supposes that he or she knows something (*le sujet-supposé-savoir*). Thus Lacan makes an ever finer distinction between the certainty that supports most speech—the master discourse he describes in *Encore* (1975b)—and a different way of using language that he calls a *genuine* teaching. This "genuine" kind of speaking awakens an insistence in those who are listening that can only be described as the desire to know. And such desire can only emerge when one has already taken the measure of ignorance as such (Lacan 1988b, 207).

Reversing the standard ideas of ignorance and knowledge, Lacan measures a *genuine* teaching by its *effects* on the listeners at the level where a question appears, instead of an answer. Ignorance appears rather than resolution. A "genuine" teacher awakens in others the desire to know what the unconscious (*$*) is trying to say. It does not seem so strange, given this point of view, that Lacan characterizes ignorance in a way that requires one to redefine knowledge. In Lacan's redefinition, knowledge no longer refers to method, theory, facts, or information. Indeed, Lacan (1988a) described ignorance as *another kind* of knowledge, not a *Wissen,* but unconscious knowledge that is not available, but must be retrieved. Retrieving unconscious knowledge, taking the measure of one's ignorance, means symbolizing the real; that is, coming to know what is not only unknown, but unsymbolized, precisely because it is unbearable to know.

Insofar as one remains ignorant in order *not to know* something about the unconscious, individuals suffer from insufficient knowledge by which to confront the Other in its demands. But why would one ignore the truth required to act on a problem? Ignorance is a passion, Lacan (1988a) says, precisely because it concerns the place of knowledge at the juncture between the symbolic and the real, thereby opening onto the division between conscious and unconscious knowledge (271). In a concrete sense, the encounter with division or loss that Lacan calls the real produces anxiety. Most people prefer ignorance to the physical pain of anxiety, experienced in any opening up of the gaps and holes in one's system of beliefs and assumptions. Thus, the knowledge that ignorance hides does not present itself naturally and easily; it can only present itself to one's consciousness insofar as it is constructed *dialectically* with regard to a virtual goal: the truth.

Lacan (1988a) tells us that ignorance is "a state of the subject in so far as he speaks. In analysis, starting from the point when we implicitly engage the subject in a search for the truth, we are beginning to constitute his ignorance. It is we [analysts] who create this situation and hence this ignorance" (167). But how can an *analyst* constitute the analysand's ignorance? Lacan argues that the analysand, speaking from his ego, ignores himself as the subject of unconscious desire although ignorance appears anyway in his analysand's denials. Ignorance is not misrecognition, then, for misrecognition gives the lie to itself, revealing that some knowledge has already been organized in order to be misrecognized. Moreover, misrecognition uses ignorance to hide the truth of experience until one can bear to know it (truths in the order of trauma: your mother did not love you; you were sexually abused by a family member; your beloved is not who you think she is; and so on). Yet, misrecognition is guided by the truth of ignorance insofar as it can enable the subject to recognize what he does not want to see (1988a, 167–68).

Love, hate, and ignorance are paths that concern *being* in terms of the three lines of division—real, symbolic, imaginary—in which any person is engaged when realizing himself symbolically in speech. Indeed, in the act of speaking, one homes in on the being of the other. Put another way, love wishes the unfolding of the being of the other, and hate, the debasement of the other's being (1988a, 276–77). But what does it mean to say that ignorance—which aims at one's own being—is a passion? Trying to describe passion, Lacan calls it "something like a third dimension, the space, or rather the volume, of human relations in the symbolic relation." "But it is only in the dimension of being, and not in that of the real," Lacan (1988a) says, "that the three fundamental passions can be inscribed—at the injunction of the symbolic and imaginary, this fault line . . . called *love*—at the junction of the imaginary and the real, *hate*— and at the junction of the real and the symbolic, ignorance" (271). Ignorance resides in language, then, as an impasse between what is said and what is known, at a point between what one can say and what one can bear to know. Insofar as passion means "to be abandoned," ignorance resides quite literally there where one is abandoned in the real, beyond the pale of the admissible in human relations.

IGNORANCE AND TRUTH

Lacan's concept of ignorance cannot be understood without reference to what he meant by truth, although Lacan did little to clarify his notion of truth except in aphoristic statements such as, "truth has the structure of fiction," "truth can only be partially said," and so on. But Lacan's (1988a) idea of truth becomes clearer in reference to his theory that ignorance

> is a dialectical notion, since it is only within the perspective of truth that it is constituted as such. If the subject does not refer himself to the truth, there is no ignorance. If the subject does not begin to ask himself the question what is and what is not, there is no reason for there to be a true and a false, nor even, beyond that, reality and appearance. . . . Let us say that ignorance is constituted in a polar fashion in relation to the virtual position of a truth to be attained. So it is a state of the subject insofar as he speaks. (167)

In his seminar of 1991–92, "De la nature des semblants," Jacques-Alain Miller (1991–92) returned to Lacan's early use of the concept of truth in the 1950s to demonstrate how that notion changed during his teaching, the category of the real progressively taking the place of Lacan's former category of truth (15 January 1992). Miller's idea of truth as a *category* makes sense in relation to the mathematical notion of "category." Defined topologically, for example, a category is a *quality* attributable to an object; a *class* wherein one can organize objects of the same nature; a principle of classification (20 November 1991). Insofar as constellations of objects (the object *a*) fill up the space Lacan configured via topology to constitute structure itself—that is, the two-dimensional structure of space that can be studied as such, in terms of its properties—an analyst knows that truth lies behind what an object (*a*) conceals.

At the beginning of his teaching, promoting the category of truth in psychoanalysis, Lacan directed the analytic experience toward the *dialectic* of truth. That is, he introduced truth as a dialectic, as something operated by changes and transformations, not by the bias where it would be One, eternal and omnitemporal. In such a view of truth, Miller points out, Lacan introduces the bias where it (truth) is marked by the factor of time. But what does *dialectic* of truth mean in relation to time? The *dialectic* means, Miller says, that *there is a truth in diachronic time* [*tn*] and another in synchronic or historical time [*n* + 1]. Indeed, the eminently political usage of the dialectical perspective comes from the second concept of time. But having promoted this dialectical notion of truth, Miller points out that Lacan gradually dethroned truth by the category of the real (15 January 1992).

But, one might wonder, what does this dialectical notion of truth have to do with ignorance? Miller (1991–92) argues that while the true (*le vrai*) actually belongs to *the state* of ignorance, placed within the category of appearance or the *semblant,* "truth" or the real resides in a dialectic inscribed uniquely in one person's unconscious. For example, an incest victim may be ignorant of the truth that her father abused her sexually in childhood. She may well believe she had a normal happy childhood. In her case, however, this supposedly true description hides a truth: that this daughter can better live a lie—keeping the truth unsymbolized, unknown—than face the consequences to her self-image that the truth will unveil. Indeed, ignorance is a kind of bliss, a defense against the unbearable real. The truth is based on what the ego *ignores* at all costs.

But one is never ignorant of the *true,* which, along with the *false,* occurs as pretense or semblance. In the example I just gave of the pretend happy family, details of "the true" continually give the lie to the myth. Moreover, as Miller points out, language itself indicates in its fashion that the true and the false are simply matters of semblance. This statement is clear, Miller argues, if one thinks about all the ingenuity that has attached itself to the problem of distinguishing the true from the false throughout the ages, for the purpose of knowing if there was a way to say the true or to hide it. It is precisely this perspective that leads Miller to put the real—and not the true—in opposition to the *semblant* (15 January 1992).

Names, masks, the sexual masquerade—all belong to the category of the true; that is, to the world of the semblants constituted by the symbolic. But the symbolic is itself the result of efforts, including those of philosophy, to apprehend the real (22 January 1992). Yet semblants do not hold up in the approach of the real from which ignorance protects us. Semblants speak in dream language, protecting us from the real by wearing the mask of appearance, until we approach the navel of the dream. We awake into the world of appearance, rather than encounter the real behind it. One might dream, for example, that one catches a reindeer with large *horns* and ties it up on top of a car, whose *horn* is implied as well. On the dreamer's awakening, the signifier "horny" may remain, may echo in the dreamer's thoughts, eventually shedding a different light on the dream images. Suddenly, the bound reindeer becomes a metaphorical substitution or semblant, standing in for the libidinal (metonymic) *quality* evoked by the signifier "horny" that refers to an actual person. Although there are no sexual innuendos in this dream, "horny" refers to an impasse in the real of one's life, one's sexual relations.

Dream words and images attempt to describe the real of the sexual (non)relation in any life, but are hampered by the imperfection of linguistic approximation. The innovative point Miller makes about noun *semblants*—such as horn—is that while they are true, they are also false. In a further distinction, Miller explains that while the true is an effect of the imaginary, of the perceptual realm of the visible, the real—a repressed trauma, not yet symbolized, even in the unconscious—lies beyond the unconscious. And the imaginary domain of ego misrecognitions, lies, dreams, and semblants, will never speak truth.

But what constitutes truth in the first place? It concerns the mother as signifier, insofar as her desire gives a conduit to the father's name as a signifier. But her unconscious desire remains an enigma. Out of this paternal metaphor—$\frac{FN}{MD}$—individuals build their sexuality out of an unconscious relation to desire, where the identificatory base is the father's name or the mother's desire. From this come the ideals and hopes any individual erects against the failures we mask with pretense and illusion. This truth, says Miller, lies on the side of "There is no Other of the Other" (15 January 1992). There is no meta-language, only language containing a truth that goes beyond itself, outside itself, included *in* language, all the same, at an intersection between the symbolic and the real. Lacan gives the real an actual *place* in the discourses of the master, the academic, the hysteric, and the analyst. In other words, the language he calls discourse—"which makes a social link"—is materialized by truth coming to a *place* in language:

agent ·	*other*
truth	production

—even though one *ignores* the details that speak it from the real (1975b, 21).

The shock of the truth behind what one ignores is this: *we knew it anyway.* "It" threads through speech and language as the half-spoken, as too loudly spoken asides, in dress, in the names we give our children, and so on. Miller (1991–92) writes: "If you reread Plato's Cave with the key that Lacan gives for Aristotle, and [for] all philosophy, you will see that it is a question only of that. When a person is invited to see the real, even in all its evidence, blindness follows anyway. And suffering continues. Plato's myth of the cave is a story of the eye and the gaze: the object *a.* One recognizes the object *a* here, Miller points out that the object *a* is, in this context, a philosophical support of being of the order of essence. That is why it has affinities with the *semblant*" (22 January 1992). For Plato, Miller continues, the essence—topologically speaking—is the original form, of which the things we perceive would only be the copy. The step Plato takes in advancing knowlege is to call the *eidos,* the image or the copy, the thing-in-itself, Lacan's object *a* or lure object. By denouncing the *eidos* or image as what lets itself be taken for the original version, Plato tells a structural truth. In Lacanian terms, the object *a* is whatever seems to fill the void. But it is, in truth, only a shadow, mis-taken for being.

Throughout history, thinkers have taken the semblant or appearance for being, have taken appearance for the original version, Miller says, yet appearance or being is precisely what pales, cannot sustain itself in an encounter with the real. But most people do not really doubt their own semblants. Lacan argued that where we think we *are*—as full of *being*— we are precisely at the point where we *are* not—in truth. Ignorance lies between (the real) and being (appearance), in the neurotic's "I don't want to know anything about it" (1988a, 73). But why would one not want to know about the real? What does one not want to know? Let us take a small detail from everyday life, a child's questioning "Why?" The child asks "why, why, why." But the purpose of the why is not to acquire an education or to be better informed, as anyone knows who has seriously attempted to answer the child's questions. The "why" is quite simply a request to be reassured in the real of the gaze that one *is . . .* loved, heard, seen: a semblance covering the void. Moreover, it is a request lodged against the ultimate referent of all requests, against the real of the void at the center of being that throws everyone offguard, making us all creatures of anxiety.

More dramatic is the daily currency of analysis: when someone learns, for example, that his father is not that man he had idealized (mythologized) him to be at all. His father is, in fact, a criminal, an adulterer, a perpetrator of incest, or any variation on what he *is* in truth, as opposed to what the analysand *believes* him to be at the level of the semblant and the signifier. Such truths are spoken in analysis when a person reconfigures data that has always been in evidence, but has remained undeciphered *because of* the power of ideals to close out the pain of truth.

The human refusal to decipher evidence might be described as a will to ignorance, bespeaking the desire of human beings to put on the best face, no matter what. Indeed, this feature of identificatory being and speaking makes adults seem like children on a playground, boasting about their own powers in the name of some marvelous figure. "I'm three supermans, five supermans," says the five-year-old boy. Children claim outrageous powers for their fathers, uncles, brothers, and sometimes for their mothers and sisters. Yet the real returns anyway, revealing a subject's relation to lack behind the object *a* in her discourse.

IGNORANCE AND THE TRANSFERENCE

While it is easy to think of love and hate as passions, Lacan insists that the analyst must not fail to recognize the primordial power of ignorance's accession to being (1988a, 278). Indeed love and hate are never present without ignorance (which is commonly neglected, although it is one of the primary components of transference). Ignorance is, moreover, the primary passion ruling any person's suffering. Analysis can only begin, Lacan argues, on the basis of a subject's placing himself in the position of one who is in ignorance (1988a, 271). But the analysand's ignorance will not appear in analysis through understanding; only through the analyst's refusal to understand. In this sense, Lacan's use of the cut to punctuate the analytic session is crucial to the functioning of analysis, precisely because the referent of the cut is the *jouissance* that keeps the analysand fixed in lies. By suspending a patient's certainties, the analyst takes up the challenge of giving her a way out of her alienations in the Other, a way to *form* her own desire. Perhaps the most enabling—although the most debilitating—of transference strategies is the analyst's use of the cut to give the patient access to the real. Only in this way does an analysand have the possibility of separating from the primary object that ensures her consistency in a fixity to the death drive. Only in this way is the path cleared to give one the chance to create new (master) signifiers that are detached from the primary *jouissance* whose hold is lethal.

Speaking of the fact that transference begins before the actual analytic relation, Lacan says:

> And yet if the [analytic] subject commits himself to searching after truth as such, it is because he places himself in the dimen-sion of ignorance—it doesn't matter whether he knows it or not. That is one of the elements making up what analysts call "readi-ness to the transference." There is a readiness to the transference in the patient solely by virtue of his placing himself in the posi-tion of acknowledging himself in speech, and searching out his truth to the end, the end which is there, in the analyst. (1988a, 277–78)

One of Lacan's unique contributions to psychoanalysis was his discov-ery that change only occurs in real time. By using time to cut into the semblants of the analysand's speech, precisely where the truth cannot be said, Lacan turned the transference away from Freudian ideas of the ego telling its story. Arguing that the transference is the only means of recov-ering one's relationship to knowledge that has been lost in the uncon-scious, Lacan reconfigured Freud's theory and practice away from the substantive idea of meaning, wherein life narratives are taken seriously at the level of semblance, and ignored at the level of truth. In narrative, we reify ourselves imaginarily, seeking to make the other recognize us, love us, feed our narcissism of ideals.

When an analyst believes the patient's narrative, he cannot help the patient constitute the ignorance his language hides. Lacan dismissed the ego in favor of Freud's intuition that the truth of what happened to one's being in the Oedipal drama is written on and in the body. Indeed, the truth of ignorance carries a limit in the body itself, a limit that concerns castration and *jouissance*. In demonstrating how Freud's Wolf Man patient had foreclosed a symbolization of the genital plane, Lacan argued convincingly that *that* constituted his being on the side of psychosis. Sexuality lies at the heart of epistemology, then, giving one questions, as in neurosis, or shutting out questions, as in psychosis. In the psychoses, Lacan taught, ignorance cannot even be constituted in analysis, precisely because there is no possible dialectic to be had with truth or the real.

Overwhelmed by the real, psychotic subjects perceive from a delusory organization of language that draws its power from *jouissance,* operating from the axes of pre-mirror or mirror-stage libidinal metonymies where the object *a* functions in the real, as *Ur*-object, cause-of-desire. Since the misrecognitions that make up the associative system of affirmations and negations in psychotic language appear in a delusory framework, petrified *jouissance* attaches itself to language, making language function like an automaton, quite unlike the movement of language that depends on the unconscious qua lack. Fantasy, on the other hand, works from the Other, via the dialectical movement of metaphorical substitutions that constitute and reconstitute the lacks that give rise to the desire one satisfies with imaginary, lure objects. Never having lost the primary object, the psychotic has never formulated a question regarding the sexual difference. Lacking lack, the psychotic's certainty teaches us, nonetheless, that ignorance can only be constructed in reference to impasses in the real, impasses that bespeak the unknown as a lack in being and in knowledge.

The notion that the psychotic is *in* language, but not in transference, is difficult to conceptualize. Moreover, the fixity of any person's ego and the solidity of words themselves make it seem that nothing lacks to anyone at the level of being or knowledge. But phenomena such as dreams, belief, prayer, and anxiety, make us suspect some other dimension to conscious knowledge, something hiding *within* our knowledge. Yet that something else is opaque, like the truth of the dream insofar as it tells us that one thing substitutes for something else, while referring to something beyond it. Put another way, the very preeminence of images in dream thought complicates the issue of knowing what dreams mean. Equating the visible with the true, people tend to believe the image is the thing in itself. Even Freud, in his final edition of *The Interpretation of Dreams,* reduced dream images to a collective symbology where image equals meaning. Instead, Lacan heeded the signifier—*not the image*—in dreams, the verbal part, showing that even as the dream hides truth, it still serves the unconscious by guiding the dreamer to the point of ignorance where images refer to language that borders on the real.

Finally, if we reconsider Freud's account of Dora, the case of a *petite hystérie,* in which he discovered transference, in light of Lacan's theory that transference only functions insofar as it bases itself on the dimension of ignorance *in the analysand,* we can see Freud as blinded by imaginarizing the transference with Dora. We can see how, by following Freud in his own terms, analysis has stayed on the wrong foot ever since, whether anchoring itself in drive theory, ego theory, object-relations theory, cognitive theory, or narrative theory. On the one hand, Freud discovered the metaphorical structure of transference: one person can stand in for another. But he had no idea that the metaphorical functioning of language—its dialectical movement—depended on the real that language tries to translate.

When Freud tells Dora what her actions mean, his interpretive action is similar to that of a Lacanian analyst. That is, he does not *understand* her. He does not believe her story. But, unlike Lacanian analysts, he does interpret her narrative at the level of content. Lacanian analysts interpret *jouissance* by making a cut or punctuation in the language of semblance, with the goal of helping the analysand break up the repetitious clusters of *jouissance* meanings that fix her in a logic of the identical, in the narrative. Such use of the cut in the analytic session has the effect of progressively evacuating the *jouissance* attached to the analysand's words and identifications. By operating on the real, by using real time, Lacan discovered that the analyst could use the transference love (or hate) to help the analysand *re-form-ulate* the identifications she lives from. Only then can one escape a life mired down in the alienating desires of someone else.

When Freud told Dora that her games with Herr K., Frau K., and her father were complicitous with the very disorder disturbing her, she stopped analysis. In "Intervention on Transference" (1951), Lacan (1985) critiqued Freud's mode of treating Dora, gradually elaborating this critique into an *ethics* of psychoanalysis itself. By charting out Dora's position in the real, by telling her what she did not want to hear, what she was not ready to know, Freud drove her away from analysis. Even more distressing, from Lacan's point of view, is the effect of such an interpretation. It does not allow the analysand herself to construct her ignorance—in the time it takes her—and it does not attenuate her suffering; worse, it fixes her in an ever firmer identification with the ignorance that already *causes* her to suffer. Dora left Freud, returning only after she had extracted a confession from the guilty parties. By playing out the game of her unhappiness at the imaginary level of guilt and blame, she remained fixated in imaginary love/hate relations. Holding onto her ignorance—passionately—Dora abandoned herself to the Other's desire. By identifying herself with the Madonna at the level of ideal ego, she sees herself as blameless, a victim, a martyr, a *belle âme,* a sufferer who believes herself morally superior to others.

By rethinking Dora's two dreams as recounted by Freud in light of the idea that she *retains* the passion of ignorance, one can argue that the interpretation of dream symbols is no more efficacious in the analytic transference than is empathy with an analysand's narrative. Dora's first dream occurs just after Herr K. has kissed her and made her a sexual proposition. The dream images of a burning house are clearly sexual, designating her as a girl *lost in her desire.* She asks her father to save her, to tell her which way to go in her encounter with *jouissance.* Her own answer to herself is "flee"; get out of the house. That is, run away from your desire. In the second dream, Dora is *lost in her words.* She tries to find direction, a place in the symbolic. She asks everyone which way she should go. Finding no place on her own and, finally, refusing the help of others—and lacking an analyst who could help her—she returned to the call of her family (her mother's command to come home). Unable to constitute her desire, to make a way, she goes home to find her father dead, picks up a book—someone else's words—and keeps her ignorance intact.

The life of Ida Bauer (Deutsch 1957) bears out this interpretation. That Ida Bauer retained her friendship with Frau K., later opening a shop with her, does nothing to change the fact that she suffered from hysterical symptoms until her death. Ida Bauer spent the rest of her life going from analyst to analyst, medical doctor to medical doctor, always sick, always complaining, *ignorant* of the concrete identifications that pinned her to the ghosts of her past (Deutsch 1957, 42). Lacan called that *place* of suffering the juncture between what she does not know in the symbolic and what she has not formulated in the real. Teaching that the analysand speaks poorly, as one who does not know what she ignores in the real, Lacan defined the real as a hole, as being *or* nothingness: "This being and this nothingness are essentially linked to the phenomenon of speech. It is within the dimension of being that the tripartition of the symbolic, the imaginary, and the real is to be found, those elementary categories without which we would be incapable of distinguishing anything within our experience" (1988a, 272).

But how does one recognize the place of ignorance in being? One answer is anxiety. The real promotes anxiety all the time, its most fundamental cause being the sexual difference itself. Another answer is *jouissance,* which bespeaks a paradox: the pleasure or displeasure of Oneness, of forced unities, of consistencies supported by fundamental fantasies. Analysis plays at the interface of lack, loss, anxiety, and *jouissance,* showing language to be a poor cousin of these forces, but the only way one has to work with them. Thus, in Lacan's exegesis of Freud, ignorance *can* become knowledge, but only once it is detached from the inertia of the passion of the real that dwells on the underside of familiar language, there where desire is imprisoned in *jouissance.* In that place where one is abandoned to the passions of suffering, identifications can be reconfigured, if one learns to speak the truth of the experiences that first gave a basis to ignorance's passion.

REFERENCES

Deutsch, Felix. 1957. "A Footnote to Freud's 'Fragment of an Analysis of a Case of Hysteria.' " In *In Dora's Case: Freud—Hysteria—Feminism,* edited by Charles Bernheimer and Claire Kahane, 35–43. New York: Columbia University Press, 1985.

Freud, Sigmund. 1901/1905. *Fragment of an Analysis of a Case of Hysteria. SE* 7:7–122.

———. 1940/1938. *An Outline of Psycho-Analysis, SE* 23:141–207.

———. 1953–1974. *The Standard Edition of the Complete Psychological Works of Sigmund Freud.* Translated and edited by James Strachey. 24 vols. London: Hogarth and the Institute of Psycho-Analysis.

Lacan, Jacques. 1966. "Intervention sur le transfert." In *Ecrits,* 215–26. Paris: Seuil, 1966.

———. 1975a. *Le Séminaire de Jacques Lacan. Livre I (1953–54): Les Ecrits techniques de Freud.* Text established by Jacques-Alain Miller. Paris: Seuil.

———. 1975b. *Le Séminaire de Jacques Lacan. Livre XX (1972–73): Encore,* 19–27. Text established by Jacques-Alain Miller. Paris: Seuil.

———. 1978. *Le Séminaire de Jacques Lacan. Livre II (1954–55): Le moi dans la théorie de Freud et dans la technique de la psychanalyse.* Text established by Jacques-Alain Miller. Paris: Seuil.

———. 1985. "Intervention of Transference." (1951/1952). In *Feminine Sexuality: Jacques Lacan and the Ecole Freudienne,* edited by Juliet Mitchell and Jacqueline Rose, translated by Jacqueline Rose, 61–73. New York: Norton.

———.1988a. *The Seminar of Jacques Lacan. Book I (1953–54): Freud's Papers on Technique.* Edited by Jacques-Alain Miller. Translated with notes by John Forrester. New York: Norton.

———. 1988b. *The Seminar of Jacques Lacan. Book II (1954–55): The Ego in Freud's Theory and in the Technique of Psychoanalysis.* Edited by Jacques-

Alain Miller. Translated by Sylvana Tomaselli, with notes by John Forrester. New York: Norton.

Miller, Jacques-Alain. 1991–92. "De la nature des semblants." Seminar of 1991–92. Course given in the Department of Psychoanalysis, University of Paris VIII. (unpublished)

Ragland-Sullivan, Ellie. 1989. "Dora and the Name-of-the-Father: The Structure of Hysteria." In *Discontented Discourses: Feminism, Textual Intervention, Psychoanalysis,* edited by Marleen Barr and Richard Feldstein, 208–40. Urbana: University of Illinois Press.

9

The Passions of Adolescent Mourning: Framing the Cadaverous Structure of Freud's *Gradiva*

GEOFF MILES

> The process of the cure is accomplished in a relapse into love, if we combine all the many components of the sexual instinct under the term "love"; and such a relapse is indispensable, for the symptoms on account of which the treatment has been undertaken are nothing other than precipitates of earlier struggles connected with repression, or the return of the repressed, and they can only be resolved and washed away by a fresh high tide of the same passions.
>
> —Sigmund Freud, "Delusions and Dreams in Jensen's 'Gradiva' "

If it is through the maternal breast and its caring representatives that passion first stirs in the subject, surely one of the most profound places through which we return to the moment of this passionate loss is in adolescence. Not quite child, not yet adult, the adolescent suffers the blow of this reawakening at the level of his or her changing body. And if it was literary criticism in the 1980s that gave us writing on the body and writing through the body, such writing could do so only in the measure that it is the very narrativity of the body which is that writing's precondition. And who experiences more the fact of an embodied writing than the adolescent? This painful transformation of subjecthood and identity is a fundamental fact of our common narrative, but it is a narrative often told through the sublimating marks of attained adulthood. This is no less true for Freud who lent to us the fact that childhood is subject to a pervasive repression, but fell short of showing us that adolescence succumbs to an equally pervasive suppression. Certainly contemporary psychoanalysis can testify to the latter insofar as adolescence remains the least examined place of its inquiry. However, in the opening of her short essay "The Adolescent Novel," Julia Kristeva (1990) makes the following suggestive remarks:

> I understand by the term "adolescent" less an age category than an open psychic structure . . . the adolescent structure opens itself to the repressed at the same time that it initiates a psychic reorganization of the individual—thanks to a tremendous loosening of the superego. The awakening of pre-genitality follows, and an attempt to integrate it within genitality. In the aftermath of the oedipal stabilization of subjective identity, the adolescent again questions his identifications, along with his capacity for speech and symbolization. The search for a new love object reactivates the depressive position and manic attempts at its resolution. (8)

If for Melanie Klein (1940; 1975, 345) the depressive position is punctuated by a profound melancholia centred around the child's fear of its destruction and potential loss of the loved object, then it is in Wilhelm Jensen's 1903 novella *Gradiva: A Pompeiian Fantasy Fragment* that we find everywhere the reemergence of this fear of destruction and loss of love-object. Contrary to Freud's rendition, Jensen's novella is one in which these fears are returned via the adolescent fantasies of its main character, Norbert Hanold. Equally if one reads "Delusions and Dreams in Jensen's 'Gradiva' " with eyes upon the text and ears attuned to the moment of Freud's writing in the summer of 1906 we find that his text too contains a strange melancholia no less profound than Norbert's own.

Long before Freud wrote his 1917 paper "The Uncanny," the uncanny worked on Freud. *Gradiva,* whose central theme involves the loss of a close friendship, was read by Freud at the same time as his long friendship with Wilhelm Fliess was painfully ending. Certainly it is uncanny that Freud, like the hero Norbert Hanold, is engaged in a bereavement in which he is forced to rework his libidinal tie to a recently lost love-object through a work of substitution that is concomitant with the work of mourning. By taking the *Gradiva* novella as an *object* of analysis at such a crucial period in his life, it is Freud's passion, Freud's desire, that is at stake in its writing. Regardless of Freud's dissimulating claim that the story was brought to him by another, it is Norbert's dreams as transference object and the object of textual transference that look at Freud "with familiar faces."[1]

During the writing of "Delusions and Dreams," Freud's death anxiety peaked again, subject as it was to the suggestion of Fleiss's periodic calculation of Freud's death at 51. Anniversaries too, as Patrick Mahony (1987, 49–50) has shown, were significant to Freud and 1906 marked the tenth anniversary of Freud's father's death. Thus Freud's reading of the *Gradiva,* a novella that has the passions of object-loss as its central theme, occurred within a discursive field of object-loss for Freud: loss of friend, loss of father, loss of self. And yet this network of losses was not content to remain outside his analysis of the novella, as purely peripheral to its writing: it became uncannily doubled in a shared biographical history between Freud and the hero Norbert Hanold. Both Sigmund and Norbert shared an investment in maintaining a passionately hyperbolic fantasy for the city of Pompeii.

Now *Gradiva* is a *Bildungsroman* and central to the theme of that genre is the youthful hero's overcoming of great obstacles brought about by the change from childhood to adulthood. And if for the *Bildungsroman* adolescence becomes the space within which the author constructs his tale, what does this say about a psychoanalytic study of such an adolescent novel? What is Freud's passion for this text at the moment of its writing? Is it only in the dreams that Jensen constructs that the text knows? Is this where Freud's passion lies? Who, via the text, is the desiring subject for Freud: adult, adolescent, infant? Indeed, is it only within what Freud recounts of the story that we can assume a position of knowledge within the text for Freud? In Freud's reading of *Gradiva: A Pompeiian Fantasy-Fragment* there is a certain disaffection between Freud's drive to know and his desire to know and it is in the space between his drive and desire to know that his interest in the novella vacillates—a vacillation between mourning and melancholia.

Let us review for a moment the gist of Jensen's story, a torturously sad tale whose basis for its sadness is not just the loss of a childhood friend in her delusional guise, no less for Freud than for Norbert, but also that terrifying loss accompanying bereavement arising from parental death. For as Freud has shown us, are not all our passions born of such a death, whether this be actual or, more to the point, symbolic and thereby constituted via the realm and rule of fantasy?

THE PRIMAL SCENES

Norbert Hanold, a young German archaeologist in his early twenties, has purchased a plaster bas-relief of a woman whose main characteristic is her beautiful walk. He names her Gradiva, "she who is splendid in walking," and gives her first Roman and later Greek ancestry. Norbert's interest in women is confined solely to the image of the bas-relief and he lives a solitary life as a scholar. One night he has a terrifying dream in which he sees Gradiva in the streets of Pompeii where, after lying down, she is slowly buried by the rain of ashes. Norbert awakes in a fright but with the feeling that Gradiva really must have lived in Pompeii. Still frightened by his dream he makes an excuse to travel to Rome but from there he finds himself continuing on to Naples and then Pompeii. While wandering the streets of the excavated city he comes across a woman whom he takes to be the ghost of Gradiva. Over the next three days he has conversations with her in the House of Meleager. On the second day we learn that her name is Zoe, who Norbert believes is able to haunt Pompeii under the heat of the noonday sun. Remarkably she speaks German and over the course of their meetings she manages to elicit from Norbert, by means of ambiguous questions and statements, the fantasies he has constructed about her while viewing the bas-relief in his study—a bas-relief that is her exact replica. During the course of their third meeting Norbert, caught in a desire to discover the nature of her corporeality, uses the happenstance of a fly that has landed on Zoe-Gradiva's hand to aid his inquiry. Slapping at the fly he discovers that, far from being ghostly, Zoe-Gradiva is a woman of flesh and blood; what is more, she knows his name even though he had not told her what it is. In fear of his discovery he escapes via the Street of Tombs to the House of Diomede only to come upon the young woman once again. Here we learn that Zoe is none other than the love of his childhood, the daughter of Professor Bertgang, whom he had abandoned during adolescence, replacing her with his love of science. We further learn that the name Gradiva is a Latin translation of her father's name, which Norbert used as a substitute when naming the bas-relief. The story closes with renewed pledges of love and promises of marriage. As they leave the city Norbert has Zoe step upon the stepping-stones of Pompeii so that he can view in reality that which had been the subject of his fantasy: her remarkable style of walking.

It will, perhaps, not go unnoticed that I have said nothing of the two other dreams that are central to the story and constitute, along with the first dream, the primary focus of Freud's analysis. However, my interest in the *Gradiva* story and its analysis is not so much about what Freud includes in his study but rather what he excludes. Indeed, the three dreams are themselves not exempt from Freud's editing, especially the dream Norbert has while in Rome. This dream is grossly neglected and underinterpreted by Freud. Careful examination reveals that it is a dream of the primal scene whose manifest content comes from the passionate sounds of newlyweds on a squeaky bed in an adjacent room. Moreover, it is a dream constructed from Norbert's childhood memory of the death and burial of his parents, particularly his mother, revealing that Norbert's hysterical delusions about Gradiva are based upon his twinning of love with death. Freud (1985) only tells us, in the most cursory form, the first half of the dream, that Norbert dreams that he is again in Pompeii during its destruction and that he sees the statue of Apollo Belvedere carry away the Capitoline Venus, "no doubt by an ironical exaltation of the couple in the next room," in a squeaky cart to a dark place (91–92). He omits to tell us of the dream's second scene where Norbert stands alone overlooking the city, which has now been buried by the ashes of Vesuvius. Here is the text from Jensen's (1962) tale.

> he fell back into a doze which transported him to Pompeii just as Vesuvius again began its eruption. A vivid throng of fleeing people caught him, and among them he saw Apollo Belvedere lift up the Capitoline Venus, take her away and place her safely upon some object in a dark shadow; it seemed to be a carriage or cart on which she was to be carried off, for a rattling sound was soon heard from that direction. This mythological occurrence did not amaze the young archaeologist, but it struck him as remarkable that the two talked German, not Greek, to each other for, as they half regained their senses, he heard them say: "My sweet Gretchen." "My only Augustus." *But after that the dream-picture changed completely. Absolute silence took the place of the confused sound, and instead of smoke and the glow of fire, bright, hot sunlight rested on the ruins of the buried city. This likewise changed gradually, became a bed on whose white linen golden beams circled upon his eyes, and Norbert Hanold awoke in the scintillating spring morning of Rome.* (165)

Between these two scenes Norbert's desire is a passionate desire to maintain his hold upon the cryptic moment in which he has witnessed the entombment of the body and memory of his dead mother. Freud does not tell us that very early on in the story we learn that for Norbert Hanold "the early deaths of his parents had left him absolutely alone (Jensen 1962, 158). The couple in the other room are therefore not the only ones in this story to have shared a marriage bed. Norbert has memories of the death and burial of his parents; moreover, his interest in antiquities came from his father who had been a collector.[2]

For one who was well versed in the workings of the unconscious occasioned by dreams, jokes, and bungled actions Freud fails to interpret the darker *grave* side of the dream. Freud misses the importance of the name "Gradiva," a perfect anagram for "Gravida" (she who is pregnant). The mother and, what is more, the mother is dead. And here now is that lack for which we must account. Why in a study on a novella whose central theme is love's passion and encounter with the pregnancy of death do we find not one word on the significance of death for the hero of the story?

The symbolics of love as death are inscribed upon almost every page of *Gradiva* but there is no mention of it in Freud's essay of 1906. In fact the male child's symbolic loss and regaining of mother, of which Freud (1977, 151–52) had so eloquently spoken earlier, is curiously absent in his discussion of Norbert's symptomatology. Only once in an aside about a young student, whose repression of sexuality led to the eroticization of mathematics, does Freud even refer to the mother's role in the constitution of sexuality. But here he tells us that he will not tell us how the young student's mathematical fantasies are connected to his mother (Freud 1985, 61). And yet very early on in the novella we find that mother's place is central to Norbert's delusional constructions. In his apartment Norbert has a hallucination in which he sees "a woman offering vegetables and fruit for sale from baskets; from a half-dozen large walnuts she had removed half of the shells to show the meat, fresh and sound, as a temptation for purchasers" (Jensen 1962, 150). Upon waking from his first dream the bas-relief took on the appearance of a *Gruftdenkmal* (a tombstone or memorial stone) and it is shortly thereafter that we learn that Norbert's parents died when he was young and that it is his inheritance from their death which allows him to live and travel in a style of comfort that few are able to achieve. Thus the tombstone status of the bas-relief of Gradiva is not simply a memorial to the forgetting of Zoe but also to the death of his parents and specifically the *Gravida* who was his mother.

Norbert's repression of Zoe and the construction of his fantasy about the bas-relief, which begins within the boundary of his adolescence, is a literary symbolic representation of the adolescent's return of the repressed. We see this not only through the return of Norbert's childhood friend Zoe, which means life—Zoe too is an anagram of the mother—in the guise of the dead Gradiva but also through the dead Gravida, the dead mother of Norbert's infancy. Gradiva is a tertiary representation of an originary representation, of the *maternal imago*.

In order to understand the significance of the maternal in this novel we must not lose sight of the fact that Norbert's journey to Pompeii is a regressive journey. So regressive, in fact that it threatens, up to the very end, to envelop the hero within the tomb of psychosis. Norbert's lost interest in science, which is nowhere more dramatically depicted than in his loss of command over language (the symbolic, the domain of the father's law), is a testimony to Norbert's regression to pre-Oedipal schizoid symptomatology. Norbert, Jensen tells us, was a brilliant philologist who had achieved some fame for deciphering the Latin graffiti found on the walls of the ruins of Pompeii. But on the second day he cannot translate the word *caupo* (innkeeper) (Jensen 1962, 178–79). We can suspect that part of the reason for his forgettings in translation is that this is not the word he sees. It is instead a displacement of the word he refuses to see: *copulo*. Here the signifier/signified copula comes under repression just as in his second dream the primal copula taking place in the adjacent room was suppressed amid the nocturnal eruption of Vesuvius in his dream. From this point on in the story Norbert's passionate jealousy and denial of third-party intervention in his relations with Gradiva are intensified. We can see the extent to which his regression to pre-Oedipal relations gets a hold of him just before his third meeting in the House of Meleager. Jensen (1962) writes:

> The thought that others might also speak with her, and sit down near her to carry on a conversation with her, made him indignant. To that he alone possessed a claim, or at any rate a privilege; for he had discoverd Gradiva, of whom no one had formerly known, had observed her daily, taken her into his life, to a degree, imparted to her his life-strength, and it seemed to him as if he had thereby again lent to her life that she would not have possessed without him. Therefore he felt that there devolved upon him a right to which he alone might make a claim and which he might refuse to share with anyone else. (209)

I suspect that we might be hard-pressed to find a more eloquent description of the "omnipotence of thought" that is characteristic of both the infant's feelings about mother and the male adolescent's passionate feelings about the first true love-object who is her representative.

ANOTHER LOCALITY, ANOTHER SCENE

Between January 1872 and October 1875, a period that spans Freud's adolescence from age fifteen to nineteen, the young Sigismund wrote a large number of letters to his friend Eduard Silberstein.[3] Within their contents we find much discussion about the nature of "principles," Sigmund and Eduard's code name for young women. Freud's principal principle was Gisela Flüss who was only twelve years old when he first met and fell in love with her during his summer visit to Freiberg, the town of his infancy. And yet it is clear that Freud's adolescent passion for the young Gisela is bound to an earlier, let us say archaic, moment of passion. In this moment of Freud's preconditioning for the reactivation of the depressive position during adolescence it is here that we find the death of his brother Julius on the ides of March 1858. Tied to this latter event is the birth of Freud's sister Anna later that year. Coterminous with these two experiences the toddler Freud witnessed the imprisonment of his nursemaid for stealing Sigismund's money and toys. For Freud the nursemaid became the other mother—the abjected mother—the core of his primal guilt by association (who we see returned through Fliess's accusations of plagiarism in 1904). To this latter event we can add Freud's consequent defense through his alliance with the good-objects of the *Gradiva* novella and its author. But let us not forget the melancholy scene of the cupboard in which Sigismund was convinced that his mother was entombed and which Freud (1978) tells us was but a screen memory of Amalia's pregnancy with Anna (90–93). "In all analyses," Freud once wrote to Fliess, "one therefore hears the same story twice: once a fantasy about the mother; the second time as a real memory of the maid (Masson 1985, 317). This is the maternal imago par excellence!

In these primal moments, just as in the *Gradiva* novella, we find a kind of primal scene in which the passion for love and death stand together: Freud's love for the mother and other mother and their death through a doubled entombment, one of whom was very much a Gravida[4] at this time. The affects associated with these scenes are returned to Freud during his adolescence and produce within him both a fascination and a fear of young women. Death is the theme that ties all the figures, the nursemaid, the mother, the sister, the brother, Gisela, and Eduard, together. And yet as Kristeva (1982) has noted, "At the limit, if someone personifies abjection without assurance of purification, it is a woman, 'any woman,' the 'woman as a whole' (85). At the center of this space of abjection is man's fear of woman's procreative power signified through blood, which accompanies both birth and menstruation: love and death as marked through the time of woman's body. This leads us back again to Freud's primal moments: among his memories Freud recalled a day when he was bathed in water stained by the menstrual blood of the nursemaid. Blood was Freud's mark of Cain, tying him to the criminality of the nursemaid and it is blood that gave rise to Freud's phobia of women, during his adolescence, a trait he shares with Norbert Hanold who in his first dream produces a city bathed in "blood red light" (Jensen 1962, 153).

Let us not forget that Freud's love for Gisela Flüss turns in the direction of its opposite, an aggressive disdain, the closer she reaches the age of sixteen, the closer she reaches womanhood and thus able to symbolize the space of abjection. This passionate reversal into the opposite is dramatically illustrated in the young Freud's stingingly satirical poem "The Epithalamium" written for the fictional occasion of Gisela's marriage and with the marriage bed as one of its central scenes:

> Spherical she appears and gloriously rounded
> Rounded her face, wittily sparkling her eyes,
> Rounded her girth, and if the poet be free
> To probe with a curious eye what is normally hidden from view,
> He will find the sphere's principle pervading the forms
> Blessed night reveals to the fortunate groom.
>
> (Freud 1990, 136)

However, Freud's ambivalance toward Gisela existed from the start, both in his calling Gisela's beauty Thracian (Freud 1990, 18) and thereby identifying her with the destructive power of the Maenads, and more especially in his naming her Ichthyosaura, the Jurassic fish-lizard.

Now this appellative is more primal than primeval. And so it appears that during their adolescence Sigmund and Norbert shared the habit of fixing or fossilizing the image of woman in stone. As Lacan has noted, "it is the stability of the standing posture, the prestige of stature, the impressiveness of statues, which set the style for the identification in which the ego finds its starting-point and leave their imprint in it for ever" (Lacan 1953, 12). Thus the bas-relief of Gradiva and the fossilized image of Ichthyosaura again lead us beyond their secondary representations in

Zoe and Gisela to the doubled maternal imago upon whose status and stature they are based. But the tertiary representation of the stone image contains within it something not immediately apparent in the intermediate model of Zoe or Gisela. In the symbolic registry of Norbert's *Gruft-denkmal* and Freud's choice of an extinct aquatic animal, what stands out is the deadness of stone more than flesh and blood. It is this statuesque passion, "the impressiveness of statues" that aptly describes Sigismund's and Norbert's identifications with, not the lost mother, but the dead mother of their infantile object relations. For both, the restructuring of ego identification, within the boundary of adolescence, meant re-megence with the dead thing of their infancy—or what we might call "the framing cadaverous structure."

NECRO-F(AM)ILIUS

The framing structure of the maternal object becomes that which André Green has called the "dead mother complex." In a descriptive metaphor of ego formation Green (1986) envisions the following:

> When conditions are favourable to the inevitable separation between the mother and the child, a decisive mutation arises in the depths of the ego. The maternal object in the form of the primary object of fusion fades away, to leave the place to the ego's own cathexes which will found his personal narcissism. Henceforth the ego will be able to cathect its own objects, distinct from the primitive object. But this effacement of the mother does not make the primitive object disappear completely. The primary object becomes a "framing-structure" for the ego, sheltering the negative hallucination of the mother. (165–66)

Here we have a description of a Saturnine structure, a Black Sun, to use Kristeva's term,[5] whose devastating potential for throwing the infant into despair and depression, for want of the lost maternal object, is defended against by the residue of that maternal object. This residue forms a framing structure for the orbiting ego, stopping it from being sucked in by the gravity of a blank space left behind by the effacement of the primary/primal love object. The latter, of course, takes place under the ideal conditions of good enough love, but Green draws our attention to a condition that impedes the development of such a framing structure. This condition is produced when the ego is not yet ready to take command of stable and stabilizing cathexes of its own objects and constitutes instead the formation of "the dead mother complex."

Now Freud (1985) tells us that Norbert knew no other love-object than Zoe, and here he may well be reading his own narrative into the story if we recall Freud's loss of the nursemaid and the position of the mother whose place, in Freud's reading, Zoe has taken. In giving Zoe a maternal identification, Freud makes Norbert, like himself, have two mothers. Green (1986) notes that Freud's dream of *My Mother and the Bird-Beaked Figures* is a dream which indicates that Freud may also have suffered from the "dead mother complex" (169–73). For Green it is the fact that Freud errs over the dating of this dream by two and a half years, and the coincidence of such a length of time with Freud's own age at the time of his brother Julius's death, that gives just cause for this suspicion. But this time period, as Green and others have noted, also marks the beginning of a series of events linked to the death of Julius: the birth of his sister Anna, and at the end of that year (1859) the loss of the other mother. In Freud's infantile representation of the maternal imago something truly would have changed.[6]

All three of these moments work in tandem for Freud's re-shaped and mis-shaped maternal imago. As Green writes, it is the "brutal change of the maternal imago" that sets the "dead mother complex" in process. In the story of *Gradiva*, as I have been describing it, we have an unconscious narrative that repeats Freud's own: pregnancy and loss (death) are indelibly linked together if we can accept the message of a dead Gravida in Jensen's tale. Alongside this we have a repetition of the dead mother lost in her own mourning, with Zoe already having taken on the part of the maternal for Norbert at the time of her mother's death. In *Gradiva* we learn that Zoe had also lost her mother when she was young.

In Norbert's first attachment to the figure of Gradiva we find that it is here that his trouble begins. Norbert, we can now understand, is marked by a space of double mourning. He mourns not only the loss of his actual mother but that of his second: Zoe the child-mother of his childhood whose mourning for her mother caused a mis-shaping to take place in the representations of the maternal imago that she had become for Norbert. Though Zoe will claim that it was Norbert who left her when they became teenagers, in fact for Norbert, she had already left him through her earlier mourning, had already become a spectral presence in his life. Her loss through his adolescent delusions is but a repetition of this former loss. Gradiva, as we can now see, is a double representation of the dead mother, a bas-relief of a bas-relief of the dead mother. At its deepest and most complex level this is where I would situate Freud's interest in the novella—an unconscious recognition of and identification with the doubling of the dead mother.

In his relations with Gisela, Freud makes of her a stone image under the name Ichthyosaura, thus producing both a petrifying and petrified image of the dead mother. Though Gisela recalls the nursemaid it is because the nursemaid's disappearance is associated with other losses— Anna's displacement of Sigismund and the death of Julius—that caused his mother to become the "dead mother," that Ichthyosaura-Gisela continuously returns Freud to all these spaces.

To address the position of the mother in the novella would require that Freud recognize his contact with the space of the dead mother, but to do so would only increase his sense of loss suffered through his break with Fliess. Freud's identification with Fliess is not simply paternal but maternal, and insofar as his correspondence re-maps that of his correspondence with Eduard Silberstein it is also fraternal. Freud, however, is unlike Norbert Hanold in this respect. His path away from the hold of the dead mother will not be so easy. No easy closure for Freud with a happy ending and identification with the fetishized object of his ocular passion. It may be in fact that his release only came at the time of his mother's own actual death: at this point the encrypted dead mother and the actual mother are once more joined together. In such a moment do we not hear a silent whisper within the pages of "The Theme of the Three Caskets"? In linking the mother to death, Freud's wish for the mother to be linked with death has behind it another wish: a wish to be released from the bondage, the passion of and for, the dead mother.[7] But at the time of writing the *Gradiva* analysis, escape from the affects that the "dead mother complex" imposes is limited to the conscious and unconscious process of dissimulation. Freud's paring down of the novella's contents allows him to sidestep the issue of death, whose trajectory is not only forward-looking but also something coming from the past.

Now death, as Jean Laplanche might call it, is the ultimate *enigmatic signifier*.[8] Death is after all the signifier to which in the first and last place we devote our most fervent passion for the mechanism of deferred action. Thus the *Gradiva* analysis can, in part, be understood as an enigmatic message returned to Freud from several moments in his life. For if the work of *Delusions and Dreams* is a work of mourning in which Freud and the hero come to mourn the loss of love and friendship, it is Only in the measure that behind such loss we find a passion ultimately far stronger than our own. Such a passion is, as Freud was fond of saying,

Ananke, the inevitable—death. But we would be blind to this inevitable if we were to assume that death inscribes itself only in our body's acquiescence. Life is marked by moments of death and this is what *Gradiva* teaches us: the melancholy passions of adolescence are only surpassed if we accept the death of childhood that it heralds. But such a death is not simply negative. In fact, the passions of adolescence offers the chance to rework the losses beset by our infantile passion for the maternal object. Moreover, adolescence affords us a second chance to do the necessary *work* of mourning. Thus loss demands its mourning; without this work, which is the work of adolescence, we can have no passion in adult life.

NOTES

1. Freud (1985, 35). Although Ernest Jones tells us that it was Jung who passed the story on to Freud, careful consideration of the Freud–Jung correspondence reveals that this was not the case. It is possible that Paul Federn had prior knowledge of the novella but as Freud states in a footnote in *The Interpretation of Dreams:* "I found by chance in *Gradiva* ... a number of artificial dreams which were perfectly correctly constructed"; Freud, *SE* 4:97 n. 1 (my emphasis).

2. It is of course well known that Freud was himself such a collector.

3. The extent and importance of this correspondence will have no equal for Freud until he repeats this experience with Fliess.

4. In accounting for why Freud misses the anagram concealed in Gradiva we can note that Freud had once made a play on words out of the word Grav—ida. The joke was about Ida Fliess, Wilhelm's wife who was pregnant; see Masson (1985, 297).

5. To quote Kristeva (1989): "the 'Black Sun' metaphor fully sums up the blinding force of the despondent mood—an excruciating, lucid affect asserts the inevitability of death, which is the death of the loved one and the self" (151).

6. Significantly, the dream of *My Mother and the Bird-Beaked Figure* is also marked by the unconscious insistence of the primal scene, the primal copula being Freud himself insofar as the dream joins him to that scene. Indeed, if Green's reflections are correct, Freud would have had this dream when he was ten and a half; that is to say, on the cusp of adolescence.

7. I draw these ideas from Green (1986, 172).

8. On the concept of the enigmatic signifier and its relation to deferred action, see Laplanche (1989, 133–39).

REFERENCES

Copjec, Joan. 1984. "Transference: Letters and the Unknown Woman." *October* 28:61–90.

Freud, Sigmund. 1953–74. *The Standard Edition of the Complete Psychological Works of Sigmund Freud.* Translated and edited by James Strachey. 24 vols. London: Hogarth and the Institute of Psycho-Analysis.

———. 1972a. "Analysis Terminable and Interminable." *SE* 23.

———. 1972b. *The Interpretation of Dreams. SE* 4.

———. 1978. *The Psychopathology of Everyday Life.* Pelican Freud Library 5. Harmondsworth: Penguin.

———. 1985. *Delusions and Dreams in Jenson's "Gradiva."* Pelican Freud Library 14:29–118. Harmondsworth: Penguin.

———. 1990. *The Letters of Sigmund Freud to Eduard Silberstein. 1871–1881.* Cambridge: Harvard University Press.

Green, André. 1986. "The Dead Mother Complex." In *On Private Madness,* 142–73. London: Hogarth.

Jacobus, Mary. 1982. "Is There a Woman in This Text?" *New Literary History* 14:117–41.

Jensen, Wilhelm. 1962. "Gradiva: A Pompeiian Fancy." Translated by Helen M. Downey. In *Delusion and Dream and Other Essays,* edited by Philip Rieff, 145–235. Boston: Beacon.

Klein, Melanie, 1940. "Mourning and Its Relation to Manic-Depressive States." In *Love, Guilt, and Reparation and Other Works,* 344–69. New York: Delacourt Press, 1975.

Kofman, Sarah. 1991. "Summarize, Interpret." In *Freud and Fiction,* 85–117. Boston: Northeastern University Press.

Kristeva, Julia. 1982. *Powers of Horror: Essays on Abjection.* New York: Columbia University Press.

———. 1989. *Black Sun: Depression and Melancholia.* New York: Columbia University Press.

———. 1990. "The Adolescent Novel." In *Abjection, Melancholia, and Love: The Work of Julia Kristeva,* 8–23. London: Routledge.

Lacan, Jacques. 1953. "Some Reflections on the Ego." *International Journal of Psychoanalysis* 34:11–17.

———. 1979. *The Four Fundamental Concepts of Psychoanalysis.* Harmondsworth: Penguin.

Laplanche, Jean. 1989. *New Foundations for Psychoanalysis.* Cambridge: Basil Blackwell.

Mahony, Patrick J. 1987. *Freud as a Writer.* New Haven: Yale University Press.

Masson, Jeffrey. 1985. *The Complete Letters of Sigmund Freud to Wilhelm Fliess.* Cambridge: The Belknap Press of Harvard University Press.

Miles, Geoff. 1992. "Gravida-Gradiva: Pregnancy and Death-Work in Freud's Pompeiian Fantasy." Ph.D. diss., York University, Toronto.

Rose, Jacqueline. 1986. "The Imaginary." In *Sexuality in the Field of Vision,* 167–98. London: Verso.

Simon-Miller, Françoise L. 1978. "Ambivalence and Identification: Freud on Literature." *Literature and Psychology* 28, nos. 1 and 4: 23–39 and 151–67.

10

Leonardo's Love of Knowledge: Freud's Passion for Error

JOHN O'NEILL

Man hat geforscht, anstatt zu leben.

—Freud

Freud may not have been a passionate man but he was certainly a man of many passions. Such a distinction, of course, results from Freud's persistent self-analysis, at least as much from his sexual ambivalence (O'Neill 1992c). From his earliest childhood, he had learned that we may well hate those whom we love, lie to those whom we owe the truth, and make ourselves quite ill with jealousy, anger, and ambition. Indeed, if Freud seems to have rendered childhood more theatrical than it had been assumed, it is because he had seen into adult character as largely driven by the "instincts" or passions of childhood. Thus Freud was not so much a philosopher of the passions—not a Platonist and not a Humean—but rather a passionate dramatist, a Sophoclean, a Shakespearean, or an Ibsenite. The two ends of Freud's insights into the passions are, then, literature for its universality, and Freud's self-analysis for its particularity. How these two lines of approach overlap might well be shown in a close account of any of the well-known case histories (O'Neill, 1996).

On this occasion, I shall take up Freud's analysis of the passion for knowledge (*Wissbegierde*) in which he loved to compare himself with Leonardo, Faust, Darwin, and Copernicus. While such comparisons may seem grandiose—quite possibly exaggerating his mother's love for him as the source of such comparative worth—Freud did, to be fair, see himself in the intellectual struggles of Little Hans, Dora, Rat Man, Wolf Man, and Schreber.

Since art gives pleasure, it might be thought that the artist is himself a man of pleasure, surrendered to sensuousness and passionate in every other aspect of his life besides art. Such a stereotype might at least hold of Leonardo da Vinci who has given the world its most enigmatic pleasure in the self-absorbed smile of the Mona Lisa. Before such a mystery, reason is halted, and the viewer suspended before the sublimity of the inarticulate harmony of a woman's presence. Any other posture could only be due to a character fault in the viewer—or to the professional deformation of the critic. Freud, therefore, had to confront at the outset of his study the hedonist tradition of art (Wollheim 1973) and the biographic tradition (Vasari 1962) on Leonardo's happy life until early manhood. Since Freud confesses his own painful childhood and, above all, his own inability to enjoy anything without analyzing the reasons for his enjoyment, he risks putting himself out of the game—establishing himself as a miserable fellow well below the genius of Leonardo and thus the despicable author of a defamatory tract, seeking to degrade a universal genius with the sexual innuendos of a sectarian science of which he himself is the mysogynistic and ambivalently homosexual author.

So Freud was obliged to carefully sift the tradition upon Leonardo in order not to lose the peculiarity (*Eigentümlichkeit*) of the combination of sense and non-sense in Leonardo's oeuvre (art, science, medicine, mathematics, physics, engineering, and practical jokes). Since Leonardo's energy had fostered the comparison with Faust—with whom Freud himself sought comparison—it was important for Freud to show particular psychoanalytic insight into Leonardo's character. The point of entry was provided by the commentary available to Freud in German and Italian (see his bibliography) on Leonardo's inability to finish his works, on their profusion and abandonment, on his lack of aggression (whatever his interest in the machinery of war). These traits suggested a difficulty on Leonardo's side in claiming intellectual property or paternity—and thus a link with his abandonment by his father if not by his mother in her marriage with another man, "Accatabriga." Along these lines, Leonardo seems to have had only a medicalized concept of reproduction and sexuality (leading to the confusion of detail in the famous cross-section coital drawing reproduced in Freud's essay, despite its ersatz origin in an illustrated handbook).

How anxious Freud was to ground his own research on Leonardo may be seen from the extraordinary textual imbalance set up in his Footnote added in 1919, which extends for three pages in the opening section of the essay. Here Freud reproduces an argument from Reitler (1917) who "in the light of" the Leonardo essay interprets Leonardo's cross-section coital drawing as evidence of Leonardo's sexual repression, fear of women, and a certain disgust with the act itself. In 1923 Freud was obliged to add a note to the effect that Reitler's arguments were based upon a sketch from Eduard Fuchs, *Sittengeschichte* (in particular, it produces part of its strained effect through the addition of feet that counterbalance the original postures). Yet the whole episode, along with Pfister's (1913) "picture-puzzle" found in Leonardo's Saint Anne with the Madonna and Child as proof of the (Freud/Leonardo) vulture fantasy (which we consider later on) is enshrined in Freud's essay.

I am drawing attention to these two remarkable "grotesques" in the Leonardo essay right at the start because I believe they demonstrate the extraordinary combination of the passion for knowledge and error (or waywardness) in Freud himself no less than in his subject: Leonardo. Thus the two men were also paired as "lefthanders," at least inasmuch as Freud treated this as a homosexual symptom—a necessary deviation in the creative person. Freud notes that Leonardo's apparently cool interest in women was offset by his preference for the company of handsome (even if devilish) boys, which resulted in a charge before the magistrates, alleging homosexual conduct. But here, I think the evidence is that Leonardo was not so much sexually sluggish as perplexed by the cunning of nature's deployment of beauty in the sexual act whose long-term pains and disappointments might otherwise lead us to consider its abandonment (Kemp 1992). Here, too, Freud is Leonardo's companion since he confesses that his own sexual life had hardly justified its pains and that his experience had in fact been a source of the psychoanalytic discovery of the psychic aspects of sexuality that remove sex from strictly medical care. Thus the two men combined in themselves a lifelong cross-fertilization of the arts and sciences under a common motto:

> Nessune cosa si può amare nè odiare,
> se prima non ha cognitio di quella.
>
> (Richter, 1952, 2:244)

> (One has no right to love or hate anything if one has not acquired a thorough knowledge of its nature.)

Freud's commentary upon Leonardo's observation deserves full citation:

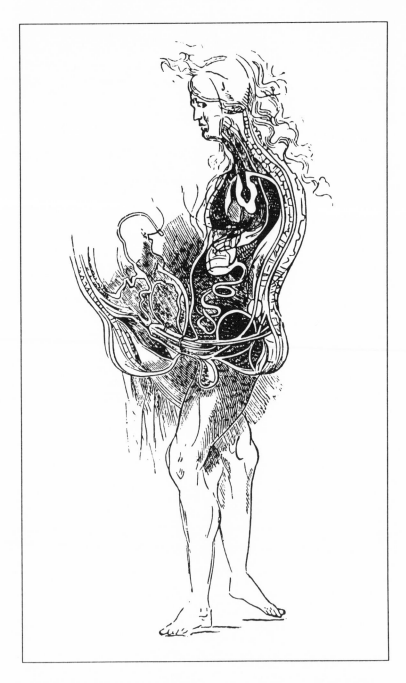

Fig. 1. Leonardo da Vinci, Coital Act. (From Eduard Fuchs, *Illustrierte Sittengeschichte,* vol. 1, *Renaissance Teil I* [Frankfurt am Main: Fischer Taschenbuch Verlag, 1985], page 73).

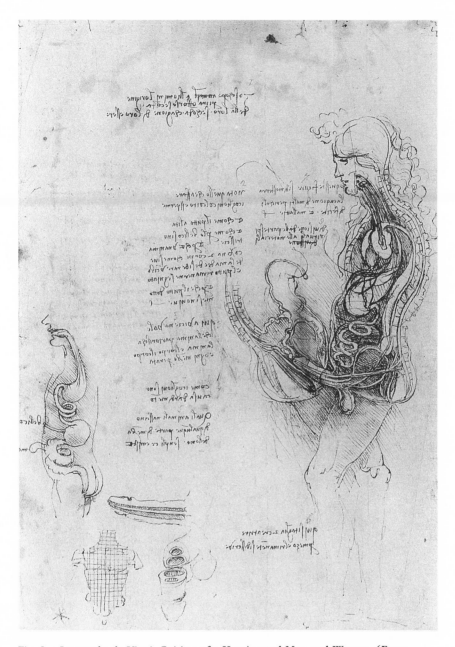

Fig. 2.   Leonardo da Vinci, Coition of a Hemisected Man and Woman. (From Martin Clayton, *The Anatomy of Man, Drawings from the Collection of Her Majesty Queen Elizabeth II,* with Commentaries on Anatomy by Ron Philo [Boston: Little, Brown, 1992], page 39).

The value of these remarks of Leonardo's is not to be looked for in their conveying an important psychological fact; for what they assert is obviously false, and Leonardo must have known this as well as we do. It is not true that human beings delay loving or hating until they have studied and become familiar with the nature of the object to which these affects apply. On the contrary they love impulsively, from emotional motives which have nothing to do with knowledge, and whose operation is at most weakened by reflection and consideration. Leonardo, then, could only have meant that the love practiced by human beings was not of the proper and unobjectionable kind: one *should* love in such a way as to hold back the affect, subject it to the process of reflection and only let it take its course when it has stood up to the test of thought. And at the same time we understand that he wishes to tell us that it happens so in his case and that it would be worthwhile for everyone else to treat love and hatred as he does. (*SE* 11:74, and Penguin Freud Library 14:163)

Leonardo's observations upon love and hatred at first sight run quite counter to what one generally observes in men and women. They would, if taken literally, undermine Leonardo's claims either to great art or to great science where the blindness and impulsivity of the passions is rather the general finding. But Leonardo is in fact offering a formula for the proper constitution of the passions (whether of love or of hatred) in their own seeming opposite, namely, knowledge. In short, Leonardo has formulated the problematic of *sublimation* ("holding back the affect") intrinsic to the constitution of great passion, however good or evil, however artistic or scientific it may be. Thus the *paradox of the passions,* as Leonardo and Freud understand them, is that they cannot be constituted except dispassionately; that is, "in cold labouring" inquiry that builds up their energy as if behind a dike, to use Freud's favorite image, until they are allowed to overflow in an outburst whose end effect is what people generally call "passion." Thus Leonardo's cold sciences are only properly to be understood as the sublimation effect of some great love greatly studied:

A conversion of psychical instinctual force into various forms of activity can perhaps no more be achieved without loss than a conversion of physical forces. The example of Leonardo teaches us how many other things we have to take into account in connection with these processes. The postponement of loving until full knowledge is acquired ends in a substitution of the latter for the former. A man who has won his way to a state of knowledge cannot properly be said to love and hate; he remains beyond love and hatred. *He has investigated instead of loving.* And that is perhaps why Leonardo's life was so much poorer in love than that of other great men, and of other artists. The stormy passions of a nature that inspires and consumes, passions in which other men have enjoyed their richest experience, appear not to have touched him. (*SE* 11:75, and Penguin Freud Library 14:165)

In keeping with Freud's own ambitions, however, it is the origins of Leonardo's dispassionate, if not desultory arts, that must be discovered if the world's love of Leonardo is to amount to anything more than an ignorant parade of gawking tourists. Thus the challenge to psychoanalysis is to show that Leonardo's "craving for knowledge" (*Wissbegierde*), without which his art is unintelligible, has its roots in the following genealogy:

1. presence of the excessive drive in early childhood;
2. fixation by a childhood imprint—
3. reinforced by early sexual instincts;
4. instincts that become part of later sexual life—so that
5. a given character is as passionate in research as another in love—to the point that
6. "He has investigated instead of loving." *Man hat geforscht, anstatt zu lieben*

The genealogy of the research passion (*Wissendrang*) results in a structural fixation whose energy is continuously fed from "below," inasmuch as sexual energy is available for sublimation, and from "above," inasmuch as scientific and artistic activity absorbs sexual energy. Thus we have the history and structure (*Characterbilde*) of the "research type" of which Leonardo (and, of course, Freud) is the prototype. Moreover, this clinical portrait must be "seen" to stand alongside the great art and literary portraits of the world; for such, I believe, is Freud's own ambition. Indeed, every clinical portrait by Freud is at the same time a portrait of Freud himself.

Having sketched his theory of sublimation, Freud can now return to his research sources on Leonardo's early life in order to locate the template for Leonardo's passion for one woman (Mona Lisa) and for the perfect two-mother/child relationship (Saint Anne with the Madonna and Child) in the details of Leonardo's father (Ser Piero da Vinci not having married his mother, Caterina, but Donna Albiera, and she having later taken Leonardo into her house). These experiences were sufficient to overdetermine Leonardo's destiny for research inasmuch as they mobilized quite early the child's "infantile sexual researches" (*infantilen Sexualforschung*) into the origins of babies, the myth of the stork, and the child's own premature theorizing of anal/fecal birth. The necessary defeat of these inquiries set up a period of sexual repression and opens the "instinct for research" *(Forschertriebe)* into three possible paths:

1. neurotic inhibition—inhibited curiosity, overlayed by religion and education;
2. sexualized thinking—brooding, overlayed with sexual pleasure and anxiety;
3. sublimated homosexuality—research activity driven by unrepressed but sublimated sexual energy.

Thus Freud claims Leonardo's soul for psychoanalysis by inscribing the psychoanalytic theory of sexuality upon the sketchy biographical details of the da Vinci family. Since Freud was so extremely excited about this possibility—his overexcitement in fact attaches him to several egregious errors of interpretation and translation that he nevertheless obstinately enshrines in the Leonardo essay—we must expand upon what drove him to his conclusions. Rather than impatiently dismiss the Leonardo study for its flawed art criticism (Maclagen 1923; Shapiro 1956) and let the issue of Freud's theory of infant sexuality sink with it, we must understand that the psychoanalytic theory of sexuality is in fact a *theory of mind* and as such it is what emboldens Freud in his peculiar approach to Leonardo's genius. To be sure, once we have explicated this claim, we shall return to the question of Freud's transgressions in the case of Leonardo's work and biography (Bass 1985; Elms 1988).

The major research question raised with respect to childhood memory—and thus the larger issue of psychobiography—is, How is sexual knowledge grafted upon the child's early sexual experience? To anticipate somewhat, How does Freud inscribe the sexualized body's experience of itself and other sexual bodies with a reflexive cognitive inquiry that is operative at the very origins of sexual awareness? In *Three Essays on Sexuality* (1905) Freud had introduced a cognitive drive (*Wisstrieb*) operative with the sexual instincts but exceeding them due to a capacity for *sublimation.* The same formulation is broached in the Leonardo essay where, as we have seen, Freud refers variously to a knowledge drive

(*Wissendrang*), an instinct for independent research (*Selbständiger Forschertrieb*) and a desire for knowledge (*Wissbegierde*). The cognitive drive appears to be both a component of the sexual drives and a supplement to the elementary drives destined to elaborate a cohesive economy of the partial drives. Thus the cognitive drive arises out of the infantile sexual history in which it originates and achieves a certain independence from it. Yet Freud speaks of the infantile sexual theorist's knowledge as largely absorbed in sexual curiosity *and* as knowledge that is virtually (i.e., potentially) independent of its origins in infantile sexuality. In Freud's text there is hardly any staging of these two dimensions of the cognitive drive, so that we have to consider *how* Freud understood the body's openness to knowledge, since his conception is remarkable for its avoidance of both Platonic and Cartesian dualism on the question.

In 1923 Freud returned to the historical schema he had employed in *Three Essays on the Theory of Sexuality* (1905) in order to revise its dependence on a simplified shaping of the sexual life of children and adults:

> Today I should no longer be satisfied with the statement that in the early period of childhood the primacy of the genitals has been effected only very incompletely or not at all. The approximation of the child's sexual life to that of the adult goes much further and is not limited solely to the coming into being of the choice of an object. Even if a proper combination of the component instincts under the primacy of the genitals is not effected, nevertheless, at the height of the course of development of infantile sexuality, interest in the genitals and in their activity acquires a dominating significance which falls little short of that reached in maturity. At the same time, the main characteristic of this "infantile genital organization" is its *difference* from the final genital organization of the adult. This consists in the fact that, for both sexes, only one genital, therefore, is not a primacy of the genitals, but a primacy of the *phallus.* (*SE* 19:142, and Penguin Freud Library 7:308)

In effect, Freud argues that sexual difference is located with the same intensity in children as adults but that the infant is obliged to think sexual difference with *his* body; that is, from the standpoint of the phallus, which he attributes to everyone around him. The infantile sexual theorist is a devotee of the half-truth of sexuality, we might say! Because of the inextricable overlap of insight and blindness (or disavowal, *Verleugnung*) generated by the infant project of the phallus, he is launched on the path toward adult sexuality from the very start of his experiences of

sexual curiosity aroused in a gendered world whose double sexual organization he systematically overlooks, yet half suspects.

The distinction between the genital and pre-genital phases of infant
sexuality, therefore, overrides the distinction between infant and adult
sexuality, while nevertheless remaining open to this final determination.
In other words, the sexual instincts are never shut up in a stage-specific
interaction. Human sexuality is historical and reflexive from its very
origin. But this means that human knowledge originates with the *sexual
body* that it is destined to think.

However, we have still to discern how Freud himself rethinks the infant
sexual drives. We find him introducing a distinction between the
erogeneity of the genital experienced in autoeroticism and its perverse
seductive experience when grafted with the outline of the Other as the
figure of the supplement of genitalized sexuality and seduction. Whereas
the operation of a drive (*Trieb*) is incapable of either self-awareness or of
any awareness of its object, in the infantile sexual drive there is outlined a
reflexivity from the sexual world of others whose original effect is, so to
speak, a seduction or perversion of the partial drive:

> Moreover, the effects of seduction do not help to reveal the early
> history of the sexual instinct; they rather confuse our view of it by
> presenting children prematurely with a sexual object for which
> the infantile sexual instinct at first shows no need. It must, how-
> ever, be admitted that infantile sexual life, in spite of the prepon-
> derating dominance of erotogenic zones, exhibits components
> which from the very first involve other people as sexual objects.
> Such are the instincts of scopophilia, exhibitionism and cruelty,
> which appear in a sense independently of erotogenic zones; these
> instincts do not enter into intimate relations with genital life until
> later, but are already to be observed in childhood as independent
> impulses, distinct in the first instance from erotogenic sexual
> activity. Small children are essentially without shame, and at some
> periods of their earliest years show an unmistakable satisfaction in
> exposing their bodies, with especial emphasis on the sexual parts.
> The counterpart of this supposedly perverse inclination, curiosity
> to see other people's genitals, probably does not become manifest
> until somewhat later in childhood, when the obstacle set up by a
> sense of shame has already reached a certain degree of develop-
> ment. (*SE* 7:191–92, and Penguin Freud Library 7:109–10)

It is important to understand that here Freud's seduction theory involves the reworking of the inside/outside of the infant body within the

outside/inside frame of other/self relations as the ultimate frame of genital sexuality, which, so to speak, awaits each of us until we recognize it. In this aspect, we already fantasize our own seduction long before we enter into it. It is the violation of this eventual articulation of our sexuality with the world of gendered others that constitutes a child seduction. Freud's seduction theory properly contains this double history so that the event of a seduction/rape constitutes the violation of originary sexuality of the victim.

The infant sexual theorist is oriented toward a world in which she is known by others around her but does not know what they know of genital sexuality. At the same time, the infant is not totally excluded from sexual knowledge since the partial drives orient her toward its acquisition as an investigative body surrounded by sexual bodies that are engaged in a double game of withholding and spilling their secret. The infant theorist suspects what everyone knows and is suspected of such precocious initiation. Thus in asking, "Where do babies come from?" the infant articulates the censored answer as the point around which adult sexuality is organized but withheld between generations that are nevertheless held to the same knowledge. By the same token, the infant demand for *knowledge about origins* is the *origin of knowledge*. It arises out of the infant's interest in the event of a sibling birth and his concern over the possible scarcity of affection that this event may portend inasmuch as it casts the shadow of a rival on the parental level as well as in the sibling order. The cognitive drive is therefore grounded in an existential rather than a purely speculative event such as the Sphinx's question; it derives from the infant's surmise that his anxieties are generated by his progenitors. Thus his question, Where do babies come from? does not arise out of ignorance but rather articulates his sexual knowledge as a demand upon the generations articulated in each generation. By the same token, it opens up the intergenerational space of child sexuality in a covenant with adult sexuality so that neither side is uniquely the sexual object of the other.

We might say that the infant sexual question opens the partial drives to an intersubjective sexuality by opening the body of drives to the body of sexuality, of knowledgeable and discursive sex. From this perspective, it is impossible to experience oneself or the other self as either a subject or an object of sexual knowledge without the corporeal overlapping of interior and exterior worlds in the embodied world at play around us. Again, the question of origins awakens the child to the possibility that his parents gave birth to others as well as himself and thereby to himself like others so that his discovery is properly one about the grammar of kinship in a gendered world that is "good" both for thought and feeling. For in raising a question of the parents under the impetus of the arrival of a sibling, the infant in fact asks for knowledge on the level of the parents vis-à-vis the *infans* who will later on come into the same question. The question of origins is therefore the origin of the closing of the generations opened up by the act of procreation.

For the infant, sexual knowledge is the knowledge he supposes the parent has and withholds from him at the same time he must appropriate it for himself—yet under pain of such precocious interests! In this predicament the infant is driven to think sexual difference in terms of the phallic body that immediately forces upon him the experience of the body-without-a-phallus. To repair the phallic generalization, he will disavow perception (of the female genital) and save his theory with the concept of castration (female event; male possibility). However this disavowal is not due to the infant's phallic generalization of the value of his own penis but to his sense that the question, Where do babies come from? must have something to do with the question of sexual difference. What is experienced by the presence/absence of the penis is an inability to integrate sexual difference and generation; that is, a *splitting* of the subject of sexual difference.

Thus the infant's alimentary, excretory, and sadistic theories of procreation represent attempts to shift gendered procreation into a parthogenesis in order to suspend the anxiety of the divided self—and to repay the debt owed with birth (O'Neill, 1996). Here is the limit of the fantasy of origins; that is, to reconceive the origin of the fantasy. One must be born, one must feel, one must speak, one must think. Because of this, one is never fully oneself, never wholly male, never wholly female, never whole.

Whereas many of the preceding comments might lead us into the aura of Leonardo's great Madonnas, we are obliged to return to Freud's passion to locate the single textual place that will once and for all ground his postulate that the key to Leonardo's genius is his ideal sublimated homosexuality:

> It seems that I was always destined to be so deeply concerned with vultures; for I recall as one of my very earliest memories that while I was in my cradle a vulture came down to me, and opened my mouth with its tail, and struck me many times with its tail against my lips. (*SE* 11:82, and Penguin Freud Library 14:172)

Freud's tack is to display his own research talent by drawing our attention to the one place in Leonardo's notebooks where he leaves the trace of a childhood memory:

Fig. 3.   Mut (Néith). (From J.-F. Champollion, *Panthéon Egyptien: Collection des personnages mythologiques de l'Ancienne Egypte* [Paris: Perséa, 1986], plate 6).

What we have here then is a childhood memory; and certainly one of the strangest sort. It is strange on account of its content and on account of the age to which it is assigned. That a person should be able to retain a memory of his suckling period is perhaps not impossible, but it cannot by any means be regarded as certain. What, however, this memory of Leonardo's asserts—namely that a vulture opened the child's mouth with its tail—sounds so improbable, so fabulous, that another view of it, which at a single stroke puts an end to both difficulties, has more to commend it to our judgement. On this view the scene with the vulture would not be a memory of Leonardo's but a phantasy, which he formed at a later date and transposed to his childhood. (*SE* 11:82, and Penguin Freud Library 14: 172–73)

To make anything of this fragment, Freud has first to dismiss the impossibility of retaining memories from the cradle—even though that is the direction he wanted to push psychoanalysis (O'Neill 1992c). He does so by revising the "memory" as a fantasy formed later but transposed to the cradle scene. Freud—harking back to his own relation with his mother (*Sig(is)mund*, the omen in the mouth)—suggests that what is involved is a mother's story of an "omen": the bird that visits a child, which Leonardo for "some secret reason" kept in mind, supplying the detail of the bird's movement and himself (*not* Freud) "dubbing" the bird a vulture whereas it was a kite! Even so, we must press on with the larger puzzle behind the detail that psychoanalysis never lets go, however much it may disgust us (dear readers). Thus what the detail of the bird-tail (*coda*) attempts to conceal is

> (a) the tail as a symbol for the male organ;
> (b) an act of *fellatio*

in short, the residues of a universal experience of "the first source of pleasure in our life," and thus hardly something we should encounter with disgust either in ourselves or in Leonardo's case:

> Now we understand why Leonardo assigned the memory of his supposed experience with the vulture to his suckling period. What the phantasy conceals is merely a reminiscence of sucking—or being suckled—at his mother's breast, a scene of human beauty that he, like so many artists, undertook to depict with his brush, in the guise of the mother of God and her child. There is indeed another point which we do not yet understand and which we must not lose sight of: this reminiscence, which has the same importance for both sexes, has been transformed by the man Leonardo into a passive homosexual phantasy. For the time being we shall put aside the question of what there may be to connect homosexuality with sucking at the mother's breast, merely recalling that tradition does in fact represent Leonardo as a man with homosexual feelings. (*SE* 11:87, and Penguin Freud Library 14:177–78)

Yet our thirst for knowledge is not yet slaked until we can fix upon the "translation" of the kite into a vulture. Freud, certainly, cannot resist the hunt; especially since it leads him into his beloved Egypt (Rosenfeld 1956) and to another of his heroes, Champollion (1986), the first man to decode hieroglyphics. Freud leaps onto the slide of signifiers:

Fig. 4. Leonardo da Vinci, *Virgin and Child with Saint Anne*. (From Ludwig Goldscheider, *Leonardo da Vinci: The Artist* [London: Phaidon Press, 1951]), plate 93).

Fig. 5.   Picture Puzzle: Sigmund Freud, Leonardo da Vinci, and a Memory of
History Childhood, in *The Standard Edition of the Complete Psychological Works
of Sigmund Freud* (London: Hogarth, 1957), page 116.

Vulture:*Mut*   :   *Nibbio*:Mother

Vultures are a self-impregnating female-species (Horapollo, *Hieroglyphica*)

Mut is represented as a female figure with breasts and a male organ in a state of erection (Roscher's *Lexicon of Greek and Roman Mythology*)

What history and mythology retain for us is also retained in the infantile sexual memory, namely, that once upon a time the mother-body must have been phallic and that her child had rested in this divine plenitude until it was broken into by the father who became the wayward Law of a Second Creation. Such is the story we are asked to read in Leonardo's divine Madonnas, at once satisfying our understanding of his art and our science of its origins:

> If it is true that the unintelligible memories of a person's child-hood and the phantasies that are built on them invariably empha-size the most important elements in his mental development, then it follows that the fact which the vulture phantasy confirms, namely that Leonardo spent the first years of his life alone with his mother, will have been of decisive influence in the formation of his inner life. An inevitable effect of this state of affairs was that the child—who was confronted in his early life with one problem more than other children—began to brood on this riddle with special intensity, and so at a tender age became a researcher, tormented as he was by the great question of where do babies come from and what the father has to do with their origin. It was a vague suspicion that his researches and the history of his child-hood were connected in this way which later prompted him to exclaim that he had been destined from the first to investigate the problem of the flight of birds since he had been visited by a vulture as he lay in his cradle. Later on it will not be difficult to show how his curiosity about the flight of birds was derived from the sexual researches of his childhood. (*SE* 11:92, and Penguin Freud Library 14:182–83)

But Freud's own flight of imagination has had its wings severely clipped, even though the theory still flies with Eissler and others (Eissler 1961; Wohl and Trossman 1955; Stites 1970). Freud's mishandling of the conventions of religious art (Baxandall 1972) cannot be overlooked, any more than his mistreatment of certain facts in Leonardo's biography and his opportunistic use of Reitler (1917) on the coital drawing and Pfister (1913) on the vulture form in the garment of Mary. Here Freud's ambition of capturing mythology and biography for psychoanalysis involved him in great transgressions of the impartiality owed to knowledge. In particular here, as elsewhere, Freud was claiming priority vis-à-vis Jung (O'Neill 1992a) and callously promoting the extraordinarily suggestive perception of Pfister over Jung's more learned but rival accounts of mythology.

This is not the occasion to develop Freud's full commentary upon the Mona Lisa and Saint Anne with the Madonna and Child except from the standpoint of Freud's insistence on what it is that makes them "uniquely" Leonardo's work. I am referring to Freud's psychoanalytic claim that the family events in Leonardo's childhood aroused in him an obsession with the lost "Kissing-pleasures" exchanged between an abandoned young mother and her child—and that this lost-object is encrypted forever on the magical smile across the two paintings and in the vulture emblem of the *Notebooks* and the Madonna's skirts:

> The painting of Leonardo's which stands nearest to the Mona Lisa in point of time is the so-called "St. Anne with Two Others," St. Anne with the Madonna and Child. In it the Leonardesque smile is most beautifully and markedly portrayed on both the women's faces. It is not possible to discover how long before or after the painting of the Mona Lisa Leonardo began to paint this picture. As both works extended over years, it may, I think, be assumed that the artist was engaged on them at the same time. It would best agree with our expectations if it was the intensity of Leonardo's preoccupation with the features of Mona Lisa which stimulated him to create the composition of St. Anne out of his phantasy. For if the Gioconda's smile called up in his mind the memory of his mother, it is easy to understand how it drove him at once to create a glorification of motherhood, and to give back to his mother the smile he had found in the noble lady. We may therefore permit our interest to pass from Mona Lisa's portrait to this other picture—one which is hardly less beautiful, and which today also hangs in the Louvre. (*SE* 11:111–12, and Penguin Freud Library 14:204)

"*Die Geierphantasie Leonardos halt uns noch immer fest.*" Freud, indeed, found it impossible to renege upon the vulture fantasy that again and again he insists upon attributing to Leonardo. So taken was he by his own invention that he inscribed it once and for all in the text on Leonardo (Footnote added 1919) in a perverse play upon his disciple Pfister's (1913) offering of an "unconscious picture puzzle" (*unbewusstes Vexierbild*)

Freud's Leonardo essay is by and large a flight of fancy, a grotesque combination of knowledge and delusion. I have tried to present the essay along with its permanent blemishes because I believe it nevertheless contains a serious research claim that the development of mind necessarily entails the sexualization of thinking in the early stages where, provided the infant is not subject to overwhelming repression, the sublimation of early sexual curiosity will later blossom into an intellectual capacity for art and science. Freud feared that he may have left us nothing more than a psychoanalytic novel rather than a true biography of Leonardo. But I believe Freud's modesty in this regard barely cloaks his less modest claim to have grounded our passion for knowledge without separating us from error by means, for example, of any such extraordinary machine as that of "Descartes' doubt" (O'Neill, 1992b).

REFERENCES

Baxandall, Michael. 1972. *Painting and Experience in Fifteenth-Century Italy.* Oxford: Clarendon Press.

Bass, Alan. 1985. "On the History of a Mistranslation and the Psychoanalytic Movement." In *Difference in Translation,* edited and with an introduction by Joseph F. Graham, 102–41. Ithaca: Cornell University Press.

Champollion, J.-F. 1986. *Panthéon Egyptien: Collection des personnages mythologiques de L'Ancienne Egypte.* Paris: Perséa.

Clayton, Martin. 1992. *Leonardo da Vinci: The Anatomy of Man. With Commentaries on Anatomy by Ron Philo.* Boston: Little, Brown.

Eissler, K. 1961. *Leonardo da Vinci: Psychoanalytic Notes on the Enigma.* New York: International Universities Press.

Elms, Alan C. 1988. "Freud as Leonardo: Why the First Psychobiography Went Wrong." *Journal of Personality* 56, no. 1:19–40.

Freud, Sigmund. 1905. *Three Essays on the Theory of Sexuality. SE* 7:125–243, and Penguin Freud Library 7:33–170.

———. 1910. *Leonardo da Vinci and A Memory of His Childhood. SE* 11:59–137, and Penguin Freud Library 14:143–231.

———. 1923. "The Infantile Genital Organization: An Interpolation into *The Theory of Sexuality,*" *SE* 19:141–48, and Penguin Freud Library 7:303–12.

Kemp, Martin. 1981. *Leonardo da Vinci: The Marvellous Works of Nature and Man.* Cambridge: J. M. Dent.

Maclagen, Eric. 1923. "Leonardo in the Consulting Room." *Burlington Magazine* 42:51–54.

O'Neill, John. 1992a. "Law and Gynesis: Freud v. Schreber." In *Shadow of Spirit: Postmodernism and Religion,* edited by Philippa Berry and Andrew Wernick, 238–49. London: Routledge.

———. 1992b. "Mecum Meditari: Descartes Demolishing Doubt, Building a Prayer." In his *Critical Conventions: Interpretation in the Literary Arts and Sciences,* 222–33. Norman: University of Oklahoma Press.

———. 1992c. "Science and Founding Self: Freud's Paternity Suit in the Case of the Wolf Man." In his *Critical Conventions: Interpretation in the Literary Arts and Sciences,* 234–48. Norman: University of Oklahoma Press.

———. 1996. *The Domestic Economy of the Soul: Freud's Five Case Histories.*

Pfister, Oskar. 1913. "Kryptolalie, Kryptographie und unbewusstes Vexierbild bei Normalen." *Jahrbuch für psychoanalytische und psychopathologische Forschung:* 146–51.

Reitler, R. 1917. "Eine anatomisch-künstlerische Fehlleistung Leonardos da Vinci." *Internationale Zeitschrift für Psychoanalyse* 4:205–7.

Richter, Irma A., ed. 1952. *Selections from the Notebooks of Leonardo da Vinci, with Commentaries.* London: The World's Classics.

Rosenfeld, Eva M. 1956. "Dreams and Vision: Some Remarks on Freud's Egyptian Bird Dream." *International Journal of Psychoanalysis* 37:97–105.

Shapiro, Meyer. 1955–56. "One Slip of Leonardo and Slip of Freud." *Psychoanalysis* 4:3–8.

———. 1956. "Leonardo and Freud: An Art Historical Study." *Journal of the History of Ideas* 17, no. 2:147–78.

Stites, Raymond S. 1948. "A Criticism of Freud's Leonardo." *College Art Journal* 7:257–67.

———. 1970. *The Sublimation of Leonardo da Vinci, with a Translation of the Codex Trivulzianus.* Washington, D.C.: Smithsonian Institution.

Trosman, H. 1985. "Comparative Views of Leonardo da Vinci and Psychoanalytic Biography." In his *Freud and the Imaginative World,* 148–72. Hillsdale, N.J.: Analytic Press.

Wohl, R. R., and H. Trosman. 1955. "A Retrospect of Freud's Leonardo." *Psychiatry* 18:27–39.

Wollheim, Richard. 1973. "Freud and the Understanding of Art." In his *On Art and the Mind: Essays and Lectures,* 202–20. London: Allen Lane.

Vasari, Giorgio. 1962. *The Essential Vasari: Biographies of the Most Eminent Architects, Painters, and Sculptors of Italy,* edited by Betty Burroughs. London: Unwin.

11

Digging Psychoanalysis

LAURENCE A. RICKELS

Freud[1] was telling us to put on our Freudian ears when he announced to his disciples that his Judaism, cigar smoking, and interest in the occult should be kept separate from the science of psychoanalysis.[2] Along the margin of his science, where the name is signed, Freud signs off with three passions that are admitted into his own case. Which of the three goes with and organizes the other two? Thematic readers have been pressing for Judaism, which is indeed, in implicit and excluded ways, at once hidden and preserved inside psychoanalysis. Certainly Freud's follow-up, from Jung to Lacan, represents a Christianization of the unconscious. But this secular/circular trajectory of the Jewish part of Freud's science already conforms to the most basic structure of melancholia (right down to the invitation Freud thus issued to identify via this un-Jewish science with the Jews, who are, however, at the same time eliminated). Can Freud's investment in the occult be convincingly historicized as the subset or even displacement of a disowned commitment to his Judaism? The cigar smoking certainly falls by the wayside of this margin, at best like one of the jokes through which Freud flexes his ethnicity. But both Freud's speculations on the origin of Judaism, for example, and his joking refusal to speculate on the phallic symbolization of his smoking habit are subsumed by the course of Freud's occult spookulations, which take us deep down inside what Freud called "the underworld of psychoanalysis."[3] This is the other place covered by psychoanalysis to which Freud's struggle with the concept of mourning guides us. It is *unmourning* that holds the margin Freud wrote off, a margin, however, that is the cutting edge of where psychoanalysis begins.

In "Transience" Freud declared mourning the central problem or riddle with which the psychologist must come to grips: "Mourning over the loss of something that we loved or admired, appears to the layman so natural, that he takes it for granted. To the psychologist, however, mourning is a vast riddle, one of those phenomena which can itself not be explained but to which other obscurities can be attributed."[4] And yet, as Freud instructs in "Our Relation to Death," the practice of these inscrutable mourning rituals remains indispensable, since the mourner's own survival—indeed, the continuation and growth of culture—would be imperiled if the period of mourning, approximately two years in duration, did not come to some definite conclusion.

Our first reaction upon the death of a loved one issues in the wish to die along with the departed. And yet already alongside this first spontaneous upsurge of solidarity, Freud adds, we also admire—and thus keep our distance from—the one who, in going on ahead, has accomplished a difficult feat. The original refusal to substitute for loss, which in turn reflects a deadlock brought on by sorrow's instant ambivalent supplementation, must itself find substitution. As Freud concludes: without proper burial of its casualties, life can only become shallow and insubstantial, "like an American flirt." The unbearable intensity of grief arising from paralyzing contemplation of irreplaceable relations would have barred man from engaging in "attempts at mechanical flight, expeditions to distant lands, and experiments with explosive substances" (*SE* 14:289–300; *SA* 9:49–60).

The neurotic impasse reflects and reverses the outcome of its primal scene: the premier passing of a loved one. Unlike the slain enemy, who bears the sheer target of exteriority, the dead loved one covers two registers to the point of bringing confusion to the distinction between life and death. Since the dearly departed is at the same time other, he remains alien and inimical; but he also takes with him what he always reflected back or embodied: the most cherished extension and part of the survivor. Following the original departure of someone close, primal man, doubled over with the first bout of ambivalence, conceived spirits and other forms of afterlife and thus anticipated, for the first time, the need to mourn. While primal man's terrible grief gave rise to the premier speculations of psychological thought, modern man's ambivalent reception of death produces, in isolation from any channel or outlet of occult or psychological reflection, only neurosis.

Enter psychoanalysis, the exploratory allegorization of the psyche in terms of Psyche, bride of death. And yet, by all accounts, psychoanalysis penetrated the underworld only to excavate and commemorate the father, and never to the point of bringing back a lost object; an object that, since capable of being lost, would not be paternal. With melancholia, Freud argued, the object is given up and the object-cathexis brought to an end; but the free libido, which is not displaced onto another object as the work of mourning demands, is withdrawn into the ego, where it serves to establish "an *identification* of the ego with the abandoned object" (*SE* 14:249; *SA* 3:203). Since the first or primal identification is always with the father (*SE* 19:31; *SA* 3:299), even melancholia remains, for Freud, lodged inside that substitutive economy of symbolic positions organized around the father, who, according to psychoanalysis, is already his own shadow when alive and then, once dead, is broadcast live. This substitutive economy, which guarantees that death will introduce no loss into the family that adoption—of the name—cannot replace, finds its backup support in the work of mourning, which puts to rest and replaces what is already at rest.

Freud always addressed the phantasmic consequences of improper burial in the course of elaborating the mechanism of projection. And yet, like a projection, the concept of projection was never analyzed inside "Mourning and Melancholia." In *Totem and Taboo* Freud explained that the ghosts and demons that haunt so-called savages are dead people who have not been properly mourned; according to the interlocked logics of ambivalence and projection, the hostility the dead, while still alive, had aroused in the still living is attributed to the phantoms of the deceased who now persecute the survivors. Without any conception of natural death these savages, like children, cannot but view the dead as murder victims who, because never at rest, must be avenged or appeased (*SE* 13:59; *SA* 9:350).

In *Totem and Taboo* Freud announced that haunting belongs in the movies: it is the projection of hostile feelings harbored even against someone close who goes away. The death of someone close is that close call that always and originally summons the first ghosts just as it creates for the first time the need to mourn. In the savage and childhood context, where there is no conception of natural death or departure—to go is to be a goner struck down by death wishes—every dead person ends up, Freud instructs, a vampire. The premier and primal response on the part of the survivor of "the nearest and dearest" is to project onto the animated image or corpse death wishes that come into focus up close as vampiric; in the long shot, at the other end of mourning, as worthy of some ancestral spirit or friendly ghost.

Even the most ancient theories of ghosts see the specter as a dead person who has been improperly buried, or to whom performance of mourning rituals and presentation of sacrificial offerings are still owed. The dead person's soul must be appeased; otherwise his phantom will return to take vengeance. Robert Burton was not alone in linking the imagination affected by melancholia to the legends of ghosts, vampires, and devils he collected as integral part of his *Anatomy of Melancholy*. But whereas Burton reserved in his vast compendium of theories and legends of melancholia one subsection for discussion of mourning disorders, Freud addressed melancholia as in essence a form of mourning. Freud's divergence from the long history of speculation on the consequences and causes of excess of black bile is thus announced in the very title of the essay: mourning *and* melancholia.

At the same time, however, Freud disconnected the telepathic call from the phantom realm only to take and answer this call in zones of theorizing that did not directly address mourning and aberrations of mourning. By keeping the theory of ghosts separate from his theory of mourning, Freud did not accord a place in his redefinition of melancholia to that which is genuinely improper to mourning. In Freud's essay the catastrophe of another's death summons mourner and melancholic alike while turning them apart: the loss that afflicts the former is conscious, whereas the occasion for the latter's interminable grieving is kept in the unconscious. Which reception of loss will be available depends upon the channel of the original object choice. Thus Freud agrees with Otto Rank that whereas the mourner disengages his ego from an object loved for its separateness and otherness, the melancholic discards a narcissistic choice by consummating the ego's rapport with this cherished object through identification, internalization, and idealization. Hence the mourner feels impoverished but not degraded, such extraordinary lowering of self-esteem being precisely the melancholic's plight.

Freud assigns work to be accomplished if libidinal investments are not to be lost; when loss of object disengages libido, substitution can be effected immediately or the detached libidinal cathexis "can return for a time to the ego" (*SE* 14:306; *SA* 10:226). Introjection and identification, the support systems of mourning that effect this return, have incorporation as corporeal, literal, or primal model: the ego "wishes to incorporate the object in a manner commensurate with the oral or cannibalistic phase of libido development, namely by devouring it" (*SE* 14:249; *SA* 3:203). Melancholia thus retains what is otherwise devoured, assimilated, and expelled by the mourning body.

Mania in turn confirms by reversing this retentive tendency of melancholia. A "festival of liberation" according to Karl Abraham, mania celebrates the ego's sudden triumph over both ego ideal and the once-loved, lost, and subsequently introjected object. Whereas in melancholia the ego is vampirized by the introjected object, in mania libido turns with ravenous hunger to the external world of objects; whatever appears before the manic's rapidly advancing probe is swallowed. But this pleasurable swallowing during the manic phase, which succeeds the melancholic's sense that he is excluded from the world of objects as though disinherited, corresponds to an equally rapid, equally pleasurable expulsion of the briefly retained objects and impressions.

In mania, then, incorporation takes over the controls of the perceptual apparatus it puts on fast-forward, thereby animating the divergent "metabolisms" that keep mourning and melancholia apart.[5] The speed and excess of mania thus anesthetize without terminating the pain of mourning. That the detachment of libido from its annihilated objects should be such a painful process, and that the libido should cling to its objects rather than relinquish them when lost, even when a surrogate is available, remained for Freud the most puzzling feature of mourning (*SE* 14:306–7; *SA* 10:226–27). "Mourning has a quite specific psychical task to perform: its function is to detach the survivors' memories and hopes from the dead. When this has been achieved, the pain grows less and with it the remorse and self-reproach" (*SE* 13:65–66; *SA* 9:356). And yet when pressed into the service of mourning, this "work of recollection," as Freud called it in *Studies on Hysteria,* which records only in order to erase, remains the most painful requirement of proper mourning. The separation from the object must be effected at each way station, before each niche within the memorial architecture.

> Mourning occurs under the influence of reality-testing, for the latter function demands categorically from the bereaved person that he should separate himself from the object, since it no longer exists. Mourning is entrusted with the task of carrying out this retreat from the object in all those situations in which it was the recipient of a high degree of cathexis. That this separation should be painful fits in with what we have just said, in view of the high and unsatisfiable cathexis of longing which is concentrated on the object by the bereaved survivor during the reproduction of the situations in which he must undo the ties that bind him to it. (*SE* 20:172; *SA* 6:308)

This inner topography of the lost object must be reassembled outside the mourner in the form of funerary rites and monuments addressed to the idealized dead. Otherwise, live burial in some internal vault must result for both living and dead. An example of successful building in the wake of death was delivered by Freud's son Ernst, who studied architecture before World War I. In a letter to Lou Andreas-Salomé dated 9 November 1915, Freud narrates Ernst's supernatural rescue in the war zone: "He happened to be away from the dug-out where the whole crew in charge of his gun had sought shelter during the battle on the Karst plateau and he was thus the only one to escape the fate of being buried alive by a direct hit." Nine days later, again in a letter to Andreas-Salomé, Freud can bring the story of accident and chance to a successful close: "The news from the front is good. My son has been invited to design the memorial for his troop; this will no doubt have been his first job as an architect."

Around this now external, now internal monument, for which premature burial serves as the occasion or model, psychoanalytic treatment of countless cases of wartime traumatic neurosis began to push the theories of haunting and melancholia into alignment, though Freud continued to give them equal but separate time. The traumatic neurotic occupies the opening threshold of *Beyond the Pleasure Principle* because he in particular exhibits the compulsion to "repeat the repressed material as a contemporary experience instead of, as the physician would prefer to see, *remembering* it as something belonging to the past" (*SE* 18:19; *SA* 3:228). Thus Ernst Simmel prescribes that, in each case of war neurosis, the "film" of the traumatizing incident must, in place of the missing recollection, be run again: "Through the hypermnesia to which the patient has recourse in hypnosis the experience can be repeated. The 'film' is let roll once again; the patient dreams the whole thing one more time, the sensitized subconscious releases the affect which in turn discharges in an adequate emotional expression and the patient is cured."[6]

On this side of Simmel's media-technical analogy, Freud introduces, in place of a link-up of his different takes on aberrant mourning, the death drive, which points to a beyond of the pleasure principle as of the work of mourning. But on the other side of the analogy with film: only a theory of ghosts can anchor this paradoxical beyond, though in a ground that will always have slipped away from the psychoanalytic theory of pathological mourning. And yet Freud compares repetition compulsion to demoniacal possession and those afflicted by traumatic neurosis to the haunted; because they seem to be under occult influence they are, in fact, "uncanny."

Freud had already reserved for future discussions of traumatic neurosis an analogy doubly registered in the zone of the uncanny. Because this neurosis was always a delayed response to the impact of specific trauma—a train accident, for example, or shell shock—Freud found it fitting to compare the intervening period to one of "incubation" (*SE* 23:67; *SA* 9:516). But alongside its designation of the uncanny stealth of infection, incubation has another meaning. In Ernest Jones's monograph *On the Nightmare,* a work sufficiently present to Freud to pop up as a prop in one of his examples of thought transference (*SE* 22:50; *SA* 1:489), incubation is examined at length in terms of its occult pedigree. Jones plugs incubation back into the incubus it contains: the incubus, which could assume the form of some animal in order to have intercourse with a living person sleeping in sacred precincts, was either the ghost of a departed ancestor or himself a god. The deep sleep that left one pregnant, often with prophecy (though most frequently with the actual offspring of phantoms), was called incubation.

To describe the secret, internal repository and meeting place that takes the place of proper mourning, Nicolas Abraham and Maria Torok set incorporation aside, at one end from cannibalistic identification with father, at the other from introjection.[7] Whereas introjection covers a metaphorical ingestion and digestion enabling the subject to internalize and comprehend objects that are discarded before they are lost, incorporation demetaphorizes this process, yielding the fantasy of an actual consumption of the lost object, which is kept not only isolated and concealed but even sealed off in a separate portion of the ego. Only in this way can the topography that loss would otherwise have displaced be conserved. The corpse thus remains inside the mourning body, though as a stranger, a living dead encrypted in a specific place in the ego. Inasmuch as this internal crypt is haunted by the phantom of the deceased, who has not been laid to rest, it doubles as transmitter through which the phantom teleguides the crypt carrier, who guards with his life its undead remains.

THE JULIUS CAESAR COMPLEX

But Freud can render the bond with the father the model of all mourning sickness only by keeping the mother in the shadow—as the shadow—of the moving target. Freud's first mention of aberrant mourning can thus be found lodged inside his first rehearsal of the Oedipus complex, which emerges as an Oedipal theory of grief: "It seems as though in sons this death wish is directed against their father and in daughters against their mother."[8] Customarily repressed upon the death of one's parents, the death wish, Freud continues, can nevertheless assert itself as a substitute for mourning. The survivor who thus believes that he has brought about the death of his parents administers self-reproach and even self-punishment, which he effects through a form of "identification" enabling him to share their fatal illness.

The occasion for such identification is always an unmournable death. In Freud's case the question of mourning or not mourning had first been posed and deposited by an infant mortality in early childhood. When Freud was nineteen months old his eight-month-old brother Julius died; in Julius's departure he had witnessed the realization of hostile impulses harbored against his rival—and god.[9] Within a series of primal recollections centered on his mother we find Freud, shortly after Julius's death, wounding himself in a fall.[10] *Trauer* (mourning) bears not only etymological association with falling, dropping, or casting down. The fall in the wake of Julius's departure left behind on Freud's face a permanent scar. The analogy with an "open wound" which Freud draws already in 1895 and later in "Mourning and Melancholia" to describe the way in which melancholia empties out the ego, remains, as the legacy of a dead child and sibling, the most vulnerable point of articulation in Freud's corpus. In a manuscript forwarded to Fliess on 7 January 1895, Freud first touched on the "wound" of melancholia. On Freud's internal scanner the inward turn of the melancholic's psychic apparatus comes into focus as an "indrawing process" or "internal bleeding" that, "in a manner analogous to pain," "operates like a wound." The "open wound" of melancholia that Freud first discloses in his correspondence with Fliess—and thus alongside his only open reference to Julius's passing—encircles an indrawing process or suction effect that doubles, at another end of its inward turn, as uncanny harbinger of Freud's cancer. The beard that identification with the father always grows covered over the scar from earliest childhood, and, after the close shave of each operation on his cancer, re-covered a traumatic origin of identification the paternal bond could not double *and* contain. The departure that leaves behind a wound that is also always, Freud confides to Fliess, "a seed of reproach," remains the primal model of Freud's theory of projection, which found its first rehearsal alongside explorations of media-technological delusions and their analogue or model: belief in ghosts. What first rebounded from the double point of impact were the *revenants* or phantoms Freud acknowledged right off, though only to the extent that he found them haunting, via transference, his closest friendships.[11]

When in *Totem and Taboo* Freud attributes the haunted rapport with

the dead—whose wind-carried seed, it is believed, remains responsible
for every pregnancy—to societies governed by matrilineal descent, he
names, though again in a context kept separate from his exploration of
melancholia, the double agent who, in the midst of hardened survivors,
also serves the interests of the dead (*SE* 13:105; *SA* 9:392). The mother is
always in a position to hide secret treasure in her child's body which she
has trained, arranged, and mapped out; she can thus deposit the unmourned corpse of one of her children in the body of another little one
who survives. The mourning that never took place is covertly and am-
biguously entrusted to a surviving child who must carry a dead sibling
and mourn in the mother's place. Whether on behalf of a dead child or in
her own absence, the mother advertises a solution that is edible, not
Oedipal. Right from the start the mother is her child's *Lebensmittel,* at
once "medium of life" and "nourishment." Karl Abraham accordingly
emphasizes that, whereas in most neurotic conditions the father is the
focus and recipient of hostile tendencies, in melancholia it is invariably
the mother who attracts the ambivalent cannibalistic impulse. Because
the trauma of loss casts the melancholic back to the early age or stage to
which he thus ever returns, repression cannot frame him for an Oedipal
past.[12] The mother alone can be received, in this stricken world, as the
melancholic's premier and perpetual station of identification.

On a train trip taken at the time of little Julius's passing Freud received
the unmourning assignment from his mother. In the compartment he saw
her for the first time nude: he looked out the window (a look through
moving frames which Freud would later direct analysts to provide their
patients as analogy for the inside view of transference that can then be
more readily described in session)[13] and saw smokestacks which he, fast on
the intake, took to be souls burning in some underworld.[14] The mother's
naked inability to sustain Julius on her own person installed the projection
booth inside little Freud. (Freud's uncle Julius, his mother's brother, died at
the time she sought to retain him in the reproduction re-cycle.)

Born, like Julius right after him, an uncle, Freud had as his first play-
mates and object-choices among his peers in age his own nephew and
niece, John and Pauline Freud. The niece was later offered to Freud in
marriage, allegedly to encourage replacement of his unprofitable intellectual pursuits with more practical ones. The offer of the niece represents
a recurrent temptation, which Freud would always resist, to enter the
death cult shaped by melancholic annihilation. Karl Abraham argues that
the incestuous attachment to cousin or niece is the libidinally impoverished choice of the melancholic, the melancholic conceived, that is, as

one who mourns his lost libido.[15] According to Abraham, in those families in which such intermarriage occurs perennial bachelors abound; to marry the niece, for example, is tantamount to marrying not at all.

According to Ernest Jones, the Pauline episode not only rehearses and repeats Freud's first experience of love in adolescence, but also already gathers fantasy momentum in early childhood as the wish or command to rape imperiled Pauline.[16] This primal fantasy had been one of gang-rape conducted together with John. It was talk of corpses and name effacement, however, that prompted Freud to recognize the reincarnation of his rapport with John in his relation to Jung. In addition to being, obviously, a way of sleeping with the person at hand, the dead faint that invariably followed Freud's recognition of John in Jung also represents, according to Freud, either self-punishment for a death wish or identification with an actual corpse.[17] The only corpse available in time to be covered by both John and Jung was Julius's little one.

It was in the course of his correspondence with Fliess, another repeat of John and recipient, at the time, of Freud's transferences, that Freud first admitted and interpreted the impact on him of Julius's death. (Fliess's dead sister was named Pauline.) In the letter to Fliess dated 3 October 1897, Freud brings Julius's death into microscopic focus on his own person, which he parasurgically opens up or reduces to sheer visibility to provide the inside view of the implant of this death, this dead one inside him: the "seed of reproach." Already on 27 March 1895, Freud could include in his letter to Fliess a citation that leaves out what Freud would ever keep in: "My heart is in the coffin here with Caesar." Freud signs the letter that thus does not bury Julius with his own mutilated, mumbled name: "Your Siegm." Alongside the Oedipus and Hamlet stories, that of Julius Caesar crowds Freud's writing. And yet, unlike Oedipus and Hamlet, Julius Caesar keeps too close to Freud to be admitted into psychoanalysis as its allegorization. As recounted in *The Interpretation of Dreams,* when nephew John returned to Vienna on a visit, he played Caesar to Freud's Brutus before an audience of children (*SE* 5:424–25, 483; *SA* 411–12, 465).

LITTLE HANS NOTE

All phobias of transportation or *Verkehr,* from railway to the street, cover access to the mother's womb, which the dead father alone can gain for, while gaining on, the son. For little Hans this speed race appears sexologically contained: his saving fantasy of marrying his mother and sending his father off to marry his own mother relieves the tension building the phobic symptoms (*SE* 10:97; *SA* 8:86). Displacement goes around and comes around as happy ending because the father's father (the trans-parent figure) is both missing and at the remote controls: his more-than-absence guarantees that this farce, in which, while he's away, all the sons can play, will call curtains on the incestuous retention of the off-limits body. His place is represented by "the Professor," for whom little Hans and his father dictate and write down the case material. The course of the analysis does not rewind the course of the neurosis's development (*SE* 10:83; *SA* 8:74) but constructs *out* of the material heading little Hans off at the impasse a transference neurosis and cure along a three-way freeway. Little Hans pounds this busy street or intersection where his life as a neurotic, the father's recording and programming of his associations, and the Professor's supervision are traffic jamming.

> [father:] 'Once he knocked on the pavement with his stick and said: [little Hans:] "I say, is there a man underneath?—someone buried?—or is that only in the cemetery?"' [Freud:] So he is occupied not only with the riddle of life but with the riddle of death. (*SE* 10:69; *SA* 8:63)

Although he thus knocks at the portals of the anal and footnote underworld where dead sausage children are the internal and eternal occasions for grieving (*SE* 10:131 n. 1; *SA* 8:110 n. 1), each return of the repressed the five-year-old rides out remains always only metaphorically "like an unlaid ghost" (*SE* 10:122; *SA* 8:104). The three-way association passes from the almost improperly buried corpse (it can still be readily restored to the cemetery, which is just a question-to-the-father away) to the box-and-cart theories of birth little Hans must apply to the riddle of his sister Hanna's arrival, the birth or death that he must metabolize: before Hanna traveled with them in the railway carriage, she was already with them in the box (*SE* 10:67ff.; *SA* 8:63ff.). When the repression of his anal eroticism and frontal masturbation first starts going down and out, ultimately as condemnation, little Hans falls to the ground, thrashing about with his legs, and spitting, like the fallen horses (= parents) he desires and dreads: as Freud reminds us elsewhere, in German *Spucken* (spitting) calls up *Spuken* (haunting) (*SE* 4:248 n. 1; *SA* 2:253 n. 1). Indeed little Hans was first in touch with his widdler, the separation index on or growing onto his own person, so that at all times he would have his little hand on the emergency break distinguishing animate from inanimate objects. The conditions for haunting, which were there for Hans, as they are in every development and transference, were nevertheless contained inside the transference neurosis and cure that the little patient could remember to forget. This forgetting which is not repression but analysis is the vanishing point of Freud's 1922 postscript: during his one-time-only follow-up visit, which is on the record, big Hans assures Freud that he did not recall his life as a neurotic nor recognize himself in the study but only began to feel the pull with the references to the family outing to Gmunden. This summer resort's place name is a last resort on the sliding scale of recall, one that regressively stammers *Munden* (tasting) and *Mund* (mouth), and at the same time thus touches on the retained wound of Freud's own dismembered name: *-mund*. In other words, the boxes and carts that stay, in Hans's case, on the one-way assembly line of interpersonal, couplified rapport with mourning through substitution and reproduction were (inside Freud and his haunted cases) the crypts crowding out and shutting down easy disposal of the separation or loss. The spit thus passes through the reversible haunting of Hans to skewer Freud's rapport with ghosts underlying his vast and ongoing work of analogy or mourning.

VAMPIRE? MUMMY? WOLFMAN!

With regard to haunted forms of grief, even those openly addressed, in the first place, to dead siblings, Freud can see the analysis through to completion only by exchanging their occult or animistic value for the guilty currency of relations with father.[18] In the case of "A Seventeenth-Century Demonological Neurosis," Freud casts the hallucinated devil as double of the dead father (*SE* 19:85ff.; *SA* 7:299ff.). Etymologically, devil embraces the meaning of double, while the morbid reception of the father's passing invariably installs in the surviving son a kind of double vision equally divided between willingness and refusal to accept a loss that, as this reception confirms, is not a loss. Thus the two men in "Fetishism" who happen not to be fetishists display instead a split in the ego resulting from their refusal to acknowledge the death of their fathers, which, paradoxically, they also accept. Hence their inclusion alongside fetishists who remain always only partially blind to the evidence of nothing there in the scanner of their desire: the bereaved sons deny that the object is lost— forever (*SE* 21:155–56; *SA* 3:386–87). The dead father is thus locked into a return trajectory at either end of which there is neither loss nor retrieval: what returns, only to the extent that it is already in place as the ego's guilty relation to the superego, is the son's repressed death wish, which must be kept both intact and undisclosed (*SE* 19:53ff.; *SA* 3:319ff.). Thus in *The Interpretation of Dreams* we find a ten-year-old boy's double take in the wake of his father's sudden death: "I know father's dead, but what I can't understand is why he doesn't come home to supper" (*SE* 4:254 n. 1; *SA* 2:259 n. 1).

Abraham and Torok turn to Freud's case study of the Wolfman, in which Freud briefly turned to the other side of this ambivalent invitation to the dead father to come to dinner only to swerve, however, from the not yet Oedipal interpretation that Wolfman's aberrant mourning invites.[19] Freud kept a brother's inability to mourn his dead sister in focus long enough to uncover in Wolfman's tearful pilgrimage to the grave of a poet—to whom his sister had often been compared—the attempt to "substitute for the missing outbursts of grief." Even though this episode seems securely buried and grounded in the case history, where the sister's seduction of Wolfman in early childhood is already in place, Freud shifts to Wolfman's father, whose specter must cover, under the aegis of ambivalence, every effort to cope with corpses. And yet Wolfman, too, invites his father to act as referee and referent of his relations with his sister, "the most dearly beloved member of his family." When she kills herself, however, Wolfman puts on a show of sorrow while coolly rejoicing "at having now become the sole heir to the property" (*SE* 17:23ff.; *SA* 8:142ff.). And yet this is too much: with respect to his beloved sister, Wolfman's calculations summon an interpretation they parody and empty out. Wolfman fakes not only sorrow but even hostility and guilt. The urge to recover and retain the lost object thus climaxes in the fantasy, articulated and camouflaged in the register of father-and-son relations, of having (had) nothing to lose. The double displacement—by Wolfman and by Freud—of inexpressible sorrow over a sister's passing nevertheless emerges alongside Freud's remark in the *Introductory Lectures on Psychoanalysis* that "there are neuroses which may be described as morbid forms of grief."[20] Indeed, "Mourning and Melancholia" follows the study of Wolfman almost, Nicolas Abraham and Torok suggest, as a delayed response to the aberrant mourning only briefly admitted in Wolfman's case.

RATMAN OR CARRION BIRD

In Freud's case study of Ratman (and in the original record of the case) we watch the competing deaths of sister and father and the survivor's omnipotence of thoughts (which, via projection, underlies a certain totemic rapport with the dead) converge. Freud concludes that it is "mourning for the father" that remains the main source of the intensity of Ratman's illness (*SE* 10:186; *SA* 7:57). But Freud also instructs that obsessional neurotics like Ratman are burdened by the guilt of mass murderers: they still subscribe to the childhood or totemistic belief in the telepathic power that enables their thoughts and wishes to bring about any and every person's death. The omnipotent death wish gives impulse to ghosts and to the technical media. But the dead father is banished to the realm down under where he must engage in a kind of slave labor that produces the media magic of wish fulfillment of Ratman's omnipotent thoughts. The dead father in effect sustains the rat economy much as his corpse nourishes the rat in the cemetery. But Ratman's real name, it turns out, is *Leichenvogel* (carrion bird), a nickname he earned among his siblings by demonstrating devotion to funerals he cannot stop attending even to the point of imagining his commiseration with survivors of yet living persons (*SE* 10:235; *SA* 7:93). Whenever Ratman catches himself thus counting on someone's death he throws himself onto the floor to show contrition—though at the same time he in effect performs his underlying identification with a corpse (*SE* 10:187; *SA* 7:58).

Before Freud makes it back to the relation to father, a relation that also always covers the next world, by pointing out that Ratman entertained thoughts of his father's death at an early age, he notes that some slightly older sister had died when Ratman was between three and four years old. In a footnote Freud concedes that the death of the sister figures in certain "epic" fantasies that he and his patient had been unable to pursue according to the terms and conditions of the analysis. But Freud does establish that the sister's death gave rise to a frenzy of misbehavior on Ratman's part culminating in that biting incident that first marked his straying away from the patronymic into the rat clan (*SE* 10:205, 207n, 235; *SA* 7:71, 73n, 93).

In his essay on the childhood recollection Goethe recorded in *Poetry and Truth,* Freud unpacks the little one's antics at the window as enacting his bond with mother to the point of magically expelling all rival siblings back through the window womb. It is this relationship—Freud refers to it in shorthand as Goethe's rapport with his mother—which, Freud concludes, is the source of Goethe's great success. And yet Freud is moved to list those missing in action: the four dead little ones who found no place in Goethe's autobiography. The first fulfillment of Goethe's death wishes was thus the departure of his younger six-year-old brother Hermann Jakob, whose death was also the original occasion for Goethe's legendary refusal to mourn.

In the wake of his first cancer operations, however, Freud emerges in his Goethe essay from the footnote underworld to add that Goethe does in fact accord Hermann Jakob passing, but conclusive, reference. It is thus Freud who can recognize the death wish against a sibling only in the absence of any outward manifestation of its casualty's inclusion in the corpus. This inclusion always opens onto a mummy's tomb. As Freud notes in the original record of the Ratman case, the one who refuses to mourn believes and practices omnipotence of thoughts, especially in the form of its primal application—the death wish—to the full extent of entertaining ideas about survival after death that "are as consistently materialistic as those of the Ancient Egyptians" (*SE* 10:297).

Although in the case study proper Freud judges endless mourning for the father to be at the bottom of Ratman's obsessional neurosis, in the footnote underworld we see Freud grant a dead sister epic significance in Ratman's fantasies (*SE* 10:207 n. 1; *SA* 7:73 n. 2). And yet, Freud concludes, the terms and conditions of the analysis had precluded exploration of the sibling's crypt. In the original record, however, the dead sister Katherine rules absolutely. Freud asks: "What is the origin of his idea of his omnipotence? I believe it dates back to the first death in his family, that of Katherine (*SE* 10:299). In the corner of every primal scene presided over, according to the public record, by Ratman's dead father, we find in the original record: Katherine was there. "He had a memory that he first noticed the difference between the sexes when he saw his deceased sister Katherine (five years his senior) sitting on the pot, or something of the sort" (*SE* 10:276). Another pot containing two rats that penetrate into or out of the anus first sends Ratman to Freud. As he listened to the officer recount this torture Ratman saw the ground heave in front of him as though there were a rat under it (*SE* 10:297). Under the case study a footnote allows that rats are chthonic animals that convey the souls of dead children.

Ratman is the name Freud bestows on his patient in a case he has recast as centering on a patronymic that emerges only to slip away like the rat out of the father's grave. Ratman's siblings call him *Leichenvogel*, carrion crow. In the original record, we find *Leichenvogel*, shortly after Katherine's departure, playing with a stuffed bird from his mother's hat: "As he was running along with it in his hands, its wings moved. He was terrified that it had come to life again, and threw it down. I thought of the connection with his sister's death . . . and I pointed out how his having thought this (about the bird) made it easier for him to believe afterwards in his father's resurrection" (*SE* 10:309). But the father's resurrection cannot subsume his son's "necrophilic phantasy" (*SE* 10:278): *Leichenvogel* heaves as though there were a rat inside of him. "It is worth recalling in this connection," Géza Róheim interjects in his case study of a hebephrenic pursued by the death wishes he launched against siblings, "that, among the Pitjentara of Australia, every second child is eaten by the siblings and parents in order to give them a kind of double strength; but if the baby survives until it acquires a name, the period of danger is over and it will not be eaten."[21] Thus it is dangerous to eat the sibling after it has acquired a name, the ticket entitling a little one to proper mourning.

As his transferences attest, Ratman allows his dangerous past or repast to emerge only by tapping into Freud's own: Ratman imagines Freud and his wife with a dead child between them: "The dead child can only be his sister Katherine, he must have gained by her death" (*SE* 10:284). But Freud, thus charged with proper burial of a dead sibling, only discerns Ratman gaining—on him. Freud thus registers this gain on the other side of his own resistance, which emerges spectacularly at the start of the original record: "I have not mentioned from earlier sessions three interrelated memories dating from his fourth year, which he describes as his earliest ones and which refer to the death of his elder sister Katherine.... (It is curious that I am not certain whether these memories are his)." In the next entry Freud continues: "My uncertainty and forgetfulness... seem to be intimately connected. The memories were really his.... (They were forgotten owing to complexes of my own.)" "Once when he was very young," Freud now remembers, "and he and his sister were talking about death, she said: 'On my soul, if you die I shall kill myself' " (*SE* 10:264).

Suicide is always committed in the office of the other: according to Freud, suicide is always a pact that allows some internal other to exact retribution for death wishes, though only to the extent that both must ultimately stay or go (*SE* 13:154 n. 1; *SA* 9:437 n. 1). The suicide pact covers that relationship to the dead Freud pursued under the rubric, borrowed from Ratman, of omnipotence of thoughts. Magic, the name, and the technical media are all applications of omnipotence of thoughts, but only to the extent that this omnipotence, which always turns around into a death wish, must be shared with a dead person (*SE* 18:85ff.; *SA* 19:374ff.).

According to Freud, the return trajectory of the force of nomination always and originally carried phantoms (*SE* 23:113–14; *SA* 9:559–60). It is the taboo attached to the name that is one of the cutting, ambivalent edges framing Freud's theory of ghosts: while other taboos would appear to offer the dead commemoration and even protection, the taboo on the name could only mean, Freud realized, that the living must in turn find protection from the vengeful return of the dead (*SE* 13:54–56; *SA* 9:345–47). Because the call of the name would wake and summon its dead bearer, the name itself must be dismembered and concealed. Mourning costume too turns out to be less a show of reverence than a retreat into camouflage; mourning rituals would then amount to desperate attempts on the part of the living to render themselves unrecognizable to the vengeful dead. Freud thus discovers in the scrambling of names the projective flight pattern of the death wish, which always brings back the dead.

In *Totem and Taboo* Freud cites Ratman as exemplary totem bearer. The totem is, like the hieroglyph, a "written sign" which is adopted as name; by succumbing—as children, for example, must—to the power of the name, the bearer identifies himself with the totem animal, which always represents the dead father. Rat is Ratman's totem only to the extent that the rat he glimpses coming out of his father's grave (where it had, he surmises, chewed on the corpse) is his own double from childhood.

The hieroglyphics of rat and rate first emerge by infiltrating the postal circulation of packages sent per *Nachnahme*: C.O.D., of course, but also per surname or *Nachname*. This scenario of the somehow unpayable C.O.D. and patronymic (which reduces the father to *Spielratte*, inveterate gambler and whoremonger who gambled with the name he risked loosening and losing) is a reversal of charges that in turn reverses the circumstances of the first emergence of the rat totem. As a young child Ratman, in the course of being punished by his father for having bitten someone, calls his father a series of indiscriminately selected names that, by thus gnawing loose the proper name, keeps Ratman henceforward in a safety zone with regard to paternal punishment and intervention, a zone shaped and safeguarded by the magical power of his words and wishes (*SE* 10:205–6; *SA* 7:71–72).

During the two-year period allotted to healthy mourning, Ratman always awaited his father's ghost at midnight. Ratman would then let out another rat (according to his hieroglyphic system) by pulling out his penis, which he showed to his father's ghost at the same time he reflected it in the mirror. The initial meetings of dead father and rat within a specular realm—which is also always, according to the logic of the reverse or backside, an anal province—do not cause the son the anguish of perpetual miscalculation until, two years after the father's death, Ratman enters his uncle's "house of mourning" only to discover that his living dead are slaves to his wishes. Ratman now realizes that his dead father must continue to pay for the son's evil thoughts and wishes, while yet living persons must, in consequence of these wishes, join the father in the crypt (which the anecdote that sends Ratman to Freud has disturbed). Ratman reports to Freud only with great difficulty the tale he heard of torture for which the criminal must sit down on a pot containing rats that—Ratman concludes just as Freud breaks through his resistance—bore their way into the anus (*SE* 10:166; *SA* 7:44).

Like Freud, who, in this case, finishes Ratman's anecdote for him, the father has always known Ratman's thoughts: from age six and on, from the time he first suffered erections (rat visitations), he has been convinced that his parents know his thoughts as though he had uttered them without himself having heard them. Such reasoning, Freud reflects, "sounds like a projection into the external world of our own hypothesis that he had thoughts without knowing anything about them; it sounds like an endopsychic perception of what has been repressed" (*SE* 10:164; *SA* 7:42). Via endopsychic perception one can watch in one's very own delusional thoughts and hallucinations the inside view of the psychic apparatus, and thus the inside-out connections passing from psyche through sensorium to the media-technological sensurround, and back again. But psychoanalysis, which is watching too, sees reflected back in delusions with endopsychic insight its own theorization of the psychic apparatus. The jamming of broadcasts superintending Ratman's thoughts—which are known without his knowing it—can only appear, together with the psychoanalytic theory, on the endopsychic scanner, and thus precisely at the intersection or threshold between the technical media and their underworld.

Freud points to the belief that, owing to their rapid movements, such animals as rats bear association with the soul's departure from the body at death. Also in *Totem and Taboo,* Freud cites a colleague who would rather leave rat phobias out of the psychoanalytic explanation of animal phobias as displacements of fear of father onto such animals as horses (*SE* 13:119, 128; *SA* 9:405, 412). In a footnote to the Ratman case Freud allows that rats, which are not so much disgusting as they are uncanny, chthonic animals, represent the souls, specifically of dead children (*SE* 10:215 n. 2; *SA* 7:79 n. 1). Ghostbusters take Ratman at his word and call him carrion bird; the part of rat goes to his dead sister. When the sister died, her brother, now carrion bird, consumed the rat he henceforward carried inside. In *Totem and Taboo* Freud refers to a certain Indian tribe in California that preserves the skin and feathers of the buzzard it murders and mourns (*SE* 13:139; *SA* 9:423–24). Birds do not die; their skin and feathers are stuffed by that which they animate and cover over. The rat under cover of the carrion bird's skin and feathers is at the controls of Ratman's death cult. Those pulled into the crypt—pot or anus—by the rat that penetrates them must slave to pay for the rat's every wish, which is their command. In exchange the rat does not convey the messages of the dead to her brother, whose thoughts are known only without his knowing it. When that rat tried to get out to vampirize someone other than her brother, the carrion bird could protect her only by creating a diversion that lasted the rest of their life. Freud comes close to—only to stop short of—letting the rat out of the bag. Like Wolfman in Nicolas Abraham and Maria Torok's reading, Ratman was yet another corpse carrier who found shelter within Freudian analysis.

DORA'S FOOT—*NOT!*

In the transferences Freud recorded (those of Ratman, for example) the absence of the mother, specifically the death of Freud's mother, is, in one of Ratman's dreams, conveyed in a letter that though legibly addressed to Freud, contains the cryptic message "p.f.": *pour feliciter* in lieu of *pour condoler,* of course, but also *pour Freud* (*SE* 10:193; *SA* 7:63). In the case study of Dora, where Freud first discovered and demarcated the context of transference, the mother is "nothing"—to husband, daughter, and Freud. Freud thus attends a bourgeois father-daughter drama where the mother has been shunted aside to reveal the encyclopedic and typographic terrain of what Freud hopes will have been Dora's transference neurosis. Dora's description of a painting depicting "Nymphae" shows Freud the way Dora has explored and penetrated a vast female body she reconstructed out of terms taken from the encyclopedia. Dora protests that she had consulted the encyclopedia only once, when, upon receipt of a letter from her uncle informing her that her cousin's appendicitis made it impossible for her to come visit, she sought the meaning of her cousin's ailment. Dora's beloved aunt, who had also been kept out of reach by her cousin's inclement health, soon died, whereupon Dora developed appendicitis.

This hysterical symptom formation confirms Freud's earliest conjectures regarding melancholia, though the ambivalence toward parents central to these conjectures has been displaced or circumvented in the avuncular context or complex of aberrant mourning. Nevertheless, there remains something that exceeds or drags behind this episode and signals to Freud its underlying Oedipal context. The niece in mourning holds onto a single symptom left over from her false appendicitis. Like Fräulein Montag in *The Trial,* Dora drags one foot. She commences dragging her foot exactly nine months after her rejection of Herr K.'s proposition. Freud is eager to find a childhood rehearsal of this foot symptom in Dora's history, and soon stumbles on the missing recollection: while yet a child Dora had in fact injured the same foot in a fall downstairs. Once fallen, Dora is left with a swollen foot, an "Oedipal" foot, which Freud translates into Dora's *Fehltritt* or faux pas. Her unconscious has thus made restitution for her seeming rejection of Herr K. by giving birth, once again, to her Oedipus. Though Freud concludes that he and Dora meet at last in one pregnant moment of transference, Dora next shuts the case and departs, still dragging a foot that does not, however, correspond to some secretly desired transgression with father and father substitute. What follows Dora's departure is a footnote in which Freud acknowledges that he had overlooked Dora's homosexual bond with Frau K., who, above and beyond any encyclopedia, was Dora's main source of sexual knowledge.

This footnote is dropped in the midst of Freud's belated recognition of the role that transference should have played in his treatment of Dora. In general, Freud later admitted, he had not taken the mother-infant relation into theoretical account because the father-transferences made onto him always blocked his view.[22] In "On the Dynamics of Transference," however, Freud allowed that a patient's transference onto the treating analyst need not always take the father as model but could also be the result of a mother or brother imago. And yet the primal transference could only be made onto the father, the father of psychoanalysis: when it came to female homosexuality Freud would advertise that he never accepted mother-transferences.

Dora's mother is granted a comeback as Frau K., the mother who owes her admission to the footnote to the text of her exclusion. According to Freud, the female homosexual couple plays mother and child as much as man and woman (*SE* 22:130; *SA* 1:560): the phallic mother remains their center of attraction. Even in heterosexual love, which Freud sees as being always out of phase, it is the man's Oedipal fixation on his mother which is attracted to the woman's pre-Oedipal bond with the phallic mother (*SE* 22:134; *SA* 1:564). As Freud teaches in his essay on Leonardo da Vinci, the so-called androgeny of certain ancient goddesses worshipped by men and women alike in fact refers in each case to a mother who comes fully equipped.

To receive funerary inscriptions the mourner puts his best foot forward, though other extremities are also offered: hence vampires suck blood as often from the soles of feet and the ears as from the throat. The appendage chosen for ritual mutilation bears association with the mother, in particular when the left hand, foot, or ear is marked by mourning tattoo. According to Freud, foot fetishism, which is predicated, however secretly, on the primal urge to smell all the sources of body odor, always recalls the maternal phallus. It is always in a footnote—in the underworld—that Freud equips the mother to claim equal rights alongside the father. In the footnote to his claim that the primal and primary identification is always with the father, Freud allows that the premier identification can also be with the phallic mother, in which case, however, Oedipal resolution would remain indefinitely postponed. Thus in Freud's study of female paranoia, just as the paranoid prepares to transfer libido to the man who courts her, the maternal bond returns, in this case as the shrouded box of the hidden camera; although her gentleman friend assures her that the ticking she hears must come from a clock, the paranoid, who cannot trust the words of one in league with her mother complex, knows that the camera has recorded evidence that will make her yield to impregnation. Dora's nonmetaphorical reception of the missing persons report filling out the maternal connection is again taken literally, indeed clitorally, by the paranoid who must overhear the pounding of the maternal and homosexual on her own person by projecting it onto the click of the photographic "box"—the all-seeing pre-Oedipal eye of mother—which the (p)unitive alliance between mother-and-father substitutes or representatives aims and shoots. The box she had kept to herself, which kept her to herself, and which the heterosexual "progress" or advance her suitor pressed upon her disturbed, now, via projective reorganization, has her covered (*SE* 14:264, 266; *SA* 7:208, 210).

SCHREBERAMA

According to Karl Abraham, mourning works both to "conserve" the relation to the deceased and to secure compensation for the loss. Melancholia results only when the ambivalence that disturbed the libidinal rapport with the object even before its departure now blocks mourning. In turn, the only method available for dislodging this blockage is rapid internalization of the lost object, whereby the hostile feelings the highly ambivalent mourner cannot but address to the departed are directed against himself. Melancholia, Abraham concludes, is simply an archaic form of mourning,[23] just as the narcissistic object choice—the hinge that keeps mourning and melancholia turning together but in different time zones—remains more ancient than any genuinely heterosexual attachment. Indeed, what is threatened with extinction during mourning is heterosexual libido itself: he who cannot stop mourning becomes the widow of his heterosexuality.

Behind these extremities of the analysis of mourning, Abraham loses the theory of ghosts among the disposable effects of repression; by assuming or anticipating that underlying the haunting of his patients is the always anticipated death—the divinization and murder—of the father, Abraham advances, in advance of any exhumation or burial to be performed, the interpretation of phantom possession as the displaced effect of repressed sexual research that can be conducted only as intercourse with ghosts at one end and, at the other, as simulation of, or in place of, sublimation.[24] This scenario corresponds, in Freud's work, to the place Leonardo da Vinci's unconsummated homosexual disposition holds: the study of da Vinci was Freud's first treatment of protracted or delayed mourning—in da Vinci's case, for his mother—already in terms of an inward, inverting turn identification takes in lieu of substitution (*SE* 11:106; *SA* 10:130–31).

This phantasmatic reading of the homosexual disposition, from which the theoretical pursuit of mourning and melancholia springs, finds a counterpart in Abraham's investigation of consanguineous marriages, which occupy an intermediate zone of "compromise" between incest and homosexuality. In his analysis of war psychosis, Victor Tausk views the psychotic state of melancholia—or melancholia-cum-paranoia—as the pathological application of detached heterosexual libido already shaped and shattered from within by the narcissistic position it occupied. Whereas detached homosexual libido is readily reabsorbed by the ego—which is already aggrandized because capable of making such investments in the first place—narcissistic libido installed in a heterosexual object cannot, once severed from itself, be recuperated by an ego that melancholia reduces and minaturizes.[25] Thus in Pausanias's version, Narcissus can enter into the suicide pact of melancholia only with his dead twin sister, whom he recognizes in place of his own reflection or double.

The psychoanalytic theory of ghosts first arose to account for Leonardo da Vinci's homoerotic disposition, and then returned within the study of Schreber's paranoia once again to address the technical media in terms of sublimation breakdown. In both cases it is the common fate of repressed homosexuality and attachment to the dead to project and pursue fantasies of technologized, mechanized conveyance and writing. Analyzing Leonardo's sole recollection from infancy in which a bird's tail passed between his lips, Freud concludes that the inventor-artist had enjoyed, unchecked by paternal censorship of his sexual researches, a bird-bond with his mother and then, as his mother, with stand-ins for himself as a boy, a bond that gave impulse to his pursuit and prophecy of mechanical flight. In this case homosexuality would embrace a testamentary structure that, even if only in anticipation, commemorates the mother's love, which can never vary, in the mode of mummification. Leonardo's retentively meticulous accounting of the expenses of his mother's funeral—comparable only to accounts he kept on expenses incurred for his pretty boy pupils—tallies the safe deposit inside him of his own early bond with mother, whose separation from him, even though effected at a very early age, could not stop asserting itself as he passed through a relay of stepmothers shadowed by infertility and early death. The homosexually disposed always retains the bundle of desires called mother or, as Freud also allows, brother as a foreign body inside him transmitting commands and wishes not proper to the host body (which must, however, mimic them).

Sandor Ferenczi discovered that the homosexual patient is, therefore, particularly susceptible to hypnosis and telepathic rapport: indeed, one of Ferenczi's homosexual patients, who repeated during analytic sessions Ferenczi's every thought from the day before, was the source of Ferenczi's and Freud's intense interest in the possibility of telepathic communication whereby Ferenczi's experience of déjà vu would refer not to the collision of unconscious and conscious impressions but to telecommunication with another life. As Jones writes of Freud's reaction to the record forwarded by Ferenczi of the homosexual's telepathic powers: "Freud, however, was deeply impressed by the data and said emphatically that they put an end to any possible remaining doubt about the reality of thought transference. Henceforward the new knowledge was to be taken for granted."[26]

Telepathic telecommunications and the homosexual bond with the dead converge in the case study of Schreber, where Freud argues that the paranoid's delusional system was not part of the pathology but represented instead an attempt at recovery and reconstruction in the wake of loss. Precipitated by the repression it culminates in, this catastrophic loss takes the form of Schreber's complete withdrawal of all libido from the world. His delusional formations are thus the very measure, measured in reverse, of the "wealth of sublimations" that "the catastrophe of the general libido withdrawal has brought to ruin" (*SE* 12:73; *SA* 7:196). Disappointment in love, erotic amplification of feelings not allowed to emerge as such—or the death of a loved one—can clog the psychosexual exhaust system, giving repression the lead over sublimation.

The corpse that dislodges sublimation cannot be found beneath "the familiar turf of the father complex" to which Freud believes his analysis of Schreber can safely return: sublimated homosexuality, that is, sublimation proper, organizes cultural institutions to the extent that it always remains behind, among the effects of proper mourning for a dead father (*SE* 12:55; *SA* 7:180).

Talking birds and eagles are part of the paranoid system that culminates in Schreber's belief that God—who, however, takes cognizance only of corpses—had chosen him as a transsexual consort to conceive with divine rays a new race of men. Birds thus hover over the machines conducting this Frankensteinian corpse construction through phantasm networks of mechanical flight, from takeoff to the recording and programming—the taking down—inside the control tower. On its own the body reverses its dependence on gravity and takes flight not only through erections and ejaculations but also by throwing up.

Complex machinery in delusional formations project the patient's genitalia. In Schreber's case, both terms of this translation are represented side by side: so that he may conceive a new race in the wake of the one he lost (he and his wife were unable to reproduce living children), Schreber acquiesces in his "emasculation" by divine rays regulated by complex celestial machinery, writing machines that, in rendering him God's consort, also make him the locus of countless inscriptions. Schreber's desire to be transformed into what he calls woman (a sexless resurrected body) is at once the desire of a writer, a *Schreiber*, to be transformed—in the absence of any verbal expression, since Schreber's organs of speech and respiration have been shut down—into a body of writing conducted and amplified by machines that take down every detail of Schreber's existence so that the rays can later read what they have, in effect, written. This process of taking off and taking down will, however, never be completed but remains the protracted consummation of pleasurable attachment to his every organ of machines which are new machine-organs. Only through the process of taking off, whereby the genitally organized body is discarded, can corpses be imitated, can one's own body serve as the resurrection of another; in keeping with his sacrificial mission Schreber must become the repository for "the poison of corpses": "There arose the almost monstrous demand that I should behave continually as if I myself were a corpse."[27]

It has been pointed out that Freud, in rushing to represent a young son's relation to a father who is also a famous physician as being of necessity one of worship, overlooked the unbalanced rigor of Schreber's father's interest in the physical well-being of children.[28] The various machines of

Schreber's delusions would thus be modeled after the makeshift harnesses and contraptions with which the father shaped his son's bearing, often through the painful consequences, built into the devices, of lax or uneven posture. But in correcting Freud, these intellectual historians neglect to reevaluate, according to the shift of emphasis they introduce, the impact of the suicide of Schreber's older brother, a loss Freud takes into full account, though only to isolate it, ultimately, over and against "yearning for the father." Though Freud meticulously uncovers the fantasy of sibling incest around which Schreber's citational system circulates, he nevertheless assigns the brother in Schreber's system the position of divine double of the father god. And yet Freud's own example of deification of the dead is that of the Caesars who, beginning with Julius, became gods upon dying (*SE* 12:53 n. 1, 53; *SA* 7:176 n. 4, 177).

The healthy regimen the father imposed on life counted among its graduates one suicidal and one delusional son. That Schreber goes delusional is the good news: his paranoid system safeguards against the quiet evacuation of libido that led to his brother's self-effacement. But the older brother was always on a suicide mission, intercepting the full force of paternal designs he deflected from Schreber. The brother continues to fulfill his mission in the phantom form every suicide leaves behind. Schreber's delusional system rescues two brothers from their father, whose death is secured through Schreber's castration, which, like his brother's suicide, is directed against the father inside them.

PLAYBACK FUNCTION

Only by tapping into the separate places occupied by Freud's theory of ghosts and his theory of pathological mourning can we begin to discern that which remains outside by substituting for mourning: the audio and video broadcasts of improper burial (analyzed in *Totem and Taboo*) that are transmitted via the crypts that (as set forth in "Mourning and Melancholia") those who are incapable of mourning must build inside for the unmourned and, hence, undead. Projection is the doubly missing link between melancholia and phantom possession. Ferenczi originally introduced introjection as one end of transference opposite projection, which covered the other end.[29] This point of cohesion is also where, in Freud, the terms must billow apart: projection or countertransference already inhabits—haunts—the highly problematical frame of transference to the extent that this frame, which comes into focus for Freud only by going out of control, harbors doubles and *revenants* from earliest childhood. Transference, which thus reads back on its counter ancient projections, is in the first place grounded in introjection or even, more literally or primally, in incorporation.

A certain standard reception or edition of Freud's thought thus claims to join Freud in only projecting the full-fledged treatment of projection. In the case study of Schreber, Freud postpones the investigation of projection until some future occasion, which prompts an editorial footnote to the effect that there "seems no trace of any such later discussion." Only "one of the missing metapsychological papers" might have been reserved for the discussion that never took place (*SE* 12:66 n. 1). In the editor's introduction to the extant metapsychological papers we find, again, mention of Freud's dissatisfaction with his own preliminary treatment of projection in the Schreber study, which had issued in the promise to return to its fuller elaboration: "This he seems never to have done, unless it was in one of these missing papers" (*SE* 14:106 n. 1). And yet the next major work to follow the Schreber study was *Totem and Taboo*, which turns on a far-reaching theory of projection developed alongside Freud's account of haunted receptions of the dead. The enigmatic force of the repression that keeps this central discussion of projection in some other—missing—place cannot but find an unwitting accomplice in Freud: in "A Metapsychological Supplement to the Theory of Dreams" Freud interrupts another discussion of projection to "defer the full treatment of projection" (*SE* 14:244). But is this the same deferral that he had earlier inserted into the Schreber study? The editor prompts from the corresponding footnote that this is in fact the case.

The point of conjunction between "Mourning and Melancholia" and "The Taboo upon the Dead" that has been thus excluded nevertheless returns via certain sets of analogy, which in turn invite the theories of projection and incorporation to conjoin by plugging into the technical media. In the margin of Tausk's presentation on projection and identification as the interlocked structuring principles of every sensorium, which thus finds its analogue, not only for the schizophrenic, in the cinematographic apparatus, Freud adds from the place of the missing paper the matching analogue for projected vision: the two-dimensional representation or projection of the body supplied by the cinematograph was also the aim and frame of mummification.[30] Freud's analogies for unconscious processes and psychoanalytic technique always shift between the technical media and the domain of archaeology. But Freud also always borrows these two sets of analogy from his patients whose delusional formations in turn already double as what Freud calls endopsychic perceptions, which always anticipate by reproducing his own theories of the psychic apparatus.

In his essay on Jensen's *Gradiva*, Freud explores the archaeological end of endopsychic perception, which recognizes excavation and exhumation of ancient relics in place of the retrieval of something from the more recent repressed past (*SE* 9:51; *SA* 10:49). Upon expressing his satisfaction in *Totem and Taboo* that psychoanalysis had penetrated behind the screen to the projection booth of haunting, Freud is suddenly reminded of Schreber, who had found reflected in his own delusional formations the links and limits of his libido (*SE* 13:92; *SA* 9:380). In that case study Freud had in turn been startled upon recognizing that, via the same endopsychic projection, his theory of libido also found reflection in Schreber's "rays of God," so startled in fact that he rushed to give evidence within his study—in a frenzy of anticipation that some might call paranoid—that he had developed his theory of paranoia before reading Schreber's memoirs (*SE* 12:79; *SA* 7:200). On the endopsychic scanner, psychotic projections, psychoanalytic conceptions of the unconscious, and the technical media converge to the point that Freud can only put through or apply his discoveries by picking up a phone. Freud thus recommends right from the start that the psychoanalyst "adjust himself to the patient as a telephone receiver is adjusted to the transmitting microphone" (*SE* 12:115–16; *SA* Ergänzungsband, 175). But Freud's telephone always also plugs into the occult. In the "New Introductory" lecture devoted to the occult Freud conceives of the telephone as telepathic medium to the extent that both the technical and the occult medium await hook-up to psychoanalysis, which alone can elucidate them. The telepathic process thus finds its analogy in "speaking and hearing by telephone": "And only think if one could get hold of this physical equivalent of the psychical act! It would seem to me that psychoanalysis, by inserting the unconscious between what is physical and what was previously called psychical, has paved the way for the assumption of such processes as telepathy" (*SE* 22:55; *SA* 1:494).

In the case study of Ratman and in Freud's own case we find the motive force of the unmournable—and doubly unacknowledged—death of child and sibling that is the rehearsal and, then, repetition of the death of the father, the guarantor of proper mourning. Thus in many cases (Ratman, Schreber, and Wolfman, for example) Freud encountered difficulties on two fronts, specifically in superimposing the dead sibling onto the father's corpse. And yet both deaths, the mournable and the unmournable, pressed to find simultaneous broadcast. Otherwise psychoanalytic theory would have been left to founder on the two deaths on which it was founded.

NOTES

1. To turn up the volume on "Freud and the Passions" and admit both melancholia and gadget love as the two other passions that get off together in Freud's name and corpus, a trip back into the crypt was required, into that double recess where my book *Aberrations of Mourning,* which first let roll the genealogy of media inside Freud's thought, was buried alive in the fast-food fields of one-stop researching. But this time all the time in the world was not along for the drive to double and contain (through plagiarism, incorporation, and disownership) the first repress release from the techno-crypt of psychoanalysis. Now there's time to take the time it takes for a work of mourning to be conducted and received. This ghost appearance *and* advance preview (a revised paperback edition is coming soon) reassembles and re-collects readings distributed throughout *Aberrations of Mourning* of the secret melancholia organizing Freud's case studies, including, in the first place, his own case.

2. Cited in Peter Gay, *Freud: A Life for Our Time* (New York: Norton, 1988), 445.

3. From the closing line of "On the History of the Psychoanalytic Movement."

4. Sigmund Freud, *The Standard Edition of the Complete Psychological Works,* ed. and trans. James Strachey (London: Hogarth and the Institute of Psycho-Analysis, 1960), 14:306; hereafter cited as *SE.* The German original can be found in Sigmund Freud, *Studienausgabe,* ed. Alexander Mitscherlich et al. (Frankfurt am Main: S. Fischer, 1975), 10:226. Hereafter cited as *SA.* Since the English translation is, as its title suggests, the standard edition of Freud's works, references are always also given to this edition. No translation policy has, however, been observed. I either offer my own translations of Freud or borrow from Strachey's translation. English translations of all other German texts, unless otherwise noted, are my own.

5. Abraham, *Gesammelte Schriften,* ed. Johannes Cremerius (Frankfurt am Main: Fischer Taschenbuch, 1982), 2:76–77.

6. Ernst Simmel, *Kriegsneurosen und "Psychisches Trauma"* (Leipzig: Otto Nemnich, 1918), 25.

7. See "Deuil ou melancolie, introjecter—incorporer," in Nicolas Abraham and Maria Torok, *L'écorce et le noyau* (Paris: Aubier-Flammarion, 1978), 259–75.

8. Letter to Fliess (31 May 1897).

9. Letter to Fliess (3 October 1897).

10. See Stephan Broser, "Kästchen, Kasten, Kastration" in *Confrontation* 8 (1982): 87–114.

11. These phantoms, ultimately of Julius, appear via Freud's ambivalent rapport with his nephew John, one year Freud's senior. He ascribes his fainting spells alongside Jung to his recognition of the return, in his relations with Jung, of this childhood rapport. But in a letter to Ferenczi, Freud also draws the ultimate connection by tying his dead faints to Julius's death; Freud was one of those wrecked by success—the success, in fact, of his death wish directed against Julius. See Ernest Jones, *The Life and Work of Sigmund Freud* (New York: Basic Books, 1953), 2:146.

12. Abraham, *Gesammelte Schriften,* 2:67–68.

13. The cinematic image hovers in the background of two overlapping Freud references: *SE* 12:135 and *SE* 2:153.

14. Jones, *The Life and Work of Sigmund Freud* 1:13. This early traveling shot, which may

have condensed several experiences separated by years, most likely occurred, according to Jones, many years after Julius's death. But Freud recollected his travel souvenir as following closely upon his brother's departure. Freud's eldest half-brother Emmanuel, father of John and Pauline, died in a train wreck; shortly thereafter Freud commenced working on "Mourning and Melancholia."

15. See "Die Stellung der Verwandtenehe in der Psychologie der Neurosen," *Gesammelte Schriften* 1:14–21.

16. Jones, *The Life and Work of Sigmund Freud* 1:3, 11, 25.

17. I am following Paul Roazen's account, in which this shift to Freud's essay on Dostoevsky was already in place. *Freud and His Followers* (New York: Knopf, 1975).

18. Freud thematizes the conversion rate dictated by the terms and conditions of analysis in a footnote to his case study of Ratman; *SE* 10:207; *SA* 7:73.

19. Nicolas Abraham and Maria Torok, *Cryptonymie: Le verbier de l'Homme aus Loups* (Paris: Aubier-Flammarion, 1976). Derrida's introduction, "Fors," provides the indispensable supplement.

20. Cited in Bowlby, "Pathological Mourning and Childhood Mourning" (530 n. 10), where a discussion of Freud's curious split reception of Wolfman's sister's death—curious also given certain contexts within which the split emerges—is already in place.

21. Róheim, *Magic and Schizophrenia* (Bloomington: Indiana University Press, 1970), 209–10.

22. See John Bowlby's section on psychoanalytic theories of the mother-infant relation in volume 2 of *Attachment and Loss* (New York: Basic Books, 1980).

23. Abraham, *Gesammelte Schriften* 2:49.

24. Abraham, *Gesammelte Schriften* 2:270 ff.

25. Victor Tausk, "Diagnostische Erörterungen auf Grund der Zustandsbilder der soge-nannten Kriegspsychosen," *Gesammelte psychoanalytische und literarische Schriften,* ed. Hans-Joachim Metzger (Vienna: Medusa, 1983), 231–35.

26. Sandor Ferenczi, *Schriften zur Psychoanalyse,* ed. Michael Balint (Frankfurt am Main: Fischer Taschenbuch, 1982), 1:189; Jones, *The Life and Work of Sigmund Freud,* 3:385.

27. Cited in Ned Lukacher, "Schreber's Juridical Opera," *Structuralist Review* 2, no. 2 (1981): 16.

28. See Lukacher, who refers to the work of Marie Balmary. See also John Bowlby's section on Schreber in volume 2 of *Attachment and Loss,* and Samuel Weber's "Die Parabel," the introduction to his edition of Schreber's *Denkwürdigkeiten* (Frankfurt am Main: Ullstein, 1973).

29. Ferenczi, *Schriften zur Psychoanalyse* 1:12–47.

30. Tausk, "Uber die Entstehung des 'Beeinflussungsapparates' in der Schizophrenie," *Gesammelte psychoanalytische und literarische Schriften,* 245–86.

Contributors

DONALD L. CARVETH is professor of sociology and social and political thought at York University, Toronto. He is also a member of the Toronto Institute of Psychoanalysis. He won the American Sociological Association Theory Prize (1984) for his article on psychoanalysis and social theory. He was co-winner of the Miguel Prados Prize (1991) awarded by the Canadian Psychoanalytic Society.

JOHN FORRESTER is lecturer in the history and philosophy of science at Cambridge University. He is the author of *Language and the Origins of Psychoanalysis* (1980) and *The Seductions of Psychoanalysis: Freud, Lacan, and Derrida* (1990).

MARY JACOBUS is professor of English and women's studies at Cornell University. She is the author of *Reading Women: Essays in Feminist Criticism* (1986) and editor of *Women Writing and Writing about Women* (1979), as well as *Body/Politics: Women and the Discourses of Science* (1990).

CLAIRE KAHANE is professor of English at the State University of New York—Buffalo, and a member of the Buffalo Center for the Psychological Study of the Arts. She is co-editor (with Charles Bernheimer) of *In Dora's Case: Freud—Hysteria—Feminism* (1985).

WILLIAM KERRIGAN is professor of English at the University of Massachusetts at Amherst and co-director of the Forum on Psychiatry and the Humanities. He is the author of *The Sacred Complex: On the Psychogenesis of Paradise Lost* (1983) and co-editor of *Interpreting Lacan* (1983) and *Taking Chances: Derrida, Psychoanalysis, and Literature* (1984), as well as several other works.

GEOFF MILES is currently training as a psychotherapist at the Clarke

Institute of Psychiatry, Toronto. His doctoral thesis "Gravida-Gradiva: Pregnancy and Death-Work in Freud's Pompeiian Phantasy" (1992) was completed at York University, Toronto.

JEROME NEU is professor of philosophy at the University of California, Santa Cruz. He is the author of *Emotion, Thought, and Therapy: A Study of Hume and Spinoza and the Relationship of Philosophical Theories of the Emotions to Psychological Theories of Therapy* (1977) and editor of *The Cambridge Companion to Freud* (1991).

JOHN O'NEILL is Distinguished Research Professor of Sociology at York University, Toronto. He is the author of *Essaying Montaigne: A Study of the Renaissance Institution of Writing and Reading* (1982), *The Communicative Body: Studies in Communicative Philosophy, Politics, and Sociology* (1989), *Critical Conventions: Interpretation in the Literary Arts and Sciences* (1992), and *The Domestic Economy of the Soul: Frued's Five Case Histories* (1996). He is a co-editor of the international quarterly *Philosophy of the Social Sciences.*

ELLIE RAGLAND is professor of English at the University of Missouri–Columbia. She is author of *Jacques Lacan and the Philosophy of Psychoanalysis* (1986), *Essays on the Pleasure of Death: From Freud to Lacan* (1995), and editor of the *Newsletter of the Freudian Field.*

LAURENCE A. RICKELS is professor in the Department of Germanic, Oriental, and Slavic Languages and Literature at the University of California, Santa Barbara. He is the author of *Aberrations of Mourning: Writing on German Crypts* (1988), *The Case of California* (1991) and editor of *Looking after Nietzsche* (1990).

KATHLEEN WOODWARD is associate professor of English and director of the Center for Twentieth-Century Studies at the University of Wisconsin–Milwaukee. She is the author of *At Last the Real Distinguished Thing: The Late Poems of Eliot, Pound, Stevens, and Williams* (1980), and co-editor (with Murray M. Schwartz) of *Memory and Desire: Aging—Literature—Psychoanalysis* (1986).

Index